MAIMONIDES'
ETHICS

MAIMONIDES' ETHICS

*The Encounter of Philosophic
and Religious Morality*

Raymond L. Weiss

The University of Chicago

Press

Chicago & London

RAYMOND L. WEISS is professor
of philosophy at the
University of Wisconsin—Milwaukee.

The University of Chicago Press, Chicago 60637
The University of Chicago Press, Ltd., London
© 1991 by The University of Chicago
All rights reserved. Published 1991
Printed in the United States of America
00 99 98 97 96 95 94 93 92 91   5 4 3 2 1

ISBN: 0-226-89152-6 (cloth)

Library of Congress Cataloging-in-Publication Data

Weiss, Raymond L.
   Maimonides' ethics : the encounter of philosophic and religious
morality / Raymond L. Weiss.
      p.   cm.
   Includes bibliographical references and index.
   1. Maimonides, Moses, 1135–1204—Ethics.   2. Ethics, Jewish—
History.   I. Title.
B759.M34W45 1991
296.3'85'092—dc20   91-13921
                                                               CIP

Contents

Acknowledgments

This book had its incubation some years ago under the guidance of Leo Strauss, who first called my attention to the importance of the distinction between wisdom and piety in Maimonides' Code. I am particularly grateful to him not only for the initial direction that he gave to the project, but also for enabling me to understand that the permanent—and hence contemporary—issues are faced by the great thinkers and works of the past. This is an essential part of his legacy in the study of Maimonides. He also introduced me to the significance of the "quarrel" between Greek philosophy and biblical religion. The apparent opposition between these two traditions in the area of ethics provides the point of departure for this book.

Other friends and colleagues have provided various kinds of encouragement and intellectual stimulation: Arthur W. H. Adkins, through his gentle but probing questioning regarding some of the issues discussed here; Monford Harris, with his fresh and independent way of looking at things; and Ralph Lerner, whose own love for Maimonides fueled his interest in my project and who made a number of useful suggestions regarding the manuscript. Joel Kraemer and R. W. Sharples also deserve an expression of gratitude. Special thanks are due to Catherine Bock; her unflagging enthusiasm for the project has been a wonderful support, and her thoughtful comments on a number of drafts have contributed greatly to the book's clarity.

I am indebted to the generosity of the Earhart Foundation, which enabled me to take time off to devote to this study. A version of the book's first chapter was originally published in the *Proceedings of the American Academy for Jewish Research* 54 (1987); I am grateful for permission to reprint.

Abbreviations
and a Note on the Text

BT   *Babylonian Talmud*
CM   *Commentary on the Mishnah*
EC   *Eight Chapters*
HD   Hilkhot Deʿot ("Laws Concerning Character Traits")
Logic   *Treatise on the Art of Logic*
MT   *Mishneh Torah* (Code of Jewish Law); also referred to as
the Code.

Although Maimonides never uses the designation *Eight Chapters*, I follow common practice in using this title, and *EC* seems a convenient abbreviation. Square brackets in the citations from the *Guide of the Perplexed* contain the pagination of the Munk edition, which is also given in the running head of the English translation by Shlomo Pines. *Ethical Writings* refers to *Ethical Writings of Maimonides*, edited by Weiss and Butterworth. For *Eight Chapters* and the *Commentary on the Mishnah* as a whole, I have used the edition by Joseph Kafih; for Hilkhot Deʿot, the edition of *Sefer ha-Maddaʿ* by Moses Hyamson. Additional information for works cited in the notes can be found in the bibliography. As for the transliteration of Hebrew passages, I follow, wherever practicable, the sound (e.g., Avot rather than Aboth), in conjunction with conventional practice.

Introduction

Matthew Arnold has set forth the terms of the opposition between Hellenism and Hebraism with a useful clarity: "The uppermost idea with Hellenism is to see things as they really are; the uppermost idea with Hebraism is conduct and obedience."[1] However valuable this view of the opposition might initially be, it does not reach the vantage point from which Maimonides regarded the matter. For Hellenism also speaks in a significant way about conduct, if not obedience, and its conception of conduct in terms of "ethics," that is, states of character, is vital not simply for "seeing" human life as it is, but also for the practice of a good human life. Hebraism is, of course, also concerned with conduct, so that the question of how a person should live becomes a central issue. Maimonides finesses the opposition or "quarrel" between the two traditions so that, at least to all appearances, a considerable harmony prevails; he tends to suppress the differences to make the introduction of Hellenism acceptable to his readers. It is pertinent also to note that he speaks not of "Hellenism" but of philosophy, and not of "Hebraism" but of the Torah. It is the apparent or real difference between philosophy and the Torah that he deals with. Nor does he, as does Arnold, speak of the "forces" of Hebraism and Hellenism that have powerfully shaped human consciousness in the West; Maimonides does not approach the matter from a historical viewpoint but as a thinker whose preoccupation is the Law.

The legal context of his discussion of both philosophic eth-

1. "Hebraism and Hellenism," in *Selections from the Prose Works of Matthew Arnold*, p. 275.

1

ics and religious morality must be kept continually in mind. If we may distinguish between a historical (or objective) treatment of ethics and a practical one required by jurisprudence, the Maimonidean discourse is emphatically practical. Directing his attention to the needs of the Jewish community, he is prone to underscore, scant, or recast material in a manner that might appear scandalous to a historical scholar. Speaking as a commentator upon, or legislator of, Jewish law, Maimonides aims at the well-being of the Jewish people in his treatment of ethics. The practical purpose of jurisprudence affects the way he interprets the relationship between Athens and Jerusalem in the domain of ethics.

One of the problems confronted by Maimonides was how to regard the moral virtues. He did not think of them as unalterably fixed; the realm of morality has a certain malleability that makes possible the adaptation of philosophic ethics to the Law and, alternatively, the accommodation of Jewish precepts to a framework that derives from philosophy.[2] In his conception of the variability of ethics, Maimonides differs from Thomas Aquinas, who takes over verbatim the enumeration of the moral virtues found in the *Nicomachean Ethics*. Aquinas argues that precisely the ones set forth there exhaust the account of the human virtues. He is able to accommodate them to Christian doctrine by distinguishing these purely human virtues from the supranatural virtues of faith, hope, and charity. Maimonides, who remains completely upon a naturalistic plane, specifies only human virtues, but he takes into account the teachings of the Law in the way that he fashions them.

We shall see that he interprets the Law on the basis of ends set by human nature, namely, man's contemplative end and his political nature; morality is instrumental to the ends established by man's twofold nature. The difference between these two perspectives upon ethics must be kept in view so that we do not ascribe unnecessary contradictions to Maimonides. When speaking about the prerequisites for the study of meta-

2. Maimonides indicates in *EC* that whereas the intellectual virtues are immutable, this is not the case with the moral virtues (chap. 4, p. 384). He himself describes the moral virtues somewhat differently in *EC* and the Code.

physics, he says that "the moral virtues are a preparation for the intellectual virtues . . . [by endowing man] with the qualities of tranquility and repose" (*Guide*, 1.34 [40a]). Before delving into metaphysical questions, a man must "completely purify his character and extinguish the desires and cravings engendered in him by his imagination" (*Guide*, 1.5 [16a]). Elsewhere, however, Maimonides says that moral perfection is "as it were, only the disposition to be useful to people; consequently, it is an instrument for someone else" (*Guide*, 3.54 [133b]). And in *Guide* 3.27, when discussing the overall purpose of the Law, he refers solely to the usefulness of instilling the right moral qualities in people for the well-being of the community. To understand Maimonides, it is necessary to attend to which point of view dominates the discussion in a given context.

Maimonides composed two main ethical works, *Eight Chapters* and Hilkhot Deʿot, each being a part of larger works on Jewish law, the *Commentary on the Mishnah* and the *Mishneh Torah* (or Code), respectively. The *Guide of the Perplexed* also contains some discussion of matters related to ethics. I shall deal with each work separately, which makes possible highlighting the distinctive features of each. The occasional repetition required by such an approach has the advantage of recapitulating some of Maimonides' own repetitions— which always introduce some new subtlety or nuance worth pondering.

I shall occasionally "travel" from one work to another to illuminate a particular issue. This procedure is, I believe, defensible because Maimonides takes fundamentally the same approach to ethical matters in all his works, although his mode of presentation is, of course, affected by the purpose of a given work. The problematic of a particular work (or subsection of a work) sometimes yields a fresh, even different, understanding of one or another topic. Thus, H. Deʿot ("Laws Concerning Character Traits") is part of a code that is intended to encompass the entire Oral Law, so that Maimonides takes into account a range of rabbinic precepts there that he does not have to consider in *Eight Chapters* (*EC*). As for the *Guide*, it has its own interlocking web of purposes, but, being devoted to the true science of the Law, it presupposes the validity of the legal-istic works. Although the *Guide* in a way transcends the legal-istic works through moving onto the plane of *theoria*, it does not hold a basically different position regarding the matters that concern us here. We shall, then, not assume that the three major works by Maimonides on the Law are hermetically sealed off from one another, but neither shall we neglect the impor-tance of the context in each case.

Maimonides understands "ethics" in the strict Aristotelian sense as referring to "character traits." This poses a difficulty at the outset, particularly in the Code (which, unlike the *Commentary on the Mishnah* and the *Guide*, was written in Hebrew), because the biblical-rabbinic tradition does not dis-tinguish a domain of ethics. Now, the Bible and rabbinic works do contain precepts concerned with what we might loosely call moral matters, but Maimonides had to so interpret these pre-cepts that they would be intelligible within a strictly "ethical" frame of reference. One of the problems that he had to solve in the Code was linguistic in nature, namely, to establish a term for "ethics." We shall see that he interprets the term *deʿah* in such a manner as to serve this purpose.

The Torah deals with commandments as distinct from eth-ics proper. Although one might think that this difference points toward a serious conflict between the Torah and philosophy, Maimonides tends to minimize the opposition between the two traditions regarding this issue: the *mitsvot* (command-ments) are useful for training a person to acquire the right char-acter. The more pressing difficulty to which he alludes, and which he addresses, is the difference between the standard of the mean and the biblical-rabbinic tendency to go toward the extreme in matters pertaining to ethics. A difficulty arises solely on the plane of ethics concerning how the Jewish pro-pensity toward the extreme can be justified.

While it is sometimes difficult to render the thought of Maimonides in a terminology faithful to the original texts, our reference to "philosophic ethics" does not pose a problem. Maimonides himself uses the expression. It is even possible that he was the first to do so; at any rate, to my knowledge, he has no predecessor in this matter. Plato and Aristotle distinguish a philosophic way of life from political virtue; thus for Aristotle in particular one might argue that he implies that there is such a thing as "philosophic ethics."[3] But it is striking that Maimonides is quite explicit, and he is so in order to differentiate the moral teachings stemming from the philosophers from those that originate with the Law. More precisely, he distinguishes "philosophic ethics" from the "moral precepts [ādāb] and admonitions of the Law." This distinction is made in two of his medical writings;[4] in his works dealing with Jewish law, Maimonides refrains from speaking of "philosophic ethics."

"Philosophic ethics" is a term of distinction; it separates one source of instruction regarding moral conduct from an alternative source. (Otherwise, why not refer simply to "ethics"?) The apparent conflict between the aforementioned sources is glossed over in the medical writings. Maimonides establishes a kinship between them through the philosophic notion of a therapy for curing the soul's diseases. Not only "philosophic ethics" but also the Law is useful as a mode of correction for moral vices. We shall see that this way of building a bridge between the apparently opposing positions plays a significant role in his interpretation of religious morality in his legal works.

Maimonides is thought to have lived in a golden age of Spanish Jewry, and while there is in a sense in which this is true, it can also be misleading. Apart from the hardship of the Exile—Maimonides as a youth was compelled to flee with his family from Muslim Spain owing to persecution by the Almohades—the Jewish community was in a state of internal crisis. Because the very law governing Jews in far-flung places was in a state of confusion, Maimonides devoted much of his life to clarifying

3. E.g., Plato, *Phaedo* 82A–B, *Republic* 430C, 485A–486D; Aristotle, *Nic. Eth.* 1178a9–b7. See also below, chap. 1, n. 5. Plato, unlike Aristotle, does not treat "ethics" as a distinct subject matter.

4. *Fī Tadbī Aṣ-Ṣiḥḥat* [*On the Management of Health*], p. 68; *Ethical Writings*, pp. 107–8; also in Bar-Sela, Hoff, and Faris, pp. 25–26. *Maqāla fī al-Rabw* [*Treatise on Asthma*], Judeo-Arabic text, Paris, Bibliothèque Nationale, MS Hébreu 1211, chap. 8; *Sefer ha-Qatseret*, p. 17.

and giving a lucid structure to Jewish law.[5] There was little hope of guidance from the preachers of his day, whom Maimonides regarded as grossly incompetent.[6] Jewish piety was in a state of decay, if not floundering upon a parochial foolishness.[7] In a letter to his disciple, Joseph ben Judah, Maimonides goes so far as to advise him to imitate the conduct of the "holy men" of their time, namely, the Sufis.[8] Maimonides implies that were no (or very few) contemporaneous models of Jewish piety for Joseph to follow. Jews frequently did not seem to know that the "duties of ethics" are part of religion;[9] there was even some justification for such ignorance owing to the uncertain status of "ethics" within the biblical-rabbinic tradition. What was required under the circumstances was the sort of enlightenment that Maimonides sought to achieve through his writings on the Law.

5. *Sefer ha-Madda^c*, p. 4b.

6. *CM*, Sanhedrin, 10.1, p. 201; *'Iggrot ha-Rambam*, p. 65 (*Ethical Writings*, p. 121); *Guide*, 2.29 [65b].

7. Maimonides, for instance, testifies that he himself has seen some pious Jews ("virtuous men") who prohibit singing Arabic songs that laud generosity and courage, but they do not object to songs in the Hebrew language praising despicable things (*CM*, Avot, 1.17, p. 419). In *EC*, he is critical of the ascetic practices of certain pious Jews (chap. 4, pp. 482–83).

8. See *'Iggrot ha-Rambam*, p. 16, and Baneth's remark, p. 10.

9. Ibid., p. 63; *Ethical Writings*, p. 120.

I
The Commentary
on the Mishnah

ONE

Eight Chapters: The Adaptation of Philosophic Ethics to the Jewish Community

The Maimonidean discussion of ethics in *Eight Chapters* can be described, broadly, as Aristotelian: "ethics" is understood in terms of character traits; the correct standard for ordering them is the mean; moral virtue is distinguished from intellectual virtue; and so on. This characterization, however, can only be a starting point. We can best bring to light certain distinctive features of *EC* by noting how it differs from the *Nicomachean Ethics*. What most evidently distinguishes *EC* is the presence of biblical and rabbinic quotations; they manifest an interplay, perhaps a tension, between the Jewish tradition and philosophy. The philosophic components themselves are not identified as Aristotelian; Maimonides says in the preface that he draws upon both Greek ("ancient") and Muslim ("modern") philosophic works. In the main body of the text he refers on occasion to "the philosophers," "Greek philosophy," and so forth. He regards the philosophers as such—and not merely Aristotle (or Alfarabi)—as having a particular point of view. He therefore refers in the medical writings simply to "philosophic ethics."[1]

It would be risky to venture an account of Maimonides' view of philosophic morality *simpliciter*. His discussion of philosophic ethics is, as we have indicated, always within the framework of a larger work whose overriding purpose affects the presentation. He highlights certain matters in one work (or section of a work) that are provisionally disregarded in another. Since he sometimes even casts doubt upon the rectitude of the mean, it is necessary to ask why the middle way is stressed in

1. See above, p. 5.

9

EC.[2] The introduction of philosophic ethics into *EC* affects how he discusses other topics, such as the reasons for the commandments and the meaning of prophecy; hence these subjects sometimes come to light in different ways in *EC* and in the *Guide*. Philosophic ethics in turn is affected by being housed in a commentary on the Law; Maimonides adapts "philosophic ethics" to the needs of the Jewish community.

As part of the *Commentary on the Mishnah*, *EC* forms the introduction to Maimonides' commentary on Pirqei Avot (he refers to the latter simply as Avot). The express purpose of *EC* is to explain the "hidden meanings" of Avot (*EC*, preface). Maimonides brings to light matters which are by no means evident from the plain meaning of the text. But since philosophy was opposed in some circles as an alien source of instruction, he proceeds cautiously: he illuminates Avot through a philosophic reflection which is itself kept in the shade. Thus, not only Avot (as interpreted by Maimonides) but *EC* itself contains an esoteric dimension; the incongruity between philosophy and the Law is muted. If the multilayered character of *EC* is not recognized, one is tempted to ascribe an extraordinary naïveté to Maimonides. A sober and usually judicious scholar has this to say: "Maimonides is an Aristotelian, and he endeavors to harmonize the intellectualism and theorism of the Stagirite with the diametrically opposed ethics and religion of the Hebrew Bible. And he is apparently unaware of the yawning gulf extending between them."[3] To think that someone with the intellectual acuity of Maimonides would have missed that abyss hardly does him justice. True, he emphasizes the similarities between philosophy and the Law, but he was compelled to do so to convince his readers that the use of philosophic concepts is not detrimental to the interests of the Jewish tradition. That he proceeds with circumspection is indicated by his express state-

2. See the discussion of ethics in the medical works cited in note 4 of the introduction. In *Guide* 1.54 [66a], Maimonides even says that "all the passions are evil." In this context he speaks of the prophet's need, in governing a city, to imitate God's attributes. Since God has no passions, it would be inappropriate for a prophetic ruler to make decisions based upon any passion; when dispensing justice he should look solely to the deserts of the individual.

3. Isaac Husik, *A History of Medieval Jewish Philosophy*, p. 300.

ment that he refrains from identifying his philosophic sources to avoid offending any of his readers (*EC*, preface).

Biblical and rabbinic quotations are sometimes deployed to conceal the philosophic content of *EC*. Maimonides conveys the impression, for instance, that the doctrine of the mean is based upon the biblical verse, "The Torah of the Lord is perfect, making wise the simple, restoring the soul" (Ps. 19.8; chap. 4, p. 383)—*EC* contains no indication of the philosophic provenance of the middle way. But such verses do not serve merely as a kind of camouflage. Maimonides treats them as having a significance in their own right, though he relies upon philosophy to make their meaning evident. Thus he interprets the verse just cited to mean that a simple person can become wise by following the commandments because they furnish a discipline for attaining the middle way. Maimonides takes quite seriously—and he makes intelligible—the psalmist's statement that the Torah makes wise the simple. The "wisdom" referred to in this instance is not theoretical in nature. But conduct that brings about an equilibrium within the soul manifests a form of wisdom that "restores" the soul.

As is evident from his treatment of the psalm, Maimonides assumes the existence of a latent content, or "hidden meaning," not only in Avot but in other Jewish sources as well. While this way of dealing with a text can have revolutionary implications, it also expresses a reverence for the tradition, a determination to unearth whatever truth is contained in the text being explicated. As a mode of interpretation, it is both radical and conservative. It is capable of bringing to light whatever implicit agreement exists between philosophy and the Law; where such agreement requires introducing philosophic terminology to become explicit, that terminology can be introduced. The assumption of an implicit meaning in the text enables Maimonides to minimize the conflict between philosophy and his Jewish sources. It also permits him to conceal the conflict where he deems that to be necessary.

Let us begin with the surface of the work. Since Maimonides underscores the similarities between philosophy and Judaism, it will be instructive to see how he regards them. The Jewish quotations sometimes reveal genuine similarities even concerning matters where differences can also be discerned. We may briefly note the following points of agreement between philosophy and the Law:

1. Wickedness is harmful to the evil-doer. Philosophy regards such harm as a disease of the soul, thus conceiving of it differently from Scripture (*EC*, chap. 3). But the Bible broadly agrees that dire consequences afflict the wicked. Proverbs, for instance, states that "[t]he way of the wicked is like darkness; they know not why they stumble" (4.19; *EC*, chap. 3). Isaiah (59.2) speaks of "sins" (not the soul's diseases) as separating man from God (*EC*, chap. 7).

2. A man should examine his way of life so that he may discover his faults and correct them. Maimonides cites a rabbinic dictum that refers to the need to "appraise" one's paths in order to attain salvation from God (*EC*, chap. 4, end). A comparable biblical view can be found in Lamentations: "Let us search and examine our ways and return to the Lord" (3.40; quoted in *EC*, chap. 8).

3. Moral perfection is impossible to sustain. Even a perfect man will at one time or another discover faults in his soul, for, as Maimonides says, "a man inevitably has defects" (*EC*, chap. 4). To show the convergence of Scripture and philosophy concerning this matter, he cites a verse from Ecclesiastes which suggests that moral perfection cannot even be attained: "There is no man who is just upon the earth, who does only good and does not sin" (7.20).

4. A good man enjoys performing the right actions. This is supported by a verse from Proverbs: "To do justice is a joy to the righteous, but dismay to evil-doers" (21.15; *EC*, chap. 6).

5. Man is free to determine his actions. The biblical view is expressed in such verses as, "See I have set before you this day life and good, death and evil . . . choose life" (Deut. 30.15, 19; *EC*, chap. 8).

The assumption of human freedom is perhaps the most clear-cut area of agreement between philosophy and the Law. At any rate, Maimonides is most emphatic about the agreement in this instance: "You should know [lit., As for you, know] that our Law and Greek philosophy agree that all of man's actions are given over to him" (*EC*, chap. 8, p. 397). The broader question here is whether a man can affect his natural temperaments through his actions, and consequently whether he is free to acquire the moral virtues. Now someone might be able to perform the right actions and yet not acquire a particular moral virtue because of the strength of a refractory temperament. Maimonides refers to such instances in the *Guide* (1.34 [40a]) but not in *EC*; he prefers to pass over such difficulties and to stress, rather, the need to make every effort to acquire the moral virtues. The extreme case, though, does not do away with the above-mentioned agreement between the Law and philosophy—which is restricted to the view that man is free to determine his actions.

The discussion of the human soul in chapter 1, where a five-part Aristotelian division of the soul is set forth, is clearly based upon philosophic sources and has no Jewish counterpart. This chapter accordingly contains almost no Jewish quotations, although the single quote at the end of the chapter is noteworthy: "Indeed, without knowledge a soul is not good" (Prov. 19.2). This quite simple statement does not at first glance seem to be of particular interest; it comes as no surprise that the need for wisdom is taught in Proverbs. But more than that is indicated by the verse, namely, that a soul devoid of knowledge is defective—a view that discloses some common ground, albeit limited, between Proverbs and Greek philosophy.

A reflection upon the human soul, taken by itself, does not yield the goal of attaining knowledge of God; hence Maimonides says nothing about this goal in chapter 1. In chapter 5, where it *is* spoken about, the basis appears to be a number of Jewish quotations. The final goal of human life, as set forth in *EC*, is affected by the need to establish an accord between philosophy and the Jewish tradition. In the *Logic*, which is his only work (besides the medical writings) that does not presuppose the validity of the Law, Maimonides refers to man's final end simply as the "apprehension of intelligibles" (chap. 9). Still, the highest subject of *theoria* may be said to be God Himself—as Maimonides indicates in a number of places. In the Introduction to *CM*, for instance, he calls the apprehension of God's unity "the greatest [or most exalted] intelligible" (p. 42). From among the possible ways to formulate the goal of philosophy, Maimonides selects one that forges some sort of bond between philosophy and the Law. To say that the goal of *theoria* is to attain knowledge of God seems unobjectionable in a commentary on the Law.

The problem of whether such knowledge is accessible to human beings might appear to go beyond what Maimonides can be expected to deal with in a work devoted to ethics. He does, however, address it in a brief but telling manner. To know that God has been apprehended, the deity would have to be known in His total difference from all other beings; it is, however, beyond man's power to be certain that such an apprehension has been attained (*EC*, chap. 7). Relying upon the verse, "You shall see My back, but My face shall not be seen" (Exod. 33.23), Maimonides compares the human predicament to that of a man who sees the back of someone in the distance whom he thinks is his friend but whom he cannot identify with certainty. Similarly, there is an ever-present possibility that one is deceived in thinking that God has been apprehended. This view regarding the limits of human knowledge is not confined to *EC*; it is fully in accord with the *Guide's* position that the essence or true reality of God cannot be known by man.[4]

4. In *Guide*, 1.37, Maimonides also cites the biblical verse, "You shall see My back, but My face shall not be seen"; he interprets the latter clause as meaning that "the true reality of My existence as it veritably is cannot be grasped." Maimonides adduces support from an interpretation of Onqelos, according to which (as glossed by Maimonides) man is capable of grasping the "true reality" (*ḥaqīqa*) only of things endowed with form and matter. It seems to me that this is an elaboration of the view that the "true reality" of the deity (and also the separate intellects) cannot be apprehended by man; it does not imply that man should limit himself to the pursuit of natural science, nor that human happiness is restricted to political matters. A radically skeptical inference is warranted only if one assumes that an intellectual apprehension (*idrāk*) that falls short of knowing the "true reality" of the deity implies that no knowledge whatsoever of God is possible for man. In the passage from *EC*, as also in various places in the *Guide*, Maimonides intimates that an enigmatic perception, lacking certainty, is possible for man. The very notion of perception (*idrāk*), as applied to intellectual cognition, implies the possibility of

Maimonides nonetheless maintains that a person should direct all the powers of his soul toward attaining knowledge of God (*EC*, chap. 5). According to *EC*, ethics is dependent upon the possibility of metaphysics (divine science). What can be known with certainty in metaphysics is admittedly limited, but without metaphysics, ethics is impossible. That is, at any rate, the vantage point from which ethical conduct is regarded in *EC*, whatever Maimonides might say elsewhere (cf. *Guide*, 2.40). If a man does not devote himself to *theoria*, he is in danger of lapsing into a hedonistic way of life (*EC*, chap. 5; see also *CM*, Ḥagigah, 2.1, p. 378). True, the middle way has a basis in what exists by nature: it enables a man to be "natural" (*EC*, chap. 4, p. 383). What is natural appears to refer here to temperaments that are well ordered, to a healthy state of the soul. The middle way produces a healthy soul, but the end of a healthy soul cannot be specified without referring to metaphysics. Ethics is intimately connected with metaphysics because training one's character is necessary to prepare oneself to attain knowledge of God.

*

The contemplative orientation of *EC* sets this work apart from Aristotle's *Nicomachean Ethics*, where ethics is closely associated with politics. Much of the *Ethics* is devoted to the gentleman as distinct from the philosopher, and the nobility of the Aristotelian gentleman is preeminently displayed in the political arena.[5] In *EC*, however, ethics is severed from the political life, that is, the life of a statesman or ruler.

---

greater and lesser degrees of certainty (cf. *Guide*, 1.59). For a different line of interpretation, see Shlomo Pines, "The Limitations of Human Knowledge According to Al-Farabi, ibn Bajja, and Maimonides," in *Studies in Medieval Jewish History and Literature*, ed. I. Twersky, pp. 82–109, esp. p. 92; idem, "The Philosophical Purport of Maimonides' Halachic Works and the Purport of *The Guide of the Perplexed*," in *Maimonides and Philosophy*, pp. 6–7.

5. The gentleman does what is noble for its own sake (e.g., *Nic. Eth.* 1105a31–32, 1120a23–29); for him, "acting well" (*eupraxia*) is an end in itself (1140b7). He possesses all the moral virtues plus practical wisdom. The philosopher, however, does not need all the moral virtues, but insofar as he is a mere man and lives with other people, he will want to have some of them (1178a22–b7). Note that because of his *political* nature, he conducts himself in accordance with moral virtue: "[I]nsofar as he is a human being and lives with

We might have expected Maimonides to discuss the moral qualities suitable for a judge in *EC*, for he says in the Introduction to *CM* that Avot contains moral precepts apposite to a judge's conduct (p. 29). But *EC*, the "Introduction to Avot," contains no such discussion. A judge is in any case only roughly a "political man." He is surely not a "political man" in the manner of the *politikos* of the *Nicomachean Ethics*, whose activities presuppose the sort of freedom that a Jewish judge does not have. The latter's range of action is carefully circumscribed by the Law; he does not possess the flexibility that is essential to the practical wisdom of the Aristotelian gentleman. Furthermore, a Jewish sage acts, so to speak, as a "private man" in settling disputes and answering questions regarding the halakhah.[6] Maimonides, at any rate, opposed the practice of making judgeships salaried positions (*CM*, Avot, 4.7). This whole matter is undoubtedly complex; but regardless of how a judge's role in the community must be finally understood, Maimonides refrains from discussing ethics from the standpoint of the needs of a judge in *EC*.

Morality is understood there as a preparation for prophecy. Is not the political dimension of prophecy manifest? What is surprising—and illuminating—is that Maimonides altogether omits political considerations from his discussion of prophecy in *EC*. Someone who devotes himself entirely to attaining knowledge of God is understood to be on the level of the prophets.[7] The prophetic way of life is interpreted here in the light of the solitary individual's quest for knowledge of God. Nothing is said in *EC* about the legislative function of prophecy—which

---

a number of people, he chooses to do virtuous acts" (1178b5–6); living with other people, such as family, friends, etc., suffices to fix man's political nature (1097b8–11). It is, however, specifically with a view to man's contemplative end that Maimonides discusses the moral virtues in *EC*.

6. Cf. the twofold classification of human tasks below, p. 18. Maimonides indicates in the passage cited there that a "knower" aims at perfecting his own soul; if he sometimes acts as a judge, this role is, as it were, incidental to his main work.

7. More precisely: "If a man happens to exist in this condition, I would not say that he is inferior to the propets. I refer to a man who directs all the powers of his soul solely toward God . . ." (*EC*, chap. 5, p. 390; *Ethical Writings*, p. 77).

is underscored in the *Guide*. Nor is anything said about the prophet's power of imagination, which the *Guide* regards as essential to his being able to instruct the people in both theoretical and practical matters. Furthermore, the *Guide* stresses a prophet's need for boldness to deal with political exigencies— Moses for instance had to be bold in order to demand that Pharaoh release the Hebrew slaves (2.38)—but *EC* contains no such discussion of this quality. It is, moreover, revealing that in *EC* Maimonides uses an emphatically nonpolitical metaphor to refer to a prophet's vices: they are "veils" that hinder the intellectual perception of the deity. An entire chapter of *EC* is devoted to the "veils" of the prophets (chap. 7). David and Solomon, those great kings of Israel, are cited as examples of prophets who had a moral vice, or "veil," that impeded but did not obviate contemplation; their political feats do not come under consideration here.[8]

EC of course contains only a partial picture of prophecy. Another aspect is highlighted in the Introduction to *CM* (pp. 11–14), where we learn that a prophet has the authority to determine which political circumstances require the temporary abrogation of a law. The examples given by Maimonides concern primarily what is called for in wartime, as when a prophet commands that the Sabbath be broken for the sake of forging weapons of war or to engage in battle. But in *EC* Maimonides says nothing about the prophet's authority to make such political judgments.

As for man's political nature, it is not entirely disregarded in *EC*, but it is treated in a peripheral manner, as a kind of adjunct to the virtue of moderation: for a man's bodily needs to be satisfied in accordance with the mean, he has to live in some community and hence ought to behave justly (chap. 4, p. 383). Maimonides glosses over the value of the moral virtues for establishing decent human relations[9]—a theme that has prom-

8. Cf. Jeffrey Macy, "The Theological-Political Teaching of *Shemonah Peraqim:* A Reappraisal of the Text and of Its Arabic Sources." Macy also takes note of the absence of any reference to the prophet's imaginative faculty in *EC*.

9. Cf. the passing reference to the meaning of *shalom* in a verse from Zechariah cited in *EC*, chap. 4, p. 384.

inence in the *Guide*. He does not use the argument that he presents in the *Guide* supporting a middle way in ethics, an argument based expressly upon man's political nature (2.40). There he contends that the standard of the mean modulates the greatly divergent natural dispositions found among people, thereby making a harmonious society possible. But in *EC* he defends the middle way as being necessary for the individual's own health of soul, which in turn is needed to devote oneself to contemplation.

The downplaying of the political domain in *EC* is not an isolated phenomenon in the *Commentary on the Mishnah*. There is no mention of the political life in some passages in other parts of *CM* where one might have expected a reference to it. Thus, in the Introduction to *CM*, Maimonides poses the following question: If the purpose of human life is to attain theoretical knowledge, but most people are unable to achieve this goal, why do they exist? The answer, much condensed, is that they practice arts needed by the city (*madīna*), such as farming, weaving, and the building of homes. The "knower," however, exists for his own sake (pp. 43–44). (The other people also exist to provide companionship for the "knower.") There is no reference to the need for a king or statesman to rule the city. This division into two classes of people is redolent of a "foundation of our Law" formulated by Maimonides to show why gambling is scorned by the Jewish tradition: A man should occupy himself (1) with acquiring knowledge by which he perfects himself, or (2) with an art of trade that is useful for preserving life (*CM*, Sanhedrin, 3.3). Again, nothing is said about the political life.

The governance of the Jewish people by the Torah partly explains the abstraction from the political life in such passages as these, as well as in *EC*. In his *Logic* Maimonides observes that philosophic works dealing with the governance of the city are superfluous "in these times" because "people are governed by divine commands" (chap. 14). According to the philosophers who possessed the greatest authority for Maimonides, the governance of the best city is through living intelligence as distinct from law.[10] Since the Jewish nation is ruled by the Torah, there is no need for works that advocate rule by human beings such as a Platonic philosopher-king or the *politikoi* of the *Nicomachean Ethics*. And because the Jewish community has no strictly "political men," Maimonides cannot assimilate ethics to the political life.

It is not simply the rule of the Torah that determines how Maimonides deals with the "political domain" in *EC*. The nature of the human soul has a decisive effect upon how political matters are envisaged. The form of man's soul is the intellect, which is theoretical in its nature (chap. 1, end); the form is understood here as the same as the end that governs the ordering of the parts. Man's contemplative end dramatically reduces the dignity of the political life. This is quite clear from the discussion of the superiority of the contemplative life in the Introduction to *CM:* "It is impossible that the end of man be that he eat or drink or engage in sexual intercourse or build a wall or *become a king* because [1] these activities are accidents in relation to him, they do not add to his substance; [2] moreover, all these activities are performed not only by him but also by some other species of animals" (p. 41, emphasis added). Political activity, then, does not enhance a man's substance; it does not concern what is truly "one's own," namely, intellection. Nor is it distinctive of human life, for some species of animals also have rulers ("kings").

But is not man's rationality revealed through speech, and is not speech indicative of man's political nature? For Maimonides, man's political nature is based upon his bodily needs rather than speech;[11] The possession of speech is not what makes man a political animal. As for the "speech" or "reason" (*nuṭq*) that distinguishes man from the other animals, it consists in "the formation [or conception] of intelligibles" (*CM*, Introd. p. 42). Intelligibles are concerned with the true and the

10. See Leo Strauss, "Maimonides' Statement on Political Science," in *What Is Political Philosophy?* pp. 163–64.

11. *EC*, chap. 4, p. 383; *CM*, Introd., pp. 43–44. Cf. *Guide* 1.72 [103a], 3.27 [59b–60a].

false as distinct from the noble and the base. The essential activity of the intellect is apprehension, which is radically private (*Guide*, 1.2, 1.68).

Thus man's rational nature has no essential connection with the life of the community. The emphatically theoretical conception of the soul's form in *EC* is the ultimate basis for the ordering of morality by the goal of contemplation. This view of the human soul is accordingly the foundation for the abstraction from the political life in *EC*.

*

The position of the Jews in the Diaspora obviously differs from the political independence taken for granted by Aristotle in his discussion of ethics or, for that matter, by Alfarabi in his political works. This, too, has to be taken into consideration to understand Maimonides' procedure in *EC*. He could hardly have set forth a morality with a view to political rule when the Jewish people lived under the subjugation of the Exile.

Maimonides does not speak of the Exile in the strictly ethical sections of *EC*, but toward the end of the work he refers to its severity, to "our being strangers and cut off" from the land of Israel; it is a time of the "victory [or domination] of the religious communities over us" (chap. 8, p. 404). Elsewhere in *CM* the Exile is evaluated from the standpoint of how it comports with human virtue: it "hinders us from acquiring all of the virtues" (Commentary on Sanhedrin, 10.1, p. 207). Maimonides was clearly not oblivious to the danger that political subjugation poses for the development of a man's virtue. But the effect of the Exile upon his discussion of morality in *EC* is not so obvious.

In the ethical section of the Code he says something about how to deal with the adversity of the Exile that is helpful for our purposes. "If all the countries that he [a man] knows or hears about follow a way that is not good, *as in our time* . . . he should dwell alone in solitude. As it is said: 'Let him dwell alone and be silent'" (HD, 6.1; Lam. 3.28; emphasis added). A morality articulated for the solitary contemplative life, such as we find in *EC* (as well as in HD, chaps. 1–4), admirably suits this counsel. I am not suggesting that the Exile is the sole factor or even the main one determining how Maimonides approaches ethics in *EC*, but that, as a master of classical political philosophy, he was not blind to the relation between ethics and politics; he could not have ignored the political circumstances of the Jewish people. The morality of *EC* meets the needs of a people living in exile.

Among the virtues set forth in *EC* are humility, modesty, and contentment (chap. 4)—qualities that are useful for dealing with a hostile environment. To take just the example of contentment, its suitability for the Exile can be seen from Maimonides' statement that a person who rejoices in his lot "is content with what the times bring him and is not pained at what they do not bring" (chap. 7). Let us also note that the contemplative life calls for keeping speech to a minimum (chap. 5), a rule of conduct useful for the Exile. In the *Epistle to Yemen* Maimonides refers to the need to endure in silence the humiliation to which Jews were subjected under Islam.[12] Further, the focus of *EC* upon moral self-correction, which is applicable on an individual level irrespective of whether Jews have political independence, is apposite to the Exile.

In the *Guide*, when speaking about the melancholia produced by the Exile, Maimonides quotes the following rabbinic statement to prove that a prophet needs a joyful frame of mind: "Prophecy does not come to rest through languor nor through sadness but through something joyful." He adds: "For what 'languor' or 'sadness' can befall a man in any state that would be stronger than that due to his being a thrall slave in bondage to the ignorant" (2.36 [80a])? In chapter 7 of *EC*, Maimonides cites that very rabbinic passage to show that sadness is detrimental to the contemplative life. In addition to the suggestive parallel with the *Guide*, there is evidence in *EC* that he wanted to counteract the despondency produced by the Exile.

That a joyful disposition should be cultivated is a recurrent theme of this work, found not only in chapter 7 but also, emphatically, in chapter 5 and, more subtly, in chapter 4. In chapter 5 we are told that "[if] the humor of black bile agitates [a

12. *Moses Maimonides' Epistle to Yemen*, p. 96 (Judeo-Arabic text), p. xviii (English trans.).

man] he should make it cease by listening to songs and various kinds of melodies, by walking in gardens, etc." Wall decorations and the like are superfluous for the contemplative man "unless he intends thereby to give delight to his soul for the sake of its health and to drive sickness from it, so that it will be clear and pure to receive the sciences" (ibid.). Looking at beautiful objects and fine buildings, listening to lovely music, having an attractive dwelling and even an attractive wife—all these are recommended by Maimonides, I suggest, to counteract the baleful effect of political subjugation. In addition, as he says, looking at beautiful objects and listening to beautiful melodies refresh a soul weary from study.

A complementary theme is to be found in chapter 4, where Maimonides fashions a forceful attack upon asceticism. He cautions against afflicting the body by fasting, rising at night for prayer, abstaining from eating meat and drinking wine, and so on. The oppressive conditions of the Exile lie in the background of his vigorous opposition to bodily affliction: the Exile makes life difficult enough, without a man taking upon himself the burden of ascetic practices. The Law itself, Maimonides says, already inclines toward the extreme; Jews should not go even further and be stricter with themselves than the Law requires.

To buttress his attack upon asceticism, he cites a number of verses from the Book of Zechariah that also indicate that the Exile lies in the background of the articulation of ethics in *EC* (chap. 4). Zechariah was asked by some people whether they should continue observing a fast that had been instituted for only one day a year. He answers by disparaging their motivation on a number of fast days, and then declares that all such days shall become times of rejoicing. The motif of joy is again apparent. Zechariah says: "Thus says the Lord of hosts: The fast of the fourth month and the fast of the fifth and the fast of the seventh and the fast of the tenth shall be for the house of Judah joy and gladness and cheerful seasons. Love truth and peace" (8.19). The same verse from the Book of Zechariah is cited in the Code to prove that the fasts associated with the

Exile will be eliminated in the Messianic era (H. Taʿaniyyot, 5.19). By citing a verse in *EC* with such a Messianic resonance and treating its message as relevant in the here and now, Maimonides intimates that fasting in the face of the troubles brought on by the Exile is inappropriate. (Jewish law requires that a fast be decreed when a special tax is placed upon Jews or when obeying one of the commandments is interdicted [ibid., 2.3].)

The effect of the Exile in tandem with the supremacy of the Law is discernible in the way in which Maimonides makes use of Alfarabi's *Selected Chapters,* an important source of the philosophic passages of *EC*.[13] The purpose of Alfarabi's work is to instruct a king or statesman; Maimonides excises the political content from the passages incorporated into *EC*.[14] According to Alfarabi, the king or statesman acts as a physician of the soul, healing the moral diseases found within the city. But in *EC* the soul's physician is a sage acting on a private basis: "Those with sick souls need to *seek out* the wise men, who are the physicians of the soul" (chap. 3, emphasis added). When

13. See Herbert Davidson, "Maimonides' *Shemonah Peraqim* and Alfarabi's *Fuṣūl al-Madanī.*" Since Davidson's article appeared, a superior critical edition of the *Fuṣūl* has been published under the title, *Fuṣūl Muntazaʿa* [*Selected Chapters*], ed. Fauzi M. Najjar. I am translating *fuṣūl* as "chapters" to bring out the connection of Alfarabi's work with Maimonides' own *fuṣūl*—as he himself sometimes refers to *EC* (in the "Commentary on Avot," for instance, he occasionally refers to it as "the preceding chapters" [e.g., 1.7, 3.17, 4.1]).

14. Davidson rightly notes that Maimonides abstracts from the political content of Alfarabi's work (Davidson, "Maimonides' *Shemonah Peraqim*," pp. 47–50). His explanation differs somewhat from the one offered here; in particular, he neglects the significance of the Exile for Maimonides' procedure. Davidson also overstates the importance of the *Fuṣūl* for *EC*. Maimonides himself says that he makes use of the works of both ancient and modern philosophers (preface). Even when Maimonides draws upon the *Fuṣūl,* the context of *EC* within the *Commentary on the Mishnah* has to be kept carefully in view. For example, as Davidson correctly observes, the enumeration of the moral virtues in chapter 4 is largely taken from the *Fuṣūl.* But Maimonides also includes the virtue of contentment (*qanāʿa*), which is omitted from the *Fuṣūl;* its presence in *EC* is dictated by the needs of an introduction to Avot as well as the Exile (see below, pp. 25–26). Davidson assumes that Maimonides had a different text of the *Fuṣūl* before him, but the critical edition of Najjar, in agreement with Dunlop's edition, omits "contentment."

comparing the treatment for the body and soul, Maimonides notes that the art of medicine treats the diseases of the body, but he does not identify the art that treats the soul's diseases (ibid.). If we consider a parallel passage in the *Selected Chapters*, we find that according to Alfarabi the art in question is the art of politics.[15] The physician of the soul in *EC* practices a truncated form of the art of politics. Since it is not exercised over the entire community, it lacks the range and flexibility of the political art. The Jewish sage can, however, take into consideration the particular needs of the individual and tailor the treatment accordingly.

At the very end of the *Commentary on the Mishnah*, Maimonides makes a pregnant remark concerning his own suffering in the Exile (he mentions it to justify asking indulgence for any errors in the work). After referring to his wanderings, he notes that perhaps he has received his reward, adding cryptically that "Exile atones for sin." The Code amplifies upon how he understands this adage: A penitent might choose to exile himself from his place of residence, for "exile atones for sin because it makes him [the penitent] subdued, humble, and lowly in spirit [*shefal ruah*]" (H. Teshuvah, 2.5; cf. 3.18). Although this statement does not expressly refer to the Exile of the Jewish people, it implies that exile as such is useful for moral self-discipline. We might add that Maimonides regards self-abasement as salutary for overcoming the vice of arrogance (*CM*, Avot, 4.4).

Whatever benefit might be salvageable from the Exile, Maimonides undoubtedly stresses its overall harmfulness. His insistence upon a middle way in ethics—despite the Law's inclination toward the extreme—aims at assisting people to become more natural under circumstances that thwart naturalness, that is, that hinder Jews from acquiring complete moral virtue. Keeping in mind the Exile's bearing upon the content of *EC* helps to explain some of the emphases of the work, not the least of which is the firm opposition to afflicting the body.

15. Ed. Najjar, no. 4; English trans. by D. M. Dunlop under the title *Aphorisms of the Statesman*, no. 3.

At the same time, Maimonides does not neglect the needs of an era of political independence. The overarching goal of attaining knowledge of God is certainly in accord with his conception of the "days of the Messiah"; the ethics of *EC* would be suitable for such a time.[16] Although in *CM* there is nothing comparable to the "Laws of Kings and Their Wars" in the *Mishneh Torah*, this only reflects the more limited horizon of a commentary on the *Mishnah*. There is reason to believe that in *CM* itself Maimonides anticipates what would be necessary at a time of political independence or to achieve independence. For example, when discussing the different kinds of friendship, Maimonides illustrates the "friendship of utility" by citing the example of a king's friendship with his army (Commentary on Avot, 1.6). Elsewhere in *CM* Maimonides even hints at the possibility of war with Islam: when explaining the meaning of the expression, "permissible war" (*milḥemet reshut*), he gives not only the conventional examples of war with Ammon and Moab but also war with Ishmael (Commentary on Sanhedrin, 1.5). In addition, we may recall that when illustrating a prophet's authority to temporarily abrogate a commandment, he refers to what is necessary in wartime. In *EC* itself, although Maimonides scants the need for courage for the contemplative life, he does single it out for special attention to show that a virtue can be acquired by the right sort of training (chap. 8, beg.). By including courage in the account of the moral virtues in chapter 4, he goes beyond what is sanctioned by the rabbinic discussion in Avot, which contains no reference to such a virtue. The "mighty man" (*gibbor*), according to Avot, is someone who conquers his evil impulse (4.1).

*

The goal of contemplation controls the discussion of the moral virtues in *EC*. But they are, secondarily, accommodated to a Jewish setting. Besides the subtle effect that the Exile has upon *EC*, its position within the *Commentary on the Mishnah* affects the discussion of morality. The moral virtues are partly

16. See also below, p. 195.

adapted to the needs of an introduction to Avot. This helps to explain why—contrary to Aristotle's discussion of the gentleman's morality in the *Nicomachean Ethics*—Maimonides includes humility, contentment, and modesty among the virtues in *EC;* they are particularly appropriate for introducing the text of Avot.

1. Humility is the subject of a number of precepts in Avot (e.g., 4.4, 4.2, and 5.17); this topic will be discussed in detail later.
2. The virtue of contentment, which lies in the mean between greed and laziness, is prescribed by the rabbinic dictum, "Who is the rich man? He who rejoices with his lot" (Avot, 4.1; *EC*, chap. 7). According to Maimonides, this virtue is also referred to by the rabbinic praise of a "good eye," the "evil eye" being indicative of greed.[17] Contentment is, moreover, needed to obey the prohibition against using the Torah as a "spade to dig with," that is, against relying upon knowledge of the Torah to obtain a means of livelihood (*CM*, Avot, 4.7). This virtue undergirds the Jewish notion of study "for its own sake"; it is also useful for the self-sufficiency appropriate to the philosophic life.
3. The virtue of modesty, or sense of shame, comports with the rabbinic praise of the man who is "shame-faced," *bosh panim* (Avot, 5.18). According to *EC*, the virtue lies between the extremes of impudence and shyness; the latter extreme is condemned by the rabbinic dictum, "The shy person does not learn" (Avot, 2.6). A sense of shame is not necessarily part of the doctrine of the mean; Maimonides does not include it in his account of the middle way in the Code (HD, 1.4). This corroborates the importance of Avot for his including modesty/sense of shame as a virtue in *EC*. In the "Commentary on Avot" (5.18), to prove that a "sense of shame," *bushah* (he uses the Hebrew term), is indeed a virtue, Maimonides cites a talmudic passage which states that

17. *CM*, Avot, 2.12. See also the "Commentary on Avot," 5.17, where Maimonides interprets Abraham's "good eye," referred to in the text of Avot, as indicative of the virtue of contentment.

having a sense of shame is one of the characteristics of the Jewish people. He also links this quality to the "fear" or awe of God that the Israelites experienced at Mt. Sinai; a form of modesty was displayed by the people in the presence of God.

As interpreted by Maimonides, modesty/sense of shame is not contrary to the pursuit of knowledge. A certain daring is necessary in the inquiry into theoretical matters, but this is not the same as the vice of impudence. Thus, in the *Guide,* Maimonides observes that Aristotle did not think that his investigation of the heavens exhibited shamelessness; he was not "obtrusive" or overly hasty in his quest for knowledge of the highest things (*Guide,* 1.5 [16a]). The virtue itself, that is, a sense of shame, can provide the impetus for a great achievement. Maimonides' own shame at the disgraceful condition into which Jewish law had fallen was a factor that motivated him to compile a well-ordered, lucid code of law. The following epigraph stands at the beginning of the *Mishneh Torah:* "Then I shall not be ashamed when I consider all of Your commandments" (Ps. 119.6).

In spite of the fact that Maimonides' account of the moral virtues is to some extent accommodated to the Jewish tradition, that account is basically identifiable as philosophic ethics. This can be substantiated by considering the above-mentioned talmudic passages justifying modesty/sense of shame as a virtue.[18] The *Talmud* refers to three characteristics of Jews: they have a sense of shame, they are compassionate, and they perform deeds of loving-kindness (or beneficence). Maimonides, however, does not specify a virtue for compassion in *EC.* A middle way with respect to mercy is not indispensable for a healthy soul; it is not a prerequisite for the contemplative life.

Most of the moral virtues adumbrated in chapter 4 of *EC* have no corresponding term in the biblical-rabbinic tradition. In his Hebrew translation of *EC,* Ibn Tibbon had to coin or refashion terms for almost all of them—the exceptions being humility and sense of shame/modesty ("shame-facedness," *bosh*

18. *CM,* Avot, 5.18; *BT,* Yevamot, 79a.

panim; see Avot, 5.18). This is not to say that the virtues themselves were completely unknown in the Jewish tradition. As
Maimonides points out, it is not necessary that there be a term
for a particular moral virtue in order for the meaning to be
grasped (*EC,* chap. 4, p. 380). For example, he regards "fear of
sin" as roughly the rabbinic equivalent of "moderation" (*CM,*
Avot, 2.10): such fear restrains certain excesses that are also
condemned from the viewpoint of the virtue of moderation.
Still, there is obviously a difference in orientation between
"fear of sin," which takes its bearings from the Law, and "moderation," which is an excellence of the human soul. Even where
there are rough equivalents of the moral virtues in the biblical-
rabbinic tradition, the precise meaning of the quality in question had to be established with the assistance of philosophy.
The schema of the mean gives a new or, at any rate, a more
sharply focused meaning to the traditional terminology.

*

Philosophic ethics is entirely subordinated in *EC* to the goal of
attaining theoretical knowledge, a conception of conduct that
is contrary to the Aristotelian gentleman's way of life. The
gentleman does what is noble for the sake of the noble (*to kalon*); the noble for him is choiceworthy for its own sake, even
though nobility also comprehends what is beneficial for human life.[19] Moral conduct, according to *EC,* is instrumental to a
higher end. This is not to say that the concept of nobility is excluded from the Maimonidean discussion of ethics. A person
who performs an action that is in accord with moral virtue
does what is noble: "noble actions" are defined as those stemming from a healthy soul (chap. 3, beg.).

In *EC* the moral virtues have a rather pedestrian cast. Consider the difference between *EC* and the *Nicomachean Ethics*
concerning the virtues pertaining to material goods. Three
such virtues are specified in *EC:* "generosity," which refers to
the right disposition in giving to others; "liberality," which is

19. Aristotle distinguishes the noble from the advantageous in *Nic. Eth.*
1104b30–34. See also n. 5, above.

the right attitude in spending money upon oneself; and "contentment," which is the right disposition toward acquiring possessions.[20] Since the latter two qualities are not intrinsically noble, Aristotle does not classify them as separate virtues; he stresses the nobility of giving in his discussion of the virtue concerned with wealth. But since for Maimonides the right dispositions toward acquiring and spending money are useful for the soul's health, he treats "contentment" and "liberality" as distinct virtues. "Liberality" is, moreover, needed by the contemplative man to acquire the goods that might be needed to make him cheerful and/or to refresh him following the fatigue from study (cf. chap. 5).

In the "Commentary on Avot" (5.18), in keeping with his espousal of an instrumental morality, Maimonides justifies the occasional use of a moral vice for attaining a worthy end. The use of impudence for rebuking a sinner is the only example he gives there. In support of this position Maimonides cites a biblical verse referring to God's use of guile when dealing with the wicked: "With the crooked You show Yourself devious" (2 Sam. 22.27). When this model for conduct is transposed to a human plane, it justifies the salutary employment of a moral vice. I leave open the question whether "deviousness" ever comports with practical wisdom as understood by Aristotle. The example given by Maimonides, that is, the intelligent use of impudence, is not opposed, however, to the general tenor of the *Nicomachean Ethics*; the great-souled man might display hubris against his enemies (1125a8–9). (It is possible that the Maimonidean interpretation of Avot 5.18—whose plain meaning seems to be the opposite of the gloss—is affected by the philosophic tradition. Avot states that "the brazen man is assigned to Gehinnom.")

Maimonides departs from the teaching in the *Nicomachean Ethics* regarding the unity of the moral virtues, which is dependent upon Aristotle's conception of practical wisdom. The lat-

20. For the meanings of "liberality" (*sakhāʾ*) and "generosity" (*karam*), see *Ethical Writings*, nn. 3 and 4 to the fourth chapter of *EC* (pp. 98–99).

ter is not divisible; for a man to possess practical wisdom, he
must be able to reason well about all matters, which requires
that he have all of the moral virtues.[21] However, according to
Maimonides, not all the moral virtues are needed for a life devoted to *theoria*. Although the contemplative life is incompatible with certain defects, such as rage and melancholia, there
are some moral vices that are not an obstacle to *theoria* (at the
highest level of prophecy, however, all the moral virtues are
necessary). A kind of hierarchy of the moral virtues emerges in
EC, some being more important for contemplation than others
(chap. 7).

The transformation of Aristotle's ethics in *EC* contains a remarkable twist that could easily go unnoticed: practical wisdom is not identified as a virtue. This omission is especially
noteworthy because Maimonides does include a number of virtues belonging to the soul's rational power, but they are all
theoretical in nature (chap. 2). The absence of the virtue of
practical wisdom sets *EC* apart not only from the *Nicomachean Ethics* but also from Alfarabi's treatment of morality in
a number of works, including the *Selected Chapters*.[22] Maimonides clearly goes his own way in this matter. The omission
is cause for wonder.

The authority of the Law poses a difficulty for including
practical wisdom as a virtue. The Law specifies what actions
are obligatory regarding all sorts of matters that for the Aristotelian gentleman would be subject to the deliberation of practical wisdom. Moreover, because the commandments incline
toward an extreme, they cannot be a guideline for Aristotelian
practical wisdom, whose deliberation is directed by the standard of the mean. It is also questionable whether the place of
experience in the formation of the gentleman's practical wisdom is entirely compatible with the Law. If experience plus the

21. Aristotle, *Nic. Eth.* 1144b32–1145a2. The goal of the gentleman's reasoning is set by the moral virtues, which enable him to recognize what is the
noble thing to do (1144a6–9).

22. See, e.g., *Selected Chapters*, ed. Najjar, nos. 33, 39, 41, 85 (Dunlop, nos.
30, 36, 38, 80).

moral virtues suffice for deliberating well about practical matters, one might wonder whether a large portion of the Law is
necessary. Maimonides not only refrains from referring to
"prudence" (ta'aqqul: phronēsis) in EC, but he also makes no
mention of the "practical intellect."[23] It is the practical intellect, according to Alfarabi, that contains the premises which
are acquired through experience and supply the guidance for
human conduct.[24]

The question arises as to why Maimonides does not identify
deliberation, when directed toward a worthy end, as a virtue.
He certainly maintains that deliberation regarding what is
needed to devote oneself to theoria is indispensable. Granted
that the practical wisdom of the gentleman is not appropriate
for EC, isn't there a form of practical wisdom that is suitable
for the contemplative life? The supremacy of the Law is germane to this issue, but there is a further explanation that deserves to be considered. Perhaps the emphatically theoretical
character of man's rational nature is decisive here: only the actualization of what makes man human is strictly a virtue of the
soul's rational part. The intellectual form of the human soul
would then determine whether practical wisdom can be construed as a virtue. If man's rational nature is constituted by the
possession of logos (in the practical sense of the term), as Aristotle speaks of man in the early part of the Nicomachean Ethics
(1098a3–4), then practical wisdom becomes a human virtue.
But because Maimonides regards man's rational nature as constituted by nous, that is, the "formation of intelligibles," he denies that practical wisdom is a virtue.[25]

*

I have thus far been mainly concerned with showing how the
philosophic tradition, duly modified, takes its place within a

23. Cf. Simon Scheyer, Das Psychologische System des Maimonides,
pp. 23–24.
24. Selected Chapters, ed. Najjar, no. 38 (Dunlop, no. 35).
25. CM, Introd., p. 42. See also below, Overview, esp. pp. 187–88. None of
the works of Maimonides specifies a virtue for practical wisdom. There is no
reference in CM to a prophet's use of practical wisdom (ta'aqqul) when he

commentary on the Law. Although we have yet to explore how the Jewish tradition is affected by the philosophic treatment of ethics in *EC*, it is already clear that the standard of the mean serves as a corrective for any excessively strict interpretation of the Law. This, however, leads to the question of how the indigenous Jewish teachings should be understood.

---

temporarily suspends a law; a prophet relies upon "theorizing" (*naẓar*) and "syllogistic reasoning" or "analogy" (*qiyās*) to determine what should be done (*CM*, Introd., p. 13). In the Code, the middle way itself is called the "measure of wisdom" (see below, p. 99 and n. 8); H De'ot does not designate practical wisdom as a separate virtue.

TWO

The Religious Morality: Piety

Through his interpretation of *hasidut*, Maimonides juxtaposes the Jewish view of morality to the doctrine of the mean. At the same time, he attempts to revivify the rabbinic teaching of piety, as is evident not only from *EC* but also from the "Commentary of Avot," where his view of piety is illuminated in the course of lengthy comments upon rabbinic sayings concerned with humility, contentment, and speech. Following his lead, I shall explore how he understands these topics, and then turn to other examples from *CM*. His discussion of these three subjects also throws light, albeit indirectly, upon the difference between exemplary Jewish practice and the nobility of the Aristotelian gentleman. First, his general view of piety must be examined.

THE MEANING OF PIETY

In the preface to *EC*, Maimonides says that "according to us"—that is, us Jews—"there is no rank above piety (*hasidut*) except for prophecy." *Hasidut* is thus emblematic of the specifically Jewish morality; it may be said to represent Jewish virtue. This sounds anomalous because there is no word in the biblical-rabbinic tradition for that seminal Greek concept, "virtue." Maimonides bridges the gap between the Jewish and the Greek views of exemplary conduct at a single stroke: he identifies the *hasidim* as "virtuous men" (*fudalāʾ*).[1] The word *hasidut* is derived from *hesed*, whose root meaning is "excess";[2] the root of

---

1. The definition of the Hebrew term *hasid* in *CM*, Avot, 5.6, is in accord with the description of the *fudalāʾ* in *EC*, chap. 4 (p. 382).
2. *CM*, Avot, 5.6; *Guide*, 3.53.

the Arabic term for virtue (*faḍīla*) also refers to excess. There are Arabic terms other than *fuḍalā*' that Maimonides could have used for designating the *ḥasidim*; Baḥya ibn Paqudah, for instance, often refers to "pious men" as *awliyā*'. By calling the *ḥasidim* "virtuous men," Maimonides quietly moves Jewish piety into the orbit of philosophy; their conduct is in fact defined in relation to the middle way in ethics.

Traditionally, pious men are understood to do more than is required by the letter of the law; they are "inside the line of the law." Maimonides, however, says that they incline a little toward one or another extreme as a precautionary measure to attain the mean (*EC*, chap. 4, p. 382). By defining piety in relation to the middle way rather than the Law, he transposes a scrupulosity in obeying Jewish law into a scrupulosity concerning moral matters—a shift in meaning that is hinted at by calling the *ḥasidim* "virtuous men."

Ḥasidut is distinguished in *CM* from *yir'ah* (fear, awe) or *yir'at shamayim* (fear of Heaven), which is the basis for a strict observance of "traditional laws" (*mitsvot shim'iyyot*), that is, laws peculiar to the Jewish nation (*CM*, Avot, 1.3; *EC*, chap. 6). Whereas *yir'ah* is justified on specifically Jewish grounds, *ḥasidut* is justified on grounds common to man as man. In *EC*, the latter form of piety, which is based upon the nature of the human soul, takes precedence. (Our use of the term "piety" will refer throughout to *ḥasidut* as distinct from *yir'ah* or *yir'at shamayim*.)

Maimonides places his discussion of *ḥasidut* into a psychotherapeutic framework according to which the cure for the soul's diseases is fundamentally the same as that for healing the body. Just as the body must be brought back to a state of equilibrium by being compelled to follow a course of treatment opposed to the disease, so too a sick soul is healed by being compelled to incline toward the extreme opposed to a particular vice or disease (*EC*, chap. 4). This view of therapy presupposes that the soul, like the body, can be healthy or sick (chap. 3). Maimonides also takes for granted a premise that is not found in *EC* but is specified in the *Guide*: the moral qualities of the soul result from the temperament of the body (3.12 [20b]); hence, basically the same treatment is suitable for the soul as for the body. The virtuous men habitually incline a little away from the worse vice or extreme related to each moral virtue so that they may counteract any tendency they have toward that vice.

The basic features of Maimonidean psychotherapy are traceable to Alfarabi, but they harken back, ultimately, to advice that Aristotle gives to potential gentlemen in the *Nicomachean Ethics.* Aristotle does not give a "physiological" basis to his account of the moral training of the soul, but he does recommend inclining a little away from the worse vice in each instance as a strategem for hitting the mean (1109a20–b26; cf. 1104b17–18). Does the Aristotelian mode of training adopted by Maimonides vitiate the Jewish content of piety? Let us reiterate that Maimonides speaks of *virtuous men* as inclining a little away from the mean; the Aristotelian gentlemen, however, typically follow the mean.[3] Moreover, the distinctive account of the moral virtues in *EC* furnishes the guideline for piety, and, as we have noted, this account is partly adapted to the Jewish tradition; it includes, for example, humility, contentment, and modesty. Further, the models for *EC* are not the Greek heroes and gentlemen who stand in the background of the *Nicomachean Ethics,* but the rabbinic sages. When Maimonides says, for instance, that the virtuous men habitually incline a little toward self-abasement and toward insensibility to pleasure, he clearly refers to certain pious Jews (chap. 4, p. 382); such conduct is foreign to the nobility of Aristotle's gentlemen.

The Jewish context of the Maimonidean teaching can be thrown into relief if we consider how Aristotle's advice of inclining toward an extreme to attain the mean would be applied in the case of magnanimity (noble pride). Aristotle's counsel in book 2 of the *Ethics* requires determining which of the extremes for a particular virtue is more unlike the mean; he recommends inclining away from the extreme that is more opposed to the virtue. Now, "smallness of soul" is "more opposed than

3. There are a few instances, though, in which it is preferable for the gentleman to depart from the mean. See *Nic. Eth.* 1120b4–6, 1125b27–29, 1136b20–22.

vanity to greatness of soul, being both more prevalent and worse" (1125a32–34). Hence, as a corrective for attaining the mean, the potential gentleman is advised to incline toward vanity! It goes without saying that Maimonides does not commend vanity as a means for attaining virtue.

There is a certain ambiguity in the account of piety in *EC* because it is patterned after an Aristotelian form of psychotherapy. Two views of piety are in fact intertwined in *EC:* piety can be a cure for the soul's diseases, or it can manifest what we might call exemplary virtue. The psychotherapeutic purpose of piety is illustrated in *EC* by certain "virtuous men" (*fuḍalāʾ*) who, to correct their vices, went to such extremes as fasting, keeping away from women, living temporarily in the desert, and so on (chap. 4, p. 382). Those who have sick souls are understood by Maimonides to be not merely continent (or self-restrained); they are "bad and defective men [who] imagine bad things as good and good things as bad" (chap. 3). Hence they must go to the opposite extreme as a cure for their vice. The virtuous men, however, more typically incline only a little toward an extreme. Piety in this respect is a "safeguard" or "precaution" (*ḥawṭa*) for the virtue that these men already possess.

Exemplary virtue can be illustrated by the behavior of the Patriarch Abraham after the victory in the War of the Nine Kings. According to the "Commentary on Avot," Abraham exhibited the "ultimate" (*ghāya*) in contentment by refusing to take any booty: "I will not take a thread nor a shoe latchet" (Gen. 14.23; *CM*, Avot, 5.17). I suggest that such behavior is indicative of conduct that inclines a little toward an extreme; the middle way for this virtue (i.e., contentment), which lies between greed and laziness, would not require the renunciation of all the spoils to which a man is entitled. Consider also what Maimonides says in the same context about Abraham's moderation. Although Abraham's wife, Sarah, was a very beautiful woman, he did not look completely at her figure until they entered Egypt and her beauty posed a threat to his life: "Behold, now I know that you are a woman of beautiful form" (Gen. 12.11). By inclining a little toward the extreme, Abraham reached the "ultimate" (*ghāya*) in moderation. The ultimate in virtue is simultaneously an expression of piety and a precautionary measure on behalf of the middle way.[4]

In the rabbinic tradition, the Jewish character of piety is evident from its close association with the "holy spirit": "piety
brings about the holy spirit" (cited in the preface to *EC*). As
interpreted in *EC*, this statement refers to the moral preparation of "virtuous men" for the contemplative life; the "holy
spirit" is, as it were, the exalted condition of the intellect that
is achieved when one has acquired the highest form of theoretical knowledge.[5]

In Maimonides' source, R. Pinehas ben Yair indicates that
upon having reached the stage of *ḥasidut*, a man ipso facto receives the holy spirit. This is quite an exalted view of *ḥasidut*,
going beyond the more circumscribed role that Maimonides ascribes to it. The rabbinic statement reads: "[H]umility brings
about fear of sin, fear of sin brings about piety, piety brings
about the holy spirit." The last clause is supported by the biblical verse, "Then You spoke in a vision to Your pious men
(*ḥasidekha*)" (Ps. 89.20); thus, *ḥasidut* is understood here as
quite literally causing the advent of the holy spirit (*Jerusalem
Talmud*, Shekalim, 3.4). In *EC*, however, Maimonides treats
piety as instrumental to moral virtue, and moral perfection itself is sharply distinguished from the intellectual apprehension
of the deity.

Piety can, of course, be followed by people who do not develop intellectual virtue; however, as a preparation for contemplation, it is appropriate for a philosopher who is a member
of the Jewish community. In the final analysis a man's allegiance cannot be both to the Torah and to philosophy, but since
man is by nature a political being, he must be a member of
a particular community. Maimonides shows how a philosopher within the Jewish community can be pious; *EC* contains
a discreet exposition of what might be called "philosophic

4. See also the reference to the "ultimate" (*ghāya*) in humility in *CM*,
Avot, 4.4 (p. 399).
5. Cf. *EC*, chap. 5. According to the Code, the "holy spirit" comes from
knowledge of the separate intellects and God's wisdom manifest in the world
(H. Yesodei ha-Torah, 7.1).

piety." This would not be possible were it not for the fact that Maimonides articulates *ḥasidut* on a completely moral plane. *Ḥasidut* does not bespeak a devout attitude toward God nor even toward the Law. By divorcing piety from matters that in some way bind the intellect, Maimonides removes the danger that it might stand in the way of the quest for the truth. At the same time, he ascribes a genuine significance to piety as a preparation for the pursuit of knowledge.

The Maimonidean interpretation of piety, or religious morality, calls to mind what al-Ghazali says about the moral training of the *falāsifa:* to purify their character traits and thus prepare themselves for the study of philosophy, they appropriated ethical teachings from Sufism.[6] Maimonides' interpretation of *ḥasidut* as a preparation for engaging in *theoria* is comparable to the appropriation of Sufi morality by the *falāsifa.* It is not irrelevant that he sometimes draws upon Sufi works to clarify the meaning of certain Jewish precepts. In the pivotal case of humility, he has recourse to a Sufi tale to clarify the meaning of self-abasement. We shall see that he also adverts to a Sufi text to explain the purpose of speech and to underscore the need for cultivating silence. Moreover, his reference to moral vices as "veils" that hinder the knowledge of God is derived from the Sufis (*EC*, chap. 7; the rabbinic prooftext does not refer to "veils." See also *Guide*, 3.9).

EXTREME HUMILITY

Although Maimonides does not directly consider how, if at all, humility comports with noble pride (greatness of soul), this question lies in the background of his discussion of the dictum by R. Levitas, "Abase yourself exceedingly," or more literally, "Be very, very lowly of spirit" (*shefal ruaḥ*) (*CM*, Avot, 4.4). To interpret this dictum Maimonides makes use of the distinction between humility (*tawāḍuʿ: ʿanavah*) and self-abasement (*takhassus: shiflut ha-ruaḥ*) that had been articulated in *EC*.

6. Al-Ghazali, *Al-Munqidh min al-Ḍalāl*, p. 86; English trans. by W. Montgomery Watt in *The Faith and Practice of Al-Ghazali*, p. 38.

Humility lies in the mean between haughtiness and self-abasement.

A haughty heart (*gova' ha-lev*) does not correspond exactly to the Greek *megalopsychia* (greatness of soul). At least some affinity between them is discernible, though; Maimonides at one point refers to the haughty man as *kabīr al-nafs* (great-souled) (*CM*, Avot, 4.4, p. 440). This is the very expression used by Alfarabi to refer to a man who has "greatness of soul"; according to both the *Virtuous City* and the *Attainment of Happiness*, it is meet for a philosopher to be *kabīr al-nafs* (great-souled). Since the great-souled man is a lover of honor, he regards doing anything disgraceful as beneath his dignity.[7] The sense of superiority that is an integral part of "greatness of soul" is redolent of what in biblical terms is called a "high" or "lofty" heart. Nevertheless, "greatness of soul" is not the same as having a haughty heart. That they differ is obvious from one of the Hebrew expressions cited by Maimonides in *CM* (Avot, 4.4) as referring to haughtiness, namely, *gasut ha-ruaḥ* (lit., coarseness of the spirit). This quality is ascribed in the Code to communal leaders who treat people in a high-handed and oppressive manner (H. Sanhedrin, 25.1–2). The tyrannical manner employed by such arrogant men is foreign to the behavior of those who are "great-souled." "Greatness of soul" in the philosophic tradition is the basis for acting nobly, which cannot be said for "haughtiness of the heart." Whereas a "great-souled" man must have all the moral virtues, this is of course not true of someone with a haughty heart. "Greatness of soul" and "haughtiness of the heart" bear only a superficial resemblance to one another.

Self-abasement (or a "lowly spirit") is, however, akin to Aristotelian "smallness of soul" (*mikropsychia*). Maimonides, like Aristotle, regards this quality as a vice. The "virtuous men" (*fuḍalāʾ*) go to the extreme of self-abasement as a "safeguard"

---

7. Alfarabi, *The Principles of the Opinions of the People of the Virtuous City*, ed. Richard Walzer (*Al-Farabi on the Perfect State*), p. 248; *Attainment of Happiness*, ed. Jafar Al-Yasin, p. 95; English trans. by Muhsin Mahdi in *Alfarabi's Philosophy of Plato and Aristotle*, sec. 60.

(ḥawṭa) to make certain that no trace of haughtiness remains in their souls. Although both extremes are vices—and hence one might think that caution should be exercised lest either vice be found in the soul—the pious men are especially concerned with eliminating haughtiness because it is so harmful a trait (CM, Avot, 4.4, p. 438). Their assessment of arrogance is in accord with the biblical-rabbinic tradition. A training in self-abasement is, moreover, useful for attaining the serenity that is conducive to the contemplative life.

To illustrate what is required by the dictum of R. Levitas to abase yourself exceedingly, Maimonides tells a story taken from a certain unnamed "book on ethics" about an unnamed "virtuous man." The book is in fact a Sufi work, and the tale was originally told about a famous Sufi master.[8] Now, the rabbinic tradition recognizes that there are "pious men of the nations of the world," and Maimonides follows that tradition. But by defining piety in relation to the mean rather than the Law, he strengthens the kinship between pious Jews and pious Gentiles. He even implies that the conduct of all pious men (fuḍalāʾ) is essentially the same: they are all scrupulous in cultivating moral virtue. Hence a virtuous non-Jew can be a model for the behavior of Jews.[9]

The story is as follows. A certain virtuous man was once asked, "On what day of your life did you have the most joy?" He replied: "One day I was traveling on a ship whose passengers included some merchants and wealthy men. My place was in the lowest part of the ship; I was wearing tattered garments. While I was lying down in my place, one of the men on board rose to urinate. He regarded me as so despicable and the condition I was in so debased that he uncovered himself and urinated upon me. I was amazed at his shamelessness. But by God, my soul was not pained at all by his deed, nor was I in the least

8. Ibrahim ibn Adham. The story is found in Al-Hujwīrī, Kashf al-Maḥjūb [Unveiling the Hidden], p. 76; English trans. by R. A. Nicholson, p. 68. Maimonides elaborates somewhat upon the story as it has been transmitted in the Kashf.

9. Joseph ben Judah, in Sefer Musar, tells the same anecdote as does Maimonides, and identifies the "virtuous man" as one of the "pious men of the nations of the world" (Commentary on Avot, 4.4).

agitated. Then I greatly rejoiced that I had reached the point where the contempt of that base man did not pain me, and I paid no heed to him."

The story suggests that self-abasement requires lowering oneself in the presence of others. The virtuous man in the tale was lying down in the lowest part of the ship; his tattered garments were visible signs of his lowliness. *Shiflut ha-ruaḥ*, the Hebrew term used by Maimonides for this extreme, also denotes lowliness. As for the opposite extreme, almost all of the terms enumerated by Maimonides (nine in all) for the opposite extreme refer in one way or another to height: a "high [or haughty] heart," "up-raised eyes," and so forth (*CM*, Avot, 4.4). Haughtiness involves assuming a posture of hauteur vis-à-vis other people. The middle way of humility, then, requires placing oneself on the same level with other people, no matter what difference there might be in intellect, in social position, and so forth. This interpretation draws support from a letter that Maimonides sent to his disciple, Joseph, who, in his controversy with the religious leadership of Babylonian Jewry, is urged to follow the example of his teacher's humility: "You know my humility [*tawāḍuʿ*] toward everyone and my *equating* myself with the most insignificant person."[10]

The irony present in the discipline of self-abasement is clear enough. The virtuous man in the story knew that he had reached a high plane of moral perfection; he certainly did not regard himself as inferior to the man who had urinated upon him. The ironic element inherent in piety is underscored in Maimonides' gloss upon the rabbinic command, "Be lowly of spirit before every man," which is interpreted to mean: "Let your conversation with him [every man] and your association with him be *as if* he were on a higher level than you. This is solely to flee from haughtiness" (*CM*, Avot, 4.12, emphasis added). The precept to abase oneself does not require that a man have a low opinion of himself, but only that he conduct himself in a lowly manner with other people.

Since lowering oneself vis-à-vis others expresses itself in a

10. *'Iggrot ha-Rambam*, p. 61 (emphasis added); *Ethical Writings*, p. 119.

respectful attitude toward them, the regimen of piety enhances decent human relations. True, this is only an incidental result of a man's training himself to "flee from haughtiness." But since moral perfection can be grasped from the standpoint of what is beneficial for society as well as for the individual, the "social utility" of self-abasement should not be neglected. Maimonides even stresses it in the above-mentioned letter to Joseph, in which Maimonides goes beyond imploring him to ignore the abuse to which he was subjected by the religious authorities in Baghdad: "May God restrain you from humiliating someone who is great in the eyes of the people. But more than that, I beseech you to treat as great whoever is insignificant in the eyes of the people."[11]

Maimonides tacitly opposes a certain strand within the Jewish tradition that requires genuine self-depreciation. He differs, for example, from Baḥya ibn Paqudah, who regards an acute awareness of one's failings as characteristic of humility. For Baḥya, humility is based upon man's inability to fulfill all of his duties to God. Consequently, if a humble man is praised for the good he has accomplished, he should reply: "Enough my brother, my good deed is nothing compared to my sins; it is like a torch of fire among the waters of the sea." For Baḥya there is no irony in extreme humility—and no difference between self-abasement and humility.[12] (Baḥya does, however, speak of the importance of cultivating equanimity in the face of praise and blame.)[13]

After telling the Sufi tale, Maimonides enters a cautionary note: one should not go completely to the extreme, but only "approach abasement."[14] A total disregard of the tokens of honor is inappropriate for the community's leaders in particular. The sages and their disciples are supposed to be honored so

11. *'Iggrot ha-Rambam*, p. 62; *Ethical Writings*, p. 119.

12. *K. al-Hidāya ilā Farā'iḍ al-Qulūb* [*Book of Guidance to the Duties of the Hearts*], 6.7, ed. Kafiḥ, pp. 294–95.

13. Ibid., 5.5, p. 264. A. S. Yahuda, in the introduction to his edition of Baḥya's *Hidāya*, traces Baḥya's view of *istiwā'* (equanimity) to the Sufis (pp. 102–3).

14. CM, Avot, 4.4, p. 338. See also ibid., p. 440: "It is not fitting to reach the point of complete abasement of the soul since it is not among the virtues."

that people will be disposed to receive instruction from them and also be prone to imitate their conduct. It would be improper for such individuals to behave like the virtuous man in the ship anecdote. The Code in fact forbids the sages and their disciples to wear shabby clothes because such garments would degrade them in the sight of the people (HD, 5.8). The Sufi's conduct is more a paradigm for showing the general purpose of self-abasement, including how to heal the sickness of the soul, than it is a model to be strictly emulated by all Jews who aspire to piety.

The discipline of self-abasement is not plagued by the critical failing that Aristotle ascribes to "smallness of soul," namely, that a small-souled man thinks himself unworthy of performing great actions. The irony inherent in piety in fact enables it to have a certain affinity with Aristotelian greatness of soul. Maimonides even speaks of himself in the *Guide* in a way that is reminiscent of greatness of soul:

> I am the man who when the concern pressed him and his way was straitened and he could find no other device by which to teach a demonstrated truth than by giving satisfaction to a single virtuous man while displeasing ten thousand ignoramuses—I am he who prefers to address that single man by himself, and I do not heed the blame of those many creatures.[15]

In the *Eudemian Ethics* Aristotle has a similar description of the great-souled man: he would heed more what one virtuous man thinks than what many ordinary people think (1232b6–7).

The desire to achieve great things is distinguishable from the desire for honor that is fundamental to the gentleman's "greatness of soul." Maimonides in effect endorses a kind of magnanimity that combines striving for great things with an indifference to the opinion of the multitude.[16] The spirit of his

15. *Guide*, Introd. [9b]. Maimonides occasionally refers to the wonderful explanation that he has given of some matter, and he speaks of his extreme predilection for the truth that led him to set forth the central perplexity of the *Guide*—rather than simply explaining what the perplexity is (*Guide*, 2.24 [54b], 3.8 [13b]; *EC*, chap 6, near end). See also below, p. 194.

16. Regarding the different ways of viewing magnanimity, cf. Miskawayh, who excludes the desire for honor from his definition of magnanimity and, presumably under a Stoic influence, classifies it under courage: "greatness of

teaching is conveyed by the following remark in a letter to Joseph accompanying the *Guide:* "The soul of a wise man seeks great things for it [his soul], and an understanding spirit seeks to ascend to remarkable heights [*ma'alot*] and distinguished [or separate] stations."[17] (My translation of the last word, *mat-savot*, follows Baneth's suggestion that it is synonymous with the *maqāmāt* that are stations on the path of the Sufi mystic. This is not to say that the term has any mystical overtones in this context.) The Jewish regimen of piety is compatible with "greatness of soul" when the latter is understood to be basically a striving for great things while being worthy of achieving them.

The "lowliness" of the pious Jew differs from the attitude toward other people that is inherent in the Aristotelian gentleman's magnanimity: the gentleman tends to show openly his sense of superiority (particularly to those of the same rank). Like the pious man, he ignores insults, but he does so because of his confidence in his virtue: the gentleman knows that they cannot be just. And while the pious Jew does not regard them as just either, he is continuously concerned with improving himself, by his own lights, so that he turns abuse to advantage and uses the opportunity to chasten pride. This is particularly salutary under the conditions of the Exile, where, as we have noted, silence in the face of insult was prudent as well as morally beneficial.

Although the gentleman regards honor in the final analysis as a "small thing," he continues to covet the great honor that is merited for rare, exceptionally notable deeds (*Nic. Eth.* 1124a19, b25–26). This is of course contrary to the utter indifference to honor required by piety. We should not forget, how-

---

soul" (*kibr al-nafs*) is "the disdain for what is insignificant, and the ability to bear honor or abasement. Whoever possesses this virtue is always preparing himself for great deeds, while being worthy of them" (*Tahdhīb al-Akhlāq* [*Refinement of Character*], ed. Zurayk [Arabic], p. 21). See also R. A. Gauthier, *Magnanimité.*

17. *'Iggrot ha-Rambam*, p. 15. The quotation alludes to knowledge of the heavenly spheres and the separate intellects. The letter is an additional epistle that Maimonides sent to Joseph, besides the one that is normally included with translations of the *Guide.*

ever, that the pious regimen of being indifferent to praise and blame is designed to eliminate haughtiness (or to test oneself to see whether any arrogance is present); the goal is the middle way, in which at least some concern with honor can be found. It is noteworthy that when Maimonides comments upon the rabbinic dictum that "honor removes a man from the world," he interprets what appears to be a total renunciation of honor as being, instead, a condemnation of the *love* of honor (*CM*, Avot, 4.27).

Extreme humility, as interpreted by Maimonides, is consonant with a philosophic way of life. In a letter to Ḥisdai Halevi, Maimonides in fact maintains that the philosophers are extremely humble. In the letter, he is intent upon showing that the ultimate moral perfection for a philosopher and a Jew is the same. To prove that this is so, he retells the ship anecdote cited above, only this time it is told about a "great philosopher."[18] The two versions differ slightly: whereas the pious man rejoiced at having reached his goal of perfect humility, the philosopher laughs when he is urinated upon. For the philosopher it was not a special occasion. He also shows more openly that the insult is a matter of indifference to him, and he turns the tables by the laughter.[19] But the letter confirms the suitability of piety for a philosopher who is a member of the Jewish community. Since Maimonides interprets extreme humility in the light of *apatheia*, he can liken the virtue of the philosopher to that of the Jew.

We cannot infer from the letter, however, that the pursuit of *theoria* necessarily requires extreme humility. What Maimonides says there about the ultimate moral perfection of the philosophers is part of an argument to convince his addressee that philosophy is not antagonistic to the Law; Maimonides attempts to prepare the ground for a favorable attitude toward

18. *Qovets Teshuvot ha-Rambam*, pt. 2, p. 24a. The copyist of the letter was sternly warned by Maimonides against showing the letter to anyone else, and seems to have gotten around that stricture (in his own eyes, at any rate) by translating the original Arabic version into Hebrew; that appears to be the meaning of the scribe's statement that he has "changed the language" (p. 23a).

19. Cf. *Treatise on Asthma* (chap. 8): a sage would look with "amusement" upon the things that most people suppose bring about happiness.

philosophy. It would therefore be rash to draw any definitive conclusions about philosophic ethics from the letter. What *is* evident is that philosophic morality can be so interpreted as to be brought into harmony with the Jewish teaching concerning self-abasement.

The Stoic Resonance

The Maimonidean teaching of self-abasement has, or appears to have, a Stoic resonance. But despite the apparent echo of Stoicism in the Sufi tale, Maimonides retains an Aristotelian schema in which the middle way is the goal. Further, he understands *apatheia* or equanimity in the light of the needs of the contemplative life (cf. *CM*, Avot, 4.4 with *EC*, chap. 5).

A consideration of the possibility of a Stoic element in Maimonides' ethical teachings requires at least a cursory examination of his medical writings. In the *Treatise on Asthma*, when he discusses how to cure the soul's diseases, Maimonides commends turning to "philosophic ethics," which, he says, aims at diminishing the passions as much as possible (chap. 8). (Note that he refers not to Stoicism but to philosophic ethics.) But here, too, he places the "Stoic" teaching, that one should retain one's composure under all circumstances, into a framework governed by the mean: A man should train himself to be neither exhilarated at good fortune nor anxious and cast down by ill fortune. Since equanimity is an equilibrium within the soul that can be construed as a middle way, an apparently "Stoic" teaching can be integrated into the doctrine of the mean. The departure from Stoicism in the medical work is, moreover, evident from the stress Maimonides places on the need to "expand" or "delight" the soul.[20] Cheerfulness is understood as having a medical purpose: it is a means for improving the body's health as well as attaining equanimity.

20. Cf. *EC*, chap. 5, p. 388. An expansive soul is a prerequisite for any serious work that requires concentrating the mind. Maimonides says that Rav Ashi was able to compose the *Talmud* because of the "expansion of the soul [*inbisāṭ al-nafs*] and love of learning" that God granted to him (*CM*, Introd., p. 34).

According to *On the Management of Health*, the right posture toward the vicissitudes of fortune is fortitude; the opposite extreme is "softness [*rakhāwa*] of the soul." Those individuals who are "truly courageous" retain their equanimity under all circumstances (Kroner, p. 68; *Ethical Writings*, p. 108). This view of fortitude bears a certain resemblance to Stoicism. Nevertheless, in his argumentation, Maimonides refers to what "the philosophers" teach—and not to a particular philosophic sect. They regard the goods of this world as bringing about only imaginary happiness. Maimonides also refers there to the need to evaluate what is good by considering the "truth of things" and the "nature of existence." He indicates that the things of this world have a transitory character; they are found wanting in comparison with what is permanent, such as man's rational form, which Maimonides views in an Aristotelian manner.

Also germane to this discussion is his gloss in *CM* on the rabbinic dictum, "A man is obliged to bless [God] for the evil just as he makes a blessing for the good." After observing that a person should accept even calamity cheerfully (lit., with joy), Maimonides states the following rule: "A man should intend with his thought and pray to God that he make everything that happens to him in this world—whether evil or good—a cause for attaining true happiness" (*CM*, Berakhot, 9.5). This is a reformulation of the premise of *EC* that all of a person's deeds should be ordered toward the contemplative life—which in some instances might issue in conduct reminiscent of Stoicism, but it is not as such a Stoic teaching.[21]

Although a Stoic influence upon Maimonides' conception of

---

21. The grounds for the rejection of the Stoic view of *apatheia* can be clarified through Alfarabi, who, like Maimonides, evaluates all things from the standpoint of whether they contribute to attaining true happiness. Alfarabi draws the inference that the passions are neither good nor bad in themselves. Even such passions as jealousy, niggardliness, and the love of honor are good if they contribute to attaining true happiness (*Selected Chapters* [*Fuṣūl Muntazaʿa*], ed. Najjar, nos. 75, 28 [Dunlop, nos. 70, 25]; see also Alfarabi's condemnation of Stoic moral teachings in *Virtuous City*, pp. 318–22. In the *Guide* Maimonides remarks that a "ruse" might be suitable for acquiring either moral or intellectual virtue (3.54 [132a]).

self-abasement cannot be ruled out, we are on firmer ground by recalling that in his explanation of the dictum of R. Levitas, Maimonides adapts a Sufi tale to a basically Aristotelian conception of how to cure the soul's diseases.

The Virtue of Contentment and Jewish Institutions

The particular care that the "virtuous men" take to cultivate the virtue of contentment, which refers to the right attitude toward acquiring money, is invaluable for obeying the rabbinic dictum in Avot that a man should not make the Torah a "spade to dig with." Maimonides interprets this precept in the strictest possible manner: scholars should not be supported by the community (CM, Avot, 4.7). He defends the "honor of the Torah," which would be debased if it were treated as a means of sustenance. He does not refer in this context to the holiness of the Torah—which is the basis for the rabbinic injunction according to Simon bar Tsemakh Duran.[22] As we shall see, however, it is not only a concern for the Torah's honor that guides the interpretation of Maimonides.

His lengthy discussion of Avot, 4.7, forms a polemic against his contemporaries, who were not averse to being supported by the community. Maimonides wanted to revivify the virtue of the rabbinic sages. He refers approvingly to a number of Mishnaic sages to prove that no matter how poor a man is, he should not exploit his knowledge of the Torah in order to be supported by the community. Hillel the elder chopped wood to earn a living; Karna, the judge of all the land of Israel, was a drawer of water; Rav Joseph carried logs for his livelihood—he rejoiced that he had an occupation that would keep him warm! These sages and others like them were "virtuous men [fuḍalāʾ] who adhere to the truth for its own sake and have faith in God and in the Law of Moses our master" (CM, Avot, 4.7, p. 443). In a parallel passage in the Code, Maimonides refers to such men as ḥasidim: "Those who support themselves by the work of their

22. Magen Avot, p. 62a.

hand are on a lofty plane; this is the measure of the early pious men [ḥasidim ha-riʾshonim] . . ." (H. Talmud Torah, 3.11).

To uphold the honor of the Torah is to avoid profaning the Name of God. If a man receives money on account of his learning, it is a "profanation of [God's] Name [ḥillul ha-shem] according to the multitude, who would suppose that [the study of] the Torah is an occupation like the occupations through which a man sustains himself; it would therefore be debased in their eyes" (CM, Avot, 4.7, p. 443). How the Torah is regarded in the Jewish community is undoubtedly an important consideration for Maimonides. Still, one wonders how much weight he gives to a reason that depends upon the opinion of the multitude. A respect for the "honor of the Torah" need not lead to so strict a reading of Avot, 4.7. His interpretation, according to R. Joseph Karo, was contrary to all the sages who preceded and who came after him. They all, Karo says, "were accustomed to receive their salary from the community."[23]

Put very succinctly, the following objections were raised against Maimonides. The Torah would fall into oblivion if scholars were not supported by the community. Even Joseph ben Judah was apprehensive about what would happen to the study of the Torah, and in his own "Commentary on Avot" he expressed a rare disagreement with his teacher regarding the passage in question. It was also argued that the rabbinic anecdotes used by Maimonides to buttress his position are subject to alternative interpretations. Further, a different conclusion could be drawn from the halakhic discussion in the Talmud, as Joseph ben Judah, among others, observed.[24] (One might think that what was evident to the student was also evident to the master.)

Without entering into the halakhic argumentation pro and con, I would note that the Talmud according to Maimonides uses dialectical reasoning, which allows alternative interpretations of contested matters to be considered (CM, Introd., p. 4).

23. Kesef Mishneh on H. Talmud Torah, 3.11.
24. Joseph Karo, ibid.; Simon bar Tsemakh Duran, Magen Avot, 4.7; Joseph ben Judah, Sefer Musar, Commentary on Avot, 4.7.

There appear to be grounds for the difference in opinion between Maimonides and his adversaries. To understand his
position, his letter to Joseph advising him not to accept any
money from the Jewish authorities in Baghdad is instructive. As
Baneth astutely observes, Maimonides does not appeal there to
Avot, 4.7; he simply says that Joseph would be degraded if he
were to accept any money from them.[25] The letter implies that
the text of Avot is not the sole basis for the Maimonidean opposition to the support of scholars.

Let us reconsider how he describes the "virtuous men" in
his commentary on Avot, 4.7: (1) they are devoted to the truth
for its own sake, and (2) they have faith in God and in the Law
of Moses. The second clause is consonant with their view that
the study of the Torah should have no ulterior motive. The first
clause, which refers simply to a devotion to the truth, alludes
to philosophic inquiry as distinct from faith in God and in the
Torah. The two clauses are related in that both philosophy and
the Torah place a premium upon learning for its own sake—the
rabbinic notion of study *lishma'* (for its own sake) is in agreement with the philosophic view that theoretical knowledge
should be sought solely for its own sake.[26] But the pursuit of
philosophy more emphatically requires independence from the
community. The importance of economic self-sufficiency for
someone like Maimonides himself is not difficult to fathom.
We need only recall the passage from the *Guide*, cited earlier,
in which he disdains caring about what ten thousand igno-
ramuses think if he can liberate a single virtuous man from his
confusion. If he had been dependent for his livelihood upon
someone like R. Samuel ben Ali, the Gaon of Baghdad, Maimonides would have been swiftly silenced in his controversy
with the Gaon.

The proposal of Maimonides would have destroyed the Yeshivot or at least have required that their structure be radically
altered, since they could no longer be supported by the com-

25. *'Iggrot ha-Rambam*, pp. 68–69 and n. 11, p. 68; *Ethical Writings*, p. 122.
26. See also *CM*, Sanhedrin, 10.1, pp. 198–99.

munity.[27] In effect he calls for scholars to act as private men so that they may be free from being muffled by any of the existing institutions. We cannot forget that Jewish institutions, governed by the Law, regulated opinions as well as actions. Maimonides moves in the direction of preferring the unencumbered quest for the truth to the communal support of the study of the *Talmud.* In fact, his own *Mishneh Torah* was intended to replace the need to study the *Talmud;* no other book had to be studied to gain knowledge of the Oral Law.[28] The Code itself was part of an ambitious program for restructuring the Jewish community.

If anyone has any doubt about whether Maimonides had in view a radical reorganization of the Jewish community, I would note that when he lists those who should receive no wages, he refers expressly to the Exilarch, the judges, the members of the Yeshivot, and those who spread (or teach) the Torah—as well as to every person who has an appointed office in the community (*CM,* Avot, 4.7, p. 442). (The teachers of children are exempt.) He appears to go beyond the simple injunction of Avot against using the Torah as a spade to dig with. At any rate, he pushes to the extreme point the notion that learning should be pursued for its own sake alone; it is at this point that the virtue of contentment becomes so important, and piety an invaluable guideline.

When to Speak and When to Be Silent

The "virtuous men" (*fuḍalāʾ*) endeavor to avoid all idle talk. Maimonides makes this observation in the course of a lengthy discussion of the rabbinic dictum, "All my days I dwelt among the sages and I found no better rule than silence" (*CM,* Avot, 1.16). A consideration of the pregnant gloss upon this dictum

27. The Yeshivot were not only courts of law; they were also centers of study. See Joseph ben Judah, *Sefer Musar,* Commentary on Avot, 4.7.

28. *Sefer ha-Maddaʿ,* p. 4b. Cf. *ʾIggrot ha-Rambam,* p. 69; *Ethical Writings,* p. 122. In *EC,* chap. 5, Maimonides mentions a number of studies that "aim at sharpening the mind and training the rational power in the method of demonstration"; he does not mention the study of the *Talmud* (p. 389).

requires us to go beyond the reference to pious conduct so that we may examine the comparison that Maimonides makes here between the Jewish and the philosophic perspectives upon speech.

He first cites a number of rabbinic statements supporting the propriety of silence; for example, if a person tends to be habitually silent, it is a sign that he comes from a good family. Maimonides also quotes Scripture, citing for instance, Kohelet's view that someone who speaks excessively is a fool. The biblical quotations do not literally refer to the suitability of silence; the rabbinic tradition appears to go beyond the Bible in this matter. In any event, the Jewish quotations show that in stressing the need to keep speech to a minimum, Maimonides taps an authentic vein of the Jewish tradition. His emphasis upon the importance of minimizing speech is also consonant with the needs of the contemplative life (*EC*, chap. 5).

To clarify when speech is suitable, Maimonides has recourse to a "book of ethics" that contains a classification of speech by one of the "practitioners of self-discipline" (*murtāḍūn*), which is a designation for the Sufis. According to Maimonides, this classification is from the viewpoint of "wisdom" (*ḥikma*), a term that can refer to philosophy. That it does indeed refer to philosophy is indicated by the fact that immediately after presenting this division of speech, he gives another one, but this time from the standpoint of "our Law." He thus juxtaposes the viewpoint of philosophy with that of the Law.

From the standpoint of philosophy, speech is classified as (1) completely harmful, (2) partly harmful and partly useful, (3) neither harmful nor useful, and (4) completely useful. A man should restrict himself to speech falling into the fourth class, and speak only when there is no ambiguity about whether it is useful to do so. The fourth class contains speech connected with (a) the sciences and the virtues, and (b) what is necessary for the preservation of life.

As for "our Law," it commands some forms of speech and prohibits others, but its assessment of speech is not limited to these two considerations. The Law classifies speech as (1) commanded, (2) forbidden, (3) loathsome, (4) laudable, and (5) permitted. What is laudable is, then, distinct from what is commanded; for example, praising a virtuous man and urging someone to acquire moral virtue are laudable but not obligatory. And what is loathsome differs from what is forbidden; idle talk is loathsome, but it is not prohibited. As for speech connected with one's livelihood, it is classified as permitted. In short, it would be incorrect to say that what the Law does not command it forbids; its prescriptions also deal with what is loathsome, laudable, or permitted.

Despite the differences between the Jewish and the philosophic views of speech, Maimonides so interprets them that they tend to converge. Both the differences and similarities will become evident if we consider examples from the Maimonidean classification of speech by the Law.

Commanded Speech

To illustrate commanded speech, Maimonides refers to speech connected with the study and the teaching of the Torah. This example invites comparison with the philosophic classification, where, under "useful speech," we find discourse concerned with the sciences. The sciences are not mentioned in the classification of speech by the Law, and the study of the Torah is of course not contained in the philosophic classification. The study of the sciences, or philosophy, and the study of the Torah are presumed to be two different activities.

One might wonder why the study of the Torah is regarded as a form of speech. Maimonides refers here to "recitation" of the Torah, that is, to reading aloud, not to the silent study that we in the modern world associate with learning. The purpose of that medieval mode of study was to facilitate memorization. For if a student "recites aloud [lit., makes his voice heard] while studying, what he learns will remain with him; but whoever [only] whispers when reading quickly forgets" (MT, H. Talmud Torah, 3.12).

The study and the teaching of the Torah, along with speech about its legal ramifications (also referred to by Maimonides), form the speech of the community constituted by the Law. These forms of speech—as distinct from the speech which is peculiar to the *polis*—sustain the singular political order of the Jewish community, what Maimonides calls in the *Guide* "the community of the adherents of the Law" (e.g., 3.21 [24b]). His own *Commentary on the Mishnah* is part of that very speech community. He occasionally refers to *CM* as a "speech," and he calls *EC* itself a "speech [*kalām*] on ethics" (chap. 1, end). Maimonides, moreover, sometimes addresses the reader of *CM* directly, as though conversing with him. The work is punctuated with such expressions as "know that," "you know that," and so on.

Forbidden Speech

"Evil speech" (*leshon ha-ra*ʿ), which is forbidden by the Law, includes not only speaking falsely about another person but also telling the truth about his defects (*CM*, Avot, 1.16, p. 420). The philosophic standpoint classifies "vilification" as "harmful," but it does not go so far as to forbid it. In *EC*—where, in agreement with the philosophic position, he discusses speech with a view to its usefulness—Maimonides commends defaming the wicked to prevent them from harming innocent people (chap. 5). There is accordingly a contradiction between the Law's emphatic condemnation of "evil speech" (*leshon ha-ra*ʿ) and the philosophic approval of speaking the truth about the wicked. This conflict is in fact reproduced in the Law's own classification of speech in the "Commentary on Avot" (1.16). For from the standpoint of the Law, speech is deemed "laudable" when it derogates the vices of evil men to show that their deeds are reprehensible.

The rabbinic tradition goes so far as to forbid a hint of defamation, which is called the "dust of evil speech," such as a statement that might induce a third party to speak ill of others. Maimonides gives the following example. There once was a man who *praised* the script of a certain scribe before a large group of people, but was chided by his teacher for speaking *leshon ha-ra*ʿ. He was told that by praising the scribe before the multitude, he would inadvertently arouse someone disliking the scribe to malign him. This typifies the extent to which religious morality goes in its scrupulosity regarding derogatory speech. Surprisingly, a somewhat similar example is to be found in the philosophic class of speech that is partly harmful and partly useful: One should not praise a man to gain some benefit from him in the presence of his enemy because the latter's anger would be aroused. (Maimonides intimates that to praise a man for the sake of deriving benefit from him is not as such wrong; for example, speech in praise of a Sultan so that the sciences might be studied in his land.)

The Law, like philosophy, opposes obscenity, though no grounds are given in the passage under discussion. In the *Guide* Maimonides presents a rather novel justification for condemning foul language. It is not simply incompatible with moral virtue; it also does not comport with intellectual perfection. Since the use of the tongue for speech is closely associated with man's final end, it is not fitting for the tongue to be debased by obscene language (3.8 [14a]). Is the tongue also degraded by lying and giving false testimony? According to the "Commentary on Avot," such speech is forbidden by the Law. Lying and giving false testimony are not, however, included in the class of speech that is completely harmful from the standpoint of philosophy. They cannot be fully condemned by the philosophic criteria for useful speech: lying or false testimony might occasionally be useful to further the virtues or the sciences, or to save one's life.

Loathsome Speech

It is in the course of discussing the Law's condemnation of loathsome speech that Maimonides refers to the practice of the "virtuous men": they go to great lengths to avoid idle conversation. In so doing, they go beyond the letter of the law; idle talk is not forbidden by the Law. The philosophers, too, endeavor to refrain from wasteful speech. They regard it, however, as superfluous rather than loathsome; it is classified as "neither harmful nor useful" in the philosophic division of speech. Although the Law is somewhat harsher in its evaluation of such speech, philosophy and the Law basically agree in this matter.

Laudable Speech

Maimonides observes that it is laudable to use rhetoric and poetry for praising the virtues or virtuous men and for deprecating the vices or wicked men. After concluding his thematic discussion of speech, he returns to the subject of rhetoric and makes a few remarks about preaching. He gives a novel explanation of the term *midrash* in the rabbinic statement, "Not the *midrash* but the deed is the essential thing." *Midrash*, he says, refers in this instance to a preacher's discourse, and the apothegm means that a preacher's deeds ought to be in harmony with his words. Only a "virtuous man" (*fāḍil*) is fit to preach, as Maimonides infers from the rabbinic statement, "Preach [*derosh*], for it is suitable that *you* preach" (emphasis added; the addressee is assumed to be a virtuous man).[29]

I have already noted that Maimonides did not have a high regard for the preachers of his day.[30] In the "Commentary on Avot" Maimonides in effect proposes to improve things by specifying the proper goal of rhetoric, namely, to move the souls of people to acquire the virtues and to shun the vices.

Hyperbole might be used to praise a virtue or a virtuous man and censure a vice or a wicked man. This rhetorical device sometimes results in contradictory statements, which are perfectly suitable for such discourse; the community's well-being takes precedence. The rabbinic use of hyperbole can be exemplified by what Maimonides says in the commentary on R. Levitas's dictum regarding the propriety of self-abasement (*CM*, Avot, 4.4). After observing that the sages (*ḥakhamim*) made various statements in "praise of humility" and in "blame of arrogance" (p. 438), he refers to their use of hyperbole in connection with the latter ("they exaggerated about this and said . . ." [p. 440]). They exaggerated when they said, "Anyone who has any [arrogance] deserves excommunication and anyone who does not have any [arrogance] deserves excommunication." In the Code, Maimonides cites this passage, but he

---

29. CM, Avot, 1.16; *BT*, Sanhedrin, 100a.
30. See the "Introduction," n. 6.

heightens the exaggeration by transforming the rabbinic statement so that it reads, "Anyone who has an arrogant spirit— even a little—deserves excommunication" (HD, 2.3). This is one of a number of statements that contradict the doctrine of the mean; it is a salutary exaggeration, a noble deception, which informs the teaching of piety regarding humility.[31]

Permissible Speech

Permissible speech encompasses conversation connected with earning a living and fulfilling one's bodily needs. To keep such conversation to a minimum is praiseworthy. Philosophy classifies speech for self-preservation as simply useful; to say that, from the Law's viewpoint, it is "permitted" shows the extent to which the Law regulates human conduct. In the philosophic division Maimonides refers to speech that is not only for the preservation of one's life but also for the "continuation of [one's] existence"; he apparently alludes to the speech that a philosopher might find necessary for remaining alive (owing to his philosophic activity), and not simply to the conversation connected with the fulfillment of his bodily needs.

In an addendum to the Law's classification of speech, Maimonides cites a rabbinic dictum calling for brevity on the part of the teacher. His own procedure in the *Mishneh Torah* was to combine "brevity with comprehensiveness" (*Book of the Commandments*, p. 2). His avowed purpose there was to summarize legal decisions and discussions diffused in a wide variety of sources. A different use of brevity can be found in his treatment of esoteric doctrines. In the *Guide,* and even occasionally in *CM* and the Code, he makes use of brevity to point toward certain hidden matters *without* dealing with them comprehensively. The lucid brevity required by a point of law differs from the giving of hints through which new questions about theoretical matters might be awakened in the student. The use of hints for purposes of instruction obviously differs from a mode of pedagogy that requires a fully articulated argument upon any given topic. A hint in one of Maimonides' works might open

31. See the discussion in chapter 5, pp. 103–4.

new worlds for the student; it is also designed to encourage a student to think for himself. All this is not to deny that Maimonides on occasion finds it useful to speak at length upon some subject, as in his citing one rabbinic statement after another to emphasize the need to follow a certain moral teaching. This is just what he does in the passage under discussion to warn the reader against engaging in "evil speech," and it contributes to making his explanation of the rabbinic dictum regarding silence among the longest in his "Commentary on Avot."

Some Further Examples of Piety

The tendency of Maimonides to abstract from the political domain in his discussion of ethics in the *Commentary on the Mishnah* is also evident from what he says about the Pharisees in scattered places in the work. They habitually refuse to eat and drink with the multitude. This practice might seem to be motivated by the desire not to be contaminated by any ritual impurity, for the *Mishnah* describes the Pharisees as eating "everyday food in purity." Maimonides, however, interprets their conduct from the therapeutic standpoint that had been limned in *EC:* their isolation is a precautionary measure on behalf of acquiring or preserving moral virtue (*CM*, Teharot, 2.2; Ḥagigah, 2.7; in the former work, to explain their conduct he refers the reader to "our discourse on Avot," that is, to *EC*). Because the multitude is a repository of various vices, the Pharisees tend to isolate themselves from the community. They are called Pharisees (Separatists), according to Maimonides, because they separate themselves "from the defects, vices, and greed for [the things of] the world found among people" (*CM*, Soṭah, 3.3). He also speaks of them as "devout virtuous men," *fuḍalāʾ warīʿūn* (*CM*, Teharot, 2.2).

In general, when the virtuous men go beyond the letter of the law in matters pertaining to the body, Maimonides describes them with the term *waraʿ* (or some variant thereof), which I am translating as "devoutness." Besides the example of the Pharisees regarding food and drink, we may instance the

fuḍalāʾ who follow the path of devoutness in the restraint that
they exercise in relation to their wives (*CM*, Sanhedrin, 7.4,
p. 178). Whereas Jewish law permits a man to do "whatever he
wishes to do with his wife" in sexual matters, the "devout virtuous men" do not take such liberties. Their conduct is "inside
the line of the law." It is also in accord with the limits set by
nature, for according to Maimonides, the natural purpose of
sexual relations is procreation (his proof is that desire and pleasure cease after the ejaculation of the sperm). The virtuous
men restrict their sexual conduct to what is in accord with nature's purpose (ibid., p. 181).

To illustrate the conduct of the "pure virtuous man," Maimonides tells a story which is taken in its general outline from
the *Talmud*. Earlier we saw that Abraham did not notice the
beauty of Sarah's figure until his life was in peril. Maimonides
now refers to a man whose wife, unlike Sarah, had "very con-
spicuous blemishes." Even during sexual intercourse, he was
not aware of them because "his thought was occupied with
what the pure virtuous men are occupied with; when he had
need of her he intended only what nature in [its] divine wisdom
intends." This is called the "path of devoutness" (ibid.; cf. *BT*,
Shabbat, 53b). It appears that purity with respect to the virtue
of moderation entails an indifference to the physical features—
be they beautiful or otherwise—of the woman.

The way of "devoutness" is also exemplified by the refusal
of the virtuous men to look with enjoyment at an unmarried
woman. The Law permits a man to look with pleasure at an
unmarried woman who is not among the women he is forbidden to marry (the *ʿarayot*), but the virtuous men refrain from
doing so. Maimonides says that they "loathe" such lack of restraint. They want to make certain that they do not transgress
the Law by mistakenly taking pleasure in looking at a married
woman; their conduct is "inside the line of the law." Because
they incline toward the extreme of insensibility to pleasure,
their conduct is also a precautionary measure with a view to the
virtue of moderation (*CM*, Sanhedrin, 7.4, p. 178).

To turn to a different subject, when the virtuous men discuss the halakhah, they might sometimes have to be concilia-

tory in a dispute. According to Maimonides, the *Mishnah* provides a model for their behavior by occasionally stating the opinion of a certain party which is then retracted; for example, the House of Hillel might take one position, the House of Shammai another, and the former then yields to the latter. The virtuous men "with much knowledge and sound intellects" do not stubbornly hold to their position when a contrary view is "finer and theoretically stronger." They might be able to save themselves with a dialectical argument, particularly if the opponent is weaker and less capable of reasoning, but the virtuous men are acquiescent and yield (*CM*, Introd., p. 23).

Although virtuous men cannot be fools, they are preoccupied with moral goodness rather than intellectual excellence. Different degrees of knowledge are therefore found among them, as Maimonides sometimes indicates by the way he qualifies his description of the virtuous men. Antigonos of Socho, for example, was a "perfect virtuous man who apprehended the truths" (*CM*, Sanhedrin, 10.1, p. 199; cf. the description of the "true Pharisee" in *CM*, Soṭah, 3.3). There are, by contrast, "the good, virtuous men from our nation" who believe in the efficacy of talismans and refrain from using them only because of a prohibition of the Law. Their erroneous view is distinguished from the correct opinion on the matter held by the "perfect philosophers" (*CM*, ʿAvodah Zarah, 4.7). In another part of *CM* he does not pass judgment but simply narrates a story about a certain "virtuous man" by the name of Nicanor, who, along with the doors he had made for the Temple courtyard, was miraculously saved in a storm (*CM*, Kippurim, 3.11). This is the only place in *CM* where Maimonides speaks of a "miracle" occurring to one of the virtuous men.

A Final Comment

In *EC* and the "Commentary on Avot" Maimonides places ḥasidut within a horizon determined by philosophy. Broadly speaking, he discusses the old question, "What is piety?" in the light of the more comprehensive question, "What is virtue?" More specifically, the meaning of piety is determined through a reflection upon how the moral virtues are acquired and preserved. *Hasidut* can therefore become, inter alia, the piety of the philosophers. At the same time, Maimonides takes into consideration the proclivity of the Jewish tradition to go toward the extreme in moral matters.

It might be tempting, with Nietzsche, to regard the saint (i.e., the *hasid*) as a man with a sick soul, who requires extreme measures to deal with his illness. Maimonides does not exclude this possibility; he even makes it prominent by interpreting *hasidut* in the light of a method for curing the soul's diseases. But, as I have indicated, he refers to a second kind of piety as well. The *hasid* may be a particularly virtuous man whose scrupulosity is a precaution for guarding his moral goodness.

The significance of the introduction of an Aristotelian mode of psychotherapy into the Jewish tradition should not be overlooked. Maimonides thereby legitimates a radically new conception of the sages: they are to become "physicians of the soul" (*EC*, chap. 3). At the same time, he maintains that the Law basically agrees with the procedure of psychotherapy because the Law can provide a discipline for training a person to acquire the moral virtues. A certain tension nonetheless exists between the Law and psychotherapy. The Law inclines toward fixed extremes that are useful for curing typical emotional diseases or moral vices found within the community, but in isolated instances psychotherapy would require inclining toward an extreme that differs from the one dictated by the Law. Maimonides prudently does not mention this difficulty in *EC*. It is, however, almost explicit in a discussion of the limits of law in the *Guide*. Referring expressly to moral qualities (also opinions), he observes that the Law takes into account what is beneficial in a majority of cases; the generality of the commandments has the result of harming some individuals (*Guide*, 3.34). The "physicians of the soul" are presumably in a position to compensate for this deficiency of the Law; they are, in principle, not restricted by the dictates of the Law.

THREE

Philosophic Ethics and the Commandments

Philosophy, for Maimonides, comprises teachings whose validity is demonstrative and which therefore have to be taken into consideration in an interpretation of the Law. The philosophic view of the human soul offers a basis for justifying the Law, but it also poses a challenge to the authority of the Law. Establishing whatever points of accommodation that he can, Maimonides underplays, but he does not altogether suppress, the "quarrel" between philosophy and the Law. While he stresses the usefulness of the commandments for acquiring the moral virtues, a certain incongruity between the Law and the doctrine of the moral virtues is evident. Other questions arise as well; for example, the theoretical nature of the soul's intellectual form poses a problem for the conception of law as such. Also problematic is how the "traditional laws" (*mitsvot shim'iyyot*), which most emphatically express the particularity of Jewish law, are related to the needs of the human soul. These are among the issues to be explored in this chapter. I begin with a consideration of the Maimonidean treatment of the commandments.

The Discipline of the Commandments (*Mitsvot*)

The mean has a basis in the needs of the human soul because the soul's appetitive power requires an equilibrium to be in a state of health. Are the commandments, then, opposed to what is good for the soul? Since they largely incline toward the extreme, do they conflict with what is right by nature? In chapter 4 of *EC*, Maimonides resolves this problem by interpreting the *mitsvot* as a discipline for attaining the middle way. However

felicitous this solution is, it undoubtedly places the commandments in a strange light. Not only do they become instrumental to philosophic ethics, but in some instances to regard them
as for the benefit of the agent himself blatantly contradicts the
original intention of the Torah. For example, the Torah commands that a corner of the field be left for the poor, a precept
that is obviously for the benefit of the poor. According to *EC*,
however, this commandment aims at instilling the virtue of
generosity in the person who leaves a portion of his crop be-
hind. To take another example, the Torah requires that a stray
animal be returned to his owner, which is clearly for the owner's benefit; *EC* treats this precept as useful for removing avarice from the heart of the person who returns the animal. In
other works and different contexts, Maimonides himself interprets as beneficial for the community some of the very commandments that in *EC* are regarded as a discipline for the
individual.[1]

According to chapter 4 of *EC*, the Law acts as a discipline for
acquiring the following moral virtues: moderation, generosity,
contentment, gentleness, and modesty/sense of shame. The
largest number of commandments enumerated in *EC* incline
a little toward insensibility to pleasure as a training for the
virtue of moderation (temperance); the next largest number incline toward prodigality, thus training a person to be generous.
I infer that the Law is especially useful for inculcating moderation and generosity.

Which moral virtues are neglected by the Torah's precepts?
No commandments are cited in *EC* as instilling the virtues of
liberality, wit, humility, and courage. The omissions are noteworthy. (1) The Torah does not train a man in liberality, that is,

1. Regarding the manifest reason for leaving a corner of the field, see
Guide, 3.39. For the Maimonidean distinction between the "manifest" (*ẓāhir*)
meaning of a biblical verse and its rabbinic interpretation, see, e.g., appendix 1,
p. 203. The *Guide*'s discussion of parables presupposes that there is a difference between the plain meaning of a biblical verse or passage and its parabolic
significance. Throughout his works, Maimonides takes for granted that there
is such a thing as the plain meaning, the *peshat*, of Scripture; I follow him (and
common sense) in the above paragraph, referring as I do to certain "obvious"
meanings in the Bible.

in the right disposition toward spending money upon himself. It is not accidental that, when discussing psychotherapy, Maimonides singles out man's being "miserly toward himself" to exemplify a disease that should be cured (chap. 4, p. 381; cf. also the extended discussion of the usefulness of possessing fine things in chap. 5). (2) The virtue of wit is not spoken about or alluded to in the Torah; that wit or "playfulness" (la‘b) is a virtue derives from the philosophers. (3) As for humility, Moses is described in the Torah as "very humble," but none of the Torah's commandments demands humility from the people of Israel. It is the rabbinic tradition rather than the Torah that specifies the duty to abase oneself. (4) The Torah does not supply a training in courage. One is reminded that Maimonides contends that the second Temple and the second kingdom were destroyed owing to a neglect of the art of war.[2] It is, then, not simply the Exile that hinders the development of the virtue of courage; the Torah itself is not provident about training men in the art of war. (In chapter 8 of EC, Maimonides pointedly uses the example of courage to show that moral virtue can be acquired by performing the right actions whether or not a man is naturally disposed toward having a particular virtue.)

The commandments that *are* discussed in chapter 4 reveal how they stand in relation to the moral virtues: they go too far in one direction or another away from the mean. Although these commandments can have a salutary effect, what they require is excessive from the standpoint of philosophic ethics. The difference between the Law and philosophy is clear, but an examination of some specifics is necessary to make the matter more concrete.

Moderation

The following laws illustrate the Torah's tendency to require conduct that inclines toward insensibility to pleasure: the forbidden foods, forbidden sexual acts, laws of marriage, and the ban on prostitution. Departing a little from the mean, these laws exemplify a Jewish approach to the regulation of bodily

2. *Letter on Astrology*, ed. Alexander Marx, p. 350; English trans. by Ralph Lerner in *Medieval Political Philosophy: A Source Book*, p. 229.

desire. For example, the Law prescribes the need for a marriage contract (*ketubah*) and betrothal (*qiddushin*); philosophic ethics refers simply to a middle way between lust and insensibility to pleasure. Judged solely from the viewpoint of the mean, marital fidelity is a training ground for acquiring or preserving the virtue of moderation. This is, of course, not Maimonides' last word on the subject of marriage; he confines himself in this context to showing how it can be justified from the standpoint of virtue.

Since the Law is interpreted here as pedagogic for curbing lust, Maimonides omits any mention in this context of the commandment "To be fruitful and multiply." Nor does he refer here to a man's duty to give his wife her "time" (*'onah*) of conjugality. Maimonides is, moreover, silent about the limited character of the self-discipline resulting from obeying the laws concerning forbidden foods and forbidden sexual acts. A person might for instance refrain from eating the forbidden foods and yet gorge himself upon food that is permissible. A comparable difficulty exists in connection with sexual conduct, as Maimonides himself implies in the "Commentary on Sanhedrin" (7.3, pp. 180–81).

Generosity

Generosity lies between prodigality and stinginess. In inclining toward the extreme, the laws of the Torah germane to this virtue "come close" to prodigality; Maimonides does not say in this instance, as he did when discussing the laws related to moderation, that they depart only "a little" from the mean. The following laws are in a sense excessive, but they are useful for training a person to acquire the virtue of generosity: the laws concerning tithes; the laws prescribing that a portion of the harvest be left for the poor (a corner of the field, etc.); the laws of the Sabbatical and the Jubilee Years, which include the obligation of releasing the poor from their debts; the giving of charity "sufficient to make up what he [someone needy] lacks" (*dei maḥsaro*). The last, based upon Deut. 15.8, encompasses the duty to clothe the naked and feed the hungry (*CM*, Pe'ah, 1.1). To repeat, the laws of the Torah dictating that help be given to the poor are "excessive" from the standpoint of the middle way. This might throw light upon the title selected by Maimonides for the section of the Code that contains most of the above commandments, namely, "Laws of Gifts for the Poor." Not only do these laws go toward the extreme related to generosity, but what the poor deserve is not deemed relevant; what is required is in effect that *gifts* be given to those in need.

Gentleness (The Middle Way Regarding Anger)

The Torah contains a number of laws that aim at "weakening" the power of rage by inclining toward servility. Among them is the prohibition against taking revenge, which, surprisingly, is interpreted as going toward an extreme. Maimonides implies that revenge is in some instances in harmony with the middle way.[3] The standard of the mean does not, however, necessarily require vengeance. We shall see that according to the Code, the middle way with respect to anger aims at preventing the recurrence of a serious misdeed; justifiable anger is not as such vengeful (HD, 1.4). As for the difficulty of obeying an absolute prohibition against vengeance, Maimonides says in his "Commentary on Pereq Ḥeleq" that "most people prefer taking revenge upon their enemies to most of the pleasures of the body" (Sanhedrin, 10.1, p. 204). This seems to suggest that the middle way is more natural than the rabbinic condemnation of any expression of anger. In *EC*, at any rate, Maimonides treats the middle way as the sole correct standard.

Besides the prohibition against taking revenge, the following two commandments are a discipline for diminishing the power of rage: (1) the duty to help an enemy lighten or unload his donkey's burden when the animal is lying prostrate under its load (Exod. 23.5), and (2) the obligation to assist a man's donkey or ox get to its feet when it has fallen down (Deut. 22.4). Although the latter law does not refer expressly to helping an enemy, Maimonides presupposes that such conduct is what this law specifies; hence it too is useful for curbing one's temper. Ac-

3. Cf. Aristotle's view of the mean in conjunction with his definition of anger, which, stated simply, is the desire for revenge (*Rhetoric* 1378a32–34).

cording to the Code, if a man has a choice between helping a friend or enemy load his beast of burden, he should aid his enemy first "to conquer [his] evil impulse" (H. Rotseaḥ Ushemirat Nafesh, 13.13).

In *EC* Maimonides gives a number of examples in which a vice is mistaken for a virtue, one being that of erroneously believing that a person who depreciates himself (*al-muhīn al-nafs*) has the virtue of gentleness (p. 381). This example is given, I suggest, because the Law inclines toward the deficient extreme, that is, the extreme of servility (*mahāna*, p. 380). hence, Jews are prone to make this mistake. (In the *Tanbīh* Alfarabi refers to a number of instances in which a vice is confused with a virtue, but he does not give this example [ed. Al-Yasin, p. 66].) Maimonides also mentions that people might think that someone who is insensible to pleasure because of the dryness of his nature possesses the virtue of moderation. The Law itself, as we have seen, inclines toward the deficient extreme.

Contentment

Contentment lies between greed and laziness. Maimonides cites a single commandment in this instance, one that opposes the temptation toward avarice: Jewish law requires a person to go to considerable lengths to return a lost object to the owner. The Torah refers literally to an obligation to return a stray animal. "You shall not see your brother's ox or his sheep driven away, and hide yourself from them; you shall surely bring them back to your brother" (Deut. 22.1). Since the commandment goes beyond the middle way, we may infer that philosophic ethics is compatible with ignoring the animal.

Modesty/Sense of Shame

In the opening chapter we saw that the account of the moral virtues in *EC* is partly adapted to a Jewish setting, a point that takes on fresh importance for our present discussion. We might ask ourselves, What moral virtue does honoring one's parents help to instil? Or the commandment to obey the teachers of the halakhah? Although these commandments have no palpable connection with any of the moral virtues discussed in Aristotle's *Nicomachean Ethics*, they can be interpreted as useful for acquiring modesty/sense of shame.

The Torah contains laws that incline toward both extremes in this instance, namely, toward shyness and impudence. Some commandments require conduct that tends toward shyness to eliminate impudence, but some incline toward impudence (!) to counteract shyness. Now, in the case of each of the other moral virtues, one of the extremes is more widespread and harmful than the other; lust is more common and harmful than insensibility to pleasure, stinginess than prodigality, and so on. But presumably shyness and impudence are equally in need of correction. Hence, there are commandments that, paradoxically, incline in both directions.

The following commandments require behavior opposed to impudence: "You shall rise before the hoary head and honor the old man" (Lev. 19.32); "Honor your father" (Exod. 20.12); "You shall not turn aside from the thing [or word] they shall tell you" (Deut. 17.11). The last verse requires obeying those who interpret the Torah, that is, the teachers of the Oral Law (*MT*, H. Mamrim, 1.1–2). As for the obligation to honor your father, Maimonides abbreviates the original injunction to honor both parents, thereby implying that the honor given to one's father, that is, the sterner parent, is more important for eliminating the tendency toward impudence. We can summarize the above three commandments as requiring that honor be given to the elderly, to one's father (or parents), and to the teachers of the Law. The bestowal of honor in these instances is advantageous to oneself, that is, to the development of one's own virtue. It is noteworthy that Maimonides subtly presents here a reason why a philosopher should honor his father and strictly obey the teachers of the Oral Law: such subservience is salutary for counteracting any tendency he might have toward impudence, which in turn is useful for contemplation (cf. the "veils" specified in chapter 7 of *EC*).

To remove the vice of shyness, the following commandments

are useful: "You shall surely rebuke your neighbor" (Lev. 19.17), and "You shall be fearful of no man" (Deut. 1.17; this precept refers to the way a judge should comport himself). The middle way does not go so far as to require that a wrong-doer be rebuked. It is the Law that lays down an obligation to administer a fraternal correction. From the vantage point of philosophic morality, the broad duty to rebuke a sinner smacks of impudence; it extends beyond the propriety of the mean.

GENERALLY ACCEPTED OPINIONS AND
THE DENIAL OF RATIONAL LAWS

Although the commandments can be defended by reason as a means for acquiring moral virtue, this is not to say that they are strictly rational. Maimonides denies that there are any "rational laws." He deals with this issue briefly, almost in passing, within the setting of an examination of the apparent conflict between philosophy and the Law regarding self-restraint (continence). The resolution of the conflict depends upon distinguishing between "generally accepted opinions" and "traditional laws." It is in this context that Maimonides differentiates the "theological" belief in the existence of rational laws from the philosophic affirmation of "generally accepted opinions" (*EC*, chap. 6). Here, as in the *Guide*, Maimonides shows his opposition to the Mutakallimūn (the theologians); the difficulty that comes to light in *EC* is that they attempt to buttress the obedience to divine law (or a part of the Law) through contending that it is rational. In identifying the belief in rational laws with the Mutakallimūn and juxtaposing such laws with "generally accepted opinions," Maimonides implies that the philosophers affirm the validity of the latter.

The context of the discussion is itself important. His immediate goal is to resolve an apparent contradiction between the philosophers and the rabbinic sages regarding how to evaluate continence. The philosophers, Maimonides says, regard the man who is simply virtuous and never wants to do wrong as superior to the man who is tempted but controls his temptation. The rabbinic sages, however, praise the man who is tempted to do wrong but restrains his evil impulse. The rabbinic praise of continence, according to Maimonides, refers to conquering the desire to transgress the "traditional laws" (shara'i' sam'iyya: mitsvot shim'iyyot), which are specific to the Jewish nation; they include such laws as the prohibitions against mixing milk with meat, wearing a mixture of wool and linen, and the illicit sexual unions. Although a virtuous Jew might be tempted to transgress such laws, he would not be tempted to transgress certain fundamental opinions that are commonly accepted by people; for example, that murder and theft are bad. He might have to conquer his evil impulse to transgress the "traditional laws," but he would have no desire to commit a breach of what is "generally accepted" (EC, chap. 6). Maimonides concludes that the Jewish tradition does not conflict with the philosophic position.

Because the "traditional laws" require stricter conduct than does the mean, a virtuous man might be tempted to transgress them. Maimonides anticipates and provides for such a case by maintaining that a virtuous individual who conquers his evil impulse is especially laudable. Two reasons are given for this praise. Because the conquest of the evil impulse is painful, the victory is meritorious; Maimonides quotes the sages as saying that "the reward is according to the pain." And if a man has to conquer his impulse, he must have a strong passion! Hence the sages say, "Whoever is greater than his friend has a greater [evil] impulse than he." The struggle involved in obeying the "traditional laws" is, however, contrary to the equanimity that is the goal of philosophic ethics. The philosophers regard a perfectly harmonious soul as superior to one that has achieved such a victory. There is not quite perfect agreement between the philosophic and the Jewish standpoints.

The "generally accepted opinions" are completely in accord with the moral virtues, that is, with philosophic ethics (this, too, implies that the philosophers affirm their existence.) According to what is "generally accepted," the following are bad: murder, theft, robbery, fraud, harming an innocent person, repaying a benefactor with evil, and degrading one's parents. A person who follows the middle way is not tempted to steal, commit fraud, harm an innocent person, and so on. If a man wants to transgress laws based upon these opinions, he has a morally defective soul (*EC*, chap. 6). The moral virtues, then, are consonant with obeying the fundamental rules essential for the well-being of any community.

The *endoxa* set forth in *EC* all have a negative form; if they were formulated in terms of law, they would all be prohibitions. Because they require no actions for the public good, they are particularly suitable for the solitary activity of contemplation.[4] They may be said to form the broad framework for the philosopher's way of life in the community.[5] They are perfectly in accord with the dictum that a man should direct all of his conduct toward the goal of attaining theoretical knowledge (chap. 5).

Those who believe in the existence of "rational laws" (more literally, "intellectual" or "intelligible" laws) are said to suffer from the sickness of the Mutakallimūn. What, precisely, is their illness? Maimonides does not tell us in chapter 6, but in chapter 1 he offers a clue: the Mutakallimūn misunderstand the nature of necessity and how it is apprehended. In the *Guide*, he indicates that they do not understand that existence is the basis for necessity (1.73 [115b]). Maimonides implies that because judgments about good and evil are not directly derivable from the nature of things, they lack the necessity required for a "rational [i.e., intellectual] law." The truths apprehended by the intellect possess necessity; this is not the case with the "generally accepted opinions," whose validity depends upon a consensus in the community (*Guide*, 1.2; *Logic*, chap. 8).

Whereas the intellect aims at apprehending the immutable truth, law basically governs conduct; the two realms cannot be joined together in perfect harmony. By denying that there are

4. *Endoxa* need not be formulated in terms of prohibitions. See, for example, *Logic*, chap. 8: It is generally accepted that compensating one's benefactor generously is noble.

5. See Leo Strauss, *Persecution and the Art of Writing*, pp. 136–37.

"intellectual laws," Maimonides alludes to the fundamental difference between *theoria* and *praxis*.[6] How to bring these two heterogeneous realms into some sort of congruence is the ongoing problem that Maimonides deals with—sometimes in diverse ways—in his works. To put the matter differently, "intellect" (ʿaql: *nous*) and "law" are incompatible terms; hence, there are no "intellectual" (rational) laws. One can, however, properly speak of "intellectual principles," which act by necessity and are responsible for the "artisanlike" activity found in natural entities (*Guide*, 3.13 [23a], 3.19 [40b]). A principle as distinct from a law establishes the orderliness of nature.[7]

The "generally accepted opinions" are concerned with *praxis* but, lacking the necessity found in intelligibles, they are not applicable under all circumstances. Maimonides gives no examples of exceptions to the rule in *EC*, but some can be plausibly gleaned from the Code. Consider, for instance, the commonly accepted view (also promulgated by the Law) that deception is wrong. In the Code, Maimonides alludes with some delicacy to an exception that might be necessary in time of war: "It is forbidden to break a covenant with them [the enemy] and to deceive them *after* they have made peace and have accepted the seven [Noahidic] commandments" (H. Melakhim, 6.3, emphasis added). To take a different sort of case, it is obligatory to deceive a poor man in desperate straits who refuses to accept any charity; he should be told that it is a gift or a loan (H. Mattenot ʿAniyyim, 7.9).

6. This issue is discussed more fully in the final chapter of the book. For a different interpretation of the question whether Maimonides affirms the existence of rational laws, see Harry A. Wolfson, *Philo*, vol. 2, pp. 310–11; see also the extended discussion of this issue and related matters by Isadore Twersky, *Introduction to the Code of Maimonides*, pp. 356–514. For objections to Twersky's position, see my article, "Some Notes on Twersky's *Introduction to the Code of Maimonides*."

7. Principles must also be distinguished from the "foundations" of law. In his commentary on "Pereq Ḥeleq," Maimonides sets forth thirteen foundations (qawāʿid) of the Law (*CM*, Sanhedrin, 10.1; pp. 210–17); he does not call them principles. Cf. the reference to the principles of the existents in *Guide*, 1.17. According to *CM*, knowledge of the principles of the existents is part of the Account of the Beginning (physics) (Ḥagigah, 2.1, p. 377).

It is "generally accepted" that it is wrong to harm an innocent person. Are there any exceptions to this rule? When discussing the prohibition against impoverishing oneself to help a
poor person, Maimonides in a way addresses this issue. He
states the following rule: "You are not obligated to remove
harm from another person except on the condition that something like the harm that you remove from him will not befall
you." (CM, Babba Metsiʿa, 2.11. To support this statement,
Maimonides cites the rabbinic dictum, "What is yours takes
precedence over that of every man" [BT, Babba Metsiʿa, 33a].)
One might, then, indirectly harm an innocent man by tending
to one's own legitimate interests.

Since the endoxa are synchronized with the mean, and the
commandments largely incline toward the extreme, the commandments are often "excessive" in comparison to what is
commonly accepted. A case in point concerns suitable conduct
toward one's parents. Whereas it is "generally accepted" that
they should not be depreciated, the Law lays down positive injunctions to honor as well as to "fear," or revere, them. Having
reverence for one's parents requires, for instance, not contra-
dicting them nor posing an argument against what they say. To
honor them requires feeding them, clothing them, and generally helping them in their old age (MT, H. Mamrim, 6.3). The
Code gives a graphic example that illustrates how far one must
go in honoring them. Even if they take your purse filled with
gold pieces and throw it into the sea, you should not put them
to shame or give them any pain or become angry at them, but
follow the "decree of Scripture" (gezeirat ha-katuv) and be silent (ibid., 6.7). By referring here to the "decree of Scripture,"
Maimonides casts doubt upon whether such extreme conduct
is useful for training oneself to acquire the virtue of modesty/
sense of shame (cf. EC, chap. 4).

The "generally accepted opinions" furnish only the minimal
guidance for human life. Acting as constraints and, in effect, as
prohibitions, they almost cry out for supplementation by positive precepts that aim at the public good. In the Jewish community this function is, of course, fulfilled by the Law. In the
"Commentary on Peʾah" (1.1), Maimonides enumerates a num-

ber of laws whose purpose is the community's well-being, including some, such as the prohibitions against theft and fraud, that are "generally accepted," but also others that are not in the list of *endoxa* in *EC*. Not only is it wrong to harm an innocent person, as in *EC*, but it is forbidden to stand idly by while harm is being done to someone else. The Code amplifies upon what is required to fulfill the commandment in question ("Not to stand idly by the blood of your neighbor"). A man must do whatever is necessary to save the victim of an attempted murder or rape, including killing the attacker; it is likewise obligatory to help a drowning man, or the victim of a robbery, or someone attacked by a wild beast (H. Rotseah Ushemirat Nafesh, 1.6–14). It is questionable whether commonly accepted opinion would suffice to lead a man to risk his life to prevent an attempted murder or rape, or even to save the victim of a drowning. In any event, the Law in all of its particularity enjoins the duties under discussion, and Maimonides emphasizes that "all Israel" is commanded to come to the aid of a fellow Jew (ibid., 1.6, 16). In all of these instances a man's responsibility would depend, of course, upon whether he can give effective assistance to the victim. "Everyone who is able to save [the victim] and does not do so, transgresses 'You shall not stand idly by the blood of your neighbor'" (ibid., 1.14).

I argued earlier that because of the overriding importance of the philosophic conception of the human soul for *EC*, there is a strong tendency within the work to abstract from man's political nature. Now we see that even the *endoxa* forming the matrix for the stability of any community are oriented toward the needs of the solitary contemplative life. I have introduced a reference to the particularity of Jewish law in this chapter to make clear how Maimonides takes into consideration outside of *EC* the need for positive injunctions for the public good. It is the Law that extends the scope of moral obligation beyond the minimalist view of those duties toward the community that are consonant with man's rational nature; the Law is indispensable chiefly from the standpoint of the needs of man's political nature.

THE CONFLICT BETWEEN "TRADITIONAL LAWS"
AND PHILOSOPHIC ETHICS

In his justification for the existence of *endoxa*, Maimonides says that they are among the laws about which the *Talmud* says, "If they were not written down, they would deserve to be written down" (*EC*, chap. 6; *BT*, Yoma', 67b). The *Talmud* includes among such laws the "illicit sexual unions" (*'arayot*). These laws specify a variety of prohibitions regarding conduct toward the women a Jew is forbidden to marry. Quietly taking exception to the talmudic view of the *'arayot*, Maimonides classifies the "illicit sexual unions" among the "traditional laws" (*mitsvot shim'iyyot*). He thereby indicates that the "illicit sexual unions," in contrast to the *endoxa*, are not synchronized with the moral virtues; a man might have the virtue of moderation and yet commit adultery, and so on. It is Jewish law that establishes the restrictions connected with the women whom he is forbidden to marry (the *'arayot*).[8] The laws related to marriage are dependent upon the Torah for their validity.[9]

If it were not for the Law, the things forbidden by the "traditional laws" would not be evil. Maimonides does not go so far as to say in *EC* that such laws, also called *huqqim* (statutes), have no reasons; he only indicates that the sages forbid investigating the reasons for them. But in the "Commentary on Berakhot," he refers more clearly to their problematic status. The prohibition against taking a mother bird together with her young is classified among the "traditional laws," which Maimonides now says lack reasons. He argues that the reason for this particular law cannot be to show mercy to the mother bird because if it were, the slaughter of the young would have been forbidden (*CM*, Berakhot, 5.3). In the Code Maimonides calls

8. Cf. *MT*, H. Teshuvah, 2.11, where the forbidden sexual acts are classified as transgressions between man and God. See also below, p. 152, concerning the basis for the refusal of the Patriarch Joseph to yield to the blandishments of Potiphar's wife. In *CM*, Hagigah, 2.1 (p. 378), Maimonides implies that the objection to adultery from the standpoint of man's rational form is solely that while committing the act, a man would be distracted from theoretical matters.

9. *MT*, H. 'Ishut, 1.1–2. Giles of Rome correctly observes that Maimonides denies that marriage is part of the natural law (*Errores Philosophorum*, p. 65).

the prohibition against taking the mother bird together with her young a "decree of Scripture," *gezeirat ha-katuv* (H. Tefillah, 9.7); there, too, he observes that it lacks a reason.

By his silence in chapter 6 of *EC* about whether the "traditional laws" have purposes (or reasons), he preserves the apparent validity of the justification given for them earlier in *EC* (chap. 4), where the "forbidden foods" and the "forbidden sexual acts" are interpreted as a discipline for acquiring the virtue of moderation. But by classifying the "illicit sexual unions" and the prohibition against mixing milk with meat as "traditional laws" in chapter 6, Maimonides obliquely questions the extent of their usefulness for moral training.[10] The statement in the "Commentary on Berakhot" that the "traditional laws" lack reasons suggests that such laws are of dubious or, at any rate, limited worth for moral discipline. We have already noted that a person might scrupulously obey the prohibitions regarding the "forbidden foods" but eat to excess a whole host of permitted food.

I shall not attempt to give a comprehensive account of the "traditional laws" (or statutes), but I tentatively suggest the following. Maimonides moves between two positions: (1) The validity of "statutes" depends upon their having been established by an authoritative source of law; no other reason exists for obeying them. This interpretation is in accord with the *Logic*, where Maimonides distinguishes statements that are "generally accepted" from those that are "received" or "traditional" (*maqbūlāt: mequbalot*), which, being set off from the *endoxa*, are identifiable as "statutes." Deriving their validity from an authoritative individual or assembly, the "received" laws are indicative of what is distinctive of a particular nation (chap. 8). (2) According to the *Guide*, the *ḥuqqim* lack an evident reason for being obeyed.[11] This leaves open the question of whether

10. In the Code, the "illicit sexual unions" and the laws concerning "forbidden foods" are regarded as a means of distinguishing the Jewish nation from the other nations (*Sefer ha-Madda'*, p. 18b). This view is in agreement with such laws being classified among the *mitsvot shim'iyyot*; they are accordingly differentiated from the commonly accepted opinions.

11. *Guide*, 3.26, 28. See also *MT*, H. Me'ilah, 8.8; H. Temurah, 4.13; H. Miqva'ot, 11.12.

any reason can be found for obeying them, and the *Guide* indicates that most, if not all, of the *ḥuqqim* have reasons. On this account the "statutes" differ from what is "generally accepted" in that the reasons for the latter, but not the former, are obvious.[12]

It is possible for a special meaning to be bestowed upon an activity so that it has a purpose (or reason) that it would not otherwise have; since the reason in such a case would not be obvious, or intrinsic to the activity, the law could be a "statute." For example, the laws of purity, identified in the Code as *ḥuqqim*, can serve as a moral discipline if the requisite actions are performed with the proper intention. Thus, with respect to the ritual immersion in water, which is a "decree of Scripture," Maimonides says that if a person "directs his heart to purify his soul from the unclean things of the soul, which are thoughts of iniquity and bad character traits [*deʿot*]," then his actions will be effective. He must resolve "in his heart" to separate himself from such evil things; everything depends upon the "intention of the heart"; the water by itself does not bring about the purification (H. Miqvaʾot, 11.12). In the case of the philosophic method of therapy, in which the repeated performance of the prescribed actions produces a change in a given character trait, the effect is intrinsic to the actions themselves.

It is not clear how far Maimonides meant to extend the mode of interpretation that he employs in connection with the laws of purity in the Code. It is certainly applicable to at least some other activities that are also classified under the heading of "decree of Scripture." He interprets the blowing of the Shofar on the High Holidays, for instance, as in effect calling people to awaken from their slumbers, to search their deeds, and to mend their ways (H. Teshuvah, 3.7) The use of a ram's horn rather than something else for this purpose is in a sense arbitrary; it is a "decree of Scripture."

12. One might think that if a "statute" does have a reason, it is never obvious. The Code, however, identifies as a *ḥoq* the law instituted by Abraham to accompany travelers (received as guests) when they depart from the city. This law—despite its being a "statute"—has a clear reason, namely, to protect strangers from harm (H. ʾEvel, 14.2–3). The law's having been promulgated by

A Note on the Intractibility of the Soul's Parts

To return to *EC*, in chapter 2 Maimonides considers the parts of the soul and how they are regarded by the Law and philosophy. The chapter's subtitle alludes to the difficulty of obeying the Law owing to the soul's nature: "On the disobedience [or intractibility] of the soul's powers and on knowledge of the part in which the virtues and the vices are primarily found."[13]

Whereas philosophy through its conception of the moral virtues regulates the soul's appetitive part, the Law governs both the sentient and the appetitive faculties. One of the points of tension concerns the restrictions placed by the Law upon the senses, as is evident from the "illicit sexual unions," the ʿarayot, which regulate conduct regarding the women whom a man is forbidden to marry (mother, sister, daughter, a married woman, and so on).[14] A Jew is forbidden to smell the perfume of such women, or to hear them sing, or to look with pleasure at their figures, and so on.[15] By contrast, the virtue of moderation is limited to the right habituation of bodily desire. Do the aforementioned restrictions upon the senses conflict with the virtue of moderation? That question, as we have seen, is in a way resolved in chapter 6: a virtuous Jew might be tempted to transgress the "traditional laws," but he controls his temptation. Still, it is dubious whether the "statutes," the ḥuqqim, can be justified from the standpoint of the rectitude of the mean.

The asymmetry between philosophy and the Law can be further illustrated by reconsidering the practices prescribed for curing melancholia and refreshing the soul of a person weary from study. Those practices, which aim at "expanding" or de-

---

an authoritative individual suffices in this instance for it to be classified as a *ḥoq*.

13. The use of the singular, "part," in the subtitle is puzzling. It may allude to the primacy of the soul's rational part—despite the fact that the appetitive part, too, contains virtues and vices.

14. They are the women with whom sexual relations are prohibited in chapter 18 of the Book of Leviticus (*MT*, H. 'Ishut, 1.5).

15. *CM*, Sanhedrin, 7.4, p. 178; *MT*, H. 'Issurei Biʾah, 21.2.

lighting the soul through activities that engage the senses, are described in two different ways in chapter 5 of *EC*. First Maimonides commends (1) listening to songs and melodies, (2) walking in gardens, and handsome buildings, and (3) sitting before beautiful "forms," that is, statues, pictures, and the like (p. 388). No biblical or rabbinic quotation is cited in support of this advice. Later in the chapter, after taking up some other topics, he advises (1) decorating walls with gold, (2) placing a gold border upon garments, and (3) looking at works of art (*nuqūshāt*)—sculpture, paintings, engravings—and beautiful objects generally. He then quotes the rabbinic statement, "An attractive dwelling, an attractive wife, attractive utensils, and a bed prepared for the disciples of the wise give delight to the mind of a man" (p. 390). This is the only Jewish quotation cited to support any of the diverse forms of therapy that are recommended in chapter 5. Thus no halakhic support is given for listening to songs and melodies, walking in gardens and handsome buildings, and looking at statues, paintings, and engravings. We cannot help but wonder whether these activities are sanctioned by the Law.

One of his responsa justifies our skepticism in connection with music. In the responsum, Maimonides cites a talmudic passage that completely forbids listening to songs and melodies (*BT*, Soṭah, 48a). The purpose of the Law's prohibition, he says, is to keep a rein upon the soul's appetitive faculty. Maimonides also observes that the Law does not take into account the rare individual whose soul would be "protected" and whose passion for "apprehending an intelligible" would be quickened through listening to the right sort of music; there might even be someone who could be helped by music to submit more easily to the demands of the Law.[16] Maimonides argues there, as in the *Guide* (3.34), that the Law is beneficial for most people, but not for all.

---

16. *Teshuvot ha-Rambam*, vol. 2, pp. 398–400. For a fuller discussion of the responsum, see Boaz Cohen, "The Responsum of Maimonides Concerning Music." The talmudic condemnation of music is reproduced in the Code, where Maimonides says that the prohibition against playing a musical instrument and listening to music is due to the destruction of the Temple (H. Taʿaniyyot, 5.14).

As for the pleasure that comes from looking at statues and paintings, there are no restrictions upon such enjoyment from the viewpoint of the contemplative life. To repeat, what we today would call an "aesthetic" sort of pleasure is justified in *EC* to restore a downcast spirit or to relax a soul weary from study. Now, from the standpoint of the needs of the human soul, it does not matter whether a beautiful statue is the image of a god or goddess. The Law, however, forbids a Jew to gaze upon an idol (*MT*, H. ʿAvodah Zarah, 2.2). Maimonides glosses over the tension between the usefulness of looking at beautiful objects and the Law's opposition to idolatry. (The Law is not oblivious to the beauty that might be found in an idolatrous figure. If a person delights in the workmanship found in the form but does not accept the idol as a god, he is not subject to punishment [ibid., 3.6].)

Whereas the Law undoubtedly regulates the soul's sentient power, Maimonides says that a "perplexity" exists regarding whether one can speak of obedience and disobedience in connection with the soul's rational power (*EC*, chap. 2). The Law requires that certain beliefs be held, but it is doubtful whether the human intellect can be commanded to subscribe to a belief. Belief is the affirmation that something exists outside of the intellect just as it is apprehended within the intellect (*Guide*, 1.50). In other words, belief requires knowledge, but the intellectual apprehension essential to knowledge is not subject to command. Is it reasonable, moreover, to require all Jews to understand the premises that are essential to grasping the beliefs required by the Law? Philosophy refers to intellectual virtues rather than commandments, thereby avoiding the problem inherent in the attempt to bring about knowledge through compulsion; there is no obligation to acquire the intellectual virtues.

As for the soul's imaginative power, Maimonides denies that man is free to control it (*EC*, chap. 2). To understand this remark, we have to keep the practical horizon of the discussion in mind; it is not intended to be a full-scale account of the imagination. Earlier in *EC*, Maimonides had implied that it is possible to exercise at least some control over the imagination in connection with theoretical matters: the Mutakallimūn mistakenly employ the imagination when they should rely upon the intellect (chap. 1); Maimonides assumes here that a person can at least control when and how the imagination is employed. But so far as ethical matters are concerned, he maintains that a person is unable to control his imagination through an act of the will ("choice") or through "thought" (r'ay, lit., "opinion"); a man cannot be held responsible for his fantasies (chap. 2). Maimonides argues the point by observing that choice and thought do not act upon the imaginative faculty in dreams.

Is not the regulation of the imagination vital to Jewish law? The *Guide* goes so far as to identify "the evil impulse" with the imagination (2.12 [26b]). There appears to be some tension between the rabbinic assumption that man can conquer his "evil impulse" and the (philosophic) view regarding the impossibility of controlling the imagination. Be that as it may, the ramifications for the halakhah of what Maimonides says in *EC* are clear: a person is not culpable if his imagination wanders to illicit matters. The following example from the Code illustrates this view of man's restricted culpability: it is forbidden to speak about business and related matters on the Sabbath, but if a man's imagination strays to such things, he has not committed a sin (H. Shabbat, 24.1).

The Maimonidean view of the imagination also raises a question about how to understand the freedom of a person with a sick soul, who is characterized in *EC* as having a corrupt imagination. Such a person imagines that what is bad is good and vice versa—and yet he cannot help himself (chap. 3). However, by repeatedly performing the actions that counteract his vice, he is able to bring the soul's appetitive power into good condition and thus meliorate his fantasy life. In general, Maimonides regards man's *actions* as subject to his control, so that by means of a proper course of conduct he can indirectly set his imagination aright.[17]

17. See, e.g., *MT*, H. Teshuvah, 5.1.

II
The Mishneh Torah

FOUR

Introduction to the Ethics
of the Code

In the *Mishneh Torah*, Maimonides takes upon himself the task of a legislator, insofar as that is possible within a community whose laws have been specified in great detail by a long chain of tradition. The Code is divided into fourteen books, each containing a number of sections, and every section includes the commandments relevant to the subject under discussion. The 613 commandments that are enjoined upon every Jew form the scaffolding upon which the Code rests. Because it contains all 613 commandments, Maimonides is in a position to justify his claim that the Code comprises the entire Oral Law. Although the *Talmud* states that there are 613 commandments, it does not specify their content.[1] Maimonides himself determines which laws are among the 613 commandments and how they are formulated. The section concerning ethics, Hilkhot Deʿot ("Laws Concerning Character Traits"), which is part of the Book of Knowledge, contains eleven commandments. In his work as a philosophic codifier, Maimonides demarcates a separate realm within the Oral Law devoted to "ethical laws" (*hilkhot deʿot*).

A few differences between Hilkhot Deʿot (HD) and *EC* may be noted at the outset. Most of the *mitsvot* in HD are simply laid down as part of a law-code to be obeyed; HD does not contain the rather extensive justification of the *mitsvot* found in *EC*. A number of the commandments included in HD are the same as those which, according to *EC*, incline toward the ex-

---

1. Makkot, 23b. Maimonides indicates in the *Book of the Commandments* (pp. 4–5) that the enumerations of the 613 commandments available in his day were not authentic; he says that they were generally based upon the erroneous list in *Halakhot Gedolot*.

treme as a discipline for attaining the mean. There is no indication in HD that this is their purpose; Maimonides does say,
however, that the middle way is the correct standard in connection with all character traits (1.4). Further, whereas *EC* describes the middle way regarding each moral virtue in a general
manner (e.g., moderation lies in the mean between lust and insensibility to pleasure), HD contains a somewhat more specific
definition for a number of qualities that lie in the mean; a more
precise delineation of suitable conduct is required by a law-
code. As befits a work on the Oral Law, HD also contains a
larger range of rabbinic and biblical citations than does *EC*. Because Maimonides takes into consideration a number of rabbinic precepts that go to the extreme, the account of piety in
HD differs to some extent from the parallel discussion in *EC*.
As we shall see, this in turn has an effect upon the description
of the extremes in HD.

Whereas in *EC*, Maimonides expressly says that he draws
upon the works of the philosophers, no comparable statement
is found in HD. In some respects, the philosophic content or
substructure of HD is more concealed than in *EC*. What is
most evident from the surface of the work is that all the commandments in HD are supported by verses from Scripture.
Broadly speaking, Maimonides adheres to the distinction between Torah and *mitsvah* found at the beginning of the Code.
The Torah, he says, is the Written Law; *mitsvah* is the "explanation" of the Torah.[2] His account of the commandments in
HD, as in the Code as a whole, is intended to be the authoritative "explanation" of the Written Law.

If, by organizing the Oral Law on the basis of the 613 commandments, Maimonides had a certain leeway in formulating
the commandments, his having to base them on the Written
Law placed an unalterable constraint upon him. Thus, he had
to justify the doctrine of the mean on the basis of the Torah,
and he grounds it on the biblical verse, "And you shall walk in
His ways" (Deut. 28.9; this justification for the mean is not

---

2. *Sefer ha-Madda'*, p. 1b. For a discussion of the distinction between Torah
and *mitsvah*, see appendix 1.

mentioned in *EC.*) As is clear from the fact that he introduces philosophic ethics into HD, he was not unduly restricted by having to give a justification from the Torah for the precepts of HD. But his interjection of philosophic concepts into a code of Jewish law precludes perfect consistency. This is quite obvious in connection with the attempt to base the teaching of the mean upon the ways of God. Although Maimonides discloses here an authentically biblical viewpoint, which repeatedly looks to the ways of God as a model for human conduct, God's ways are not strictly in accordance with the mean. The middle way includes, for example, a definition of the mean in anger, but God does not have the passion of anger (H. Yesodei ha-Torah, 1.8).

The procedure of Maimonides suggests that consistency cannot be the decisive criterion for a codifier who, relying upon philosophic premises, reconstitutes the received opinions of the community. The overall good of the community takes precedence. In HD different purposes govern the discussion of various parts of the work so that the demands of philosophy and the community's well-being can be met. The resultant composition contains some asymmetries and an occasional contradiction. The tensions and contradictions are indicative not only of a philosophic viewpoint but also of indigenous Jewish teachings.

While radically reorienting the whole discussion of ethics in the Jewish community, Maimonides proceeds with circumspection. His caution can be exemplified by the manner in which he speaks of the ways of God: he prudently omits any indication that they are not to be understood literally. In the *Book of the Commandments*—a work that was much less exposed than the Code—he says that in HD he speaks metaphorically (or through "similitude") when referring to the ways of God (positive precept no. 8).

Maimonides does what he can to mitigate the difficulties that arise from the incorporation of philosophic concepts into the Code. A brief comment on how he deals with the following issues will illuminate his procedure.

1. The subject of ethics (lit., character traits) is on the face of it incompatible with the notion of obligation. Can a person be *commanded* to have certain states of character? Maimonides interprets the obligation to follow the middle way as requiring that a man *assess* his character traits on the basis of the mean and that he make his *goal* the attainment of the mean (HD, 1.4). Further, a person is obliged to *habituate* himself in such a manner that he acquires the right moral qualities (1.6–7).

2. One might wonder whether having a particular passion can be dictated by the Law. For example, is it reasonable to command a person to feel love for his neighbor? Maimonides resolves the difficulty by interpreting the commandment to love your neighbor as yourself as requiring that a person have a concern for the honor and the possessions of his neighbor (6.3); there is no obligation to feel the emotion of love. A comparable difficulty exists in connection with some other precepts of the Torah. A man is forbidden, for instance, to be fearful in time of war. The commandment is formulated as follows in the enumeration of precepts in the Code's Introduction: "Men engaged in warfare shall not fear nor be terrified of their enemies at the time of battle. As it is said, 'You shall not tremble nor be frightened because of them'" (negative precept no. 58). Maimonides solves the problem in this instance by saying that a man is forbidden to *think* about his wife and children at the time of battle; a man's thought, as distinct from the passion of fear, is presumed to be under his control. "Whoever begins to think and reflect [about them] during warfare transgresses a negative commandment . . ." (H. Melakhim, 7.15).

3. Can every Jew be reasonably commanded to train his character in accordance with the strict standard of the mean? To use the idiom of the philosophers we may ask whether it is reasonable to require all people to possess the moral virtues. Although the command to adhere to the mean is enjoined upon all Jews, Maimonides quietly indicates that most people are not expected actually to adhere to the sage's morality: "Just as the wise man is identified by his wisdom and

his character traits, which distinguish him from the rest of the people . . ." (HD, 5.1). The morality of the mean is de facto that of the wise men.

To make the Code as reasonable as possible Maimonides sometimes addresses different individuals or groups in different parts of the work. A rational code has to be cognizant of the inequalities found among human beings; it has to take account of the different capacities and interests of diverse individuals, without neglecting what is necessary for the community as a whole. This view of law, inherent in the work of Maimonides, is applicable to ethics insofar as different moral paths are deemed suitable for different people. In HD, separate precepts are laid down for the following (though some overlap exists): the wise men, the pious men, the "disciple of wise men," the people in general. If we consider the Code as a whole, the list would extend to prophets, judges, and *parnasim* (communal leaders) among others. What is incumbent upon a judge, for example, is not identical with what is necessary for a man to be a prophet— nor, for that matter, are the judge's moral prerequisites exactly the same as those of a wise man.

There is no term in the biblical-rabbinic tradition corresponding to "ethics"; Maimonides fashioned the term *deʿah* to serve his purposes. The ordinary meaning of *deʿah* is "opinion" or "knowledge," but in H. Deʿot it refers to something like a state of character. At the beginning of the work he establishes its meaning by describing two habits with respect to anger: one man is rarely angry, another is irascible. Maimonides thereby alludes to Avot (4.10), where the term *deʿah* is used roughly in the sense of "character trait" (a number of attitudes with respect to anger are described). Maimonides extends the range of characteristics covered by *deʿah*, but its use in Avot gave him a wedge for dealing with moral phenomena in terms of "ethics" (*ēthē:* characters).[3]

3. Biblical law does not neatly conform to the philosophic conception of ethics. The difficulty can seen by comparing Maimonides' account of "ethics" in HD with the classification of law given in the *Book of the Commandments* (which is written in Arabic), where he observes that law regulates the following: (1) opinions, (2) actions, (3) character traits (*akhlāq*) and (4) speech. The

His choice of this term for the discussion of ethics is none-theless puzzling. There are other words that he might have used, or refashioned, such as *middot,* which became the stan-dard Hebrew word for this subject after the time of Maimoni-des. Earlier in the Code, prior to his thematic discussion of "ethics," he in fact uses *middot* when describing the moral qualities of a prophet. We are told that a prophet must be a "mighty man in his characteristics [*middot*]." It is also note-worthy that Maimonides uses the term *yetser* here: "His [the prophet's] impulse [*yetser*] shall never overcome him in any-thing but he shall always overcome his impulse with his mind" (H. Yesodei ha-Torah, 5.1). The word *yetser* is another term fundamental to the rabbinic view of moral phenomena, yet it is almost completely absent from HD. Maimonides uses it only once there: a man who is wise conquers his "impulse" (*yetser*) for certain foods that are tasty but are harmful to the body (4.10).

Prior to HD, his use of the term *de‘ah* stays close to the in-tellectual denotation in the word's root, "to know." The form of the human soul is identified as intellect (*de‘ah*), and the sepa-rate intelligences are called *de‘ot* (H. Yesodei ha-Torah, 4.8–9). In other words, *de‘ah* is initially used as the Hebrew equivalent of the Greek *nous,* and later to designate "character"! I suggest that he alludes to the intellectual component in moral quali-ties by referring to them as *de‘ot.*

A reconsideration of what he says about the human soul in *EC* throws light upon his choice of this term. In *EC,* as in HD, he regards the intellect as the form of man's soul. He stresses that the subrational parts of the human soul differ from the comparable parts found in the souls of beasts; the form of each species decisively affects all the parts of the soul. In the case of man, the subrational parts are, as it were, the matter for the

---

prohibitions against gossip and calumny are placed in the last class; they are not treated as part of ethics (Root 9, pp. 32–33). In the Code, however, the pro-hibition against speaking ill of other people is found in the "Laws Concerning Character Traits" (H. De‘ot). Maimonides uses the term *de‘ah* in the Code to cover a large range of moral phenomena. Regarding the comprehensive con-notation of the term *de‘ah,* see, for example, H. Teshuvah, 4.7: the habits of having evil thoughts and befriending the wrong people are designated as bad *de‘ot.*

soul's intellectual form (chap. 1, near end). The intellect, then, has a certain effect upon the soul's appetitive part, and moral qualities can accordingly be depicted by a term that alludes to the presence of an intellectual element.[4]

Opinions are implicit in the character traits described in HD. Thus, the middle way in bodily desire requires having the right opinion about what foods to eat and in what quantity (cf. 1.4 with chap. 4 of HD, which contains a lengthy enumeration of which foods are healthful and which harmful); the middle way with respect to anger requires knowing that anger is justifiable only if it aims at preventing a future misdeed; the mean regarding the desire for money requires knowing that a livelihood should be pursued only to the point of having sufficient money to meet one's immediate needs; and so on (1.4). Elsewhere in the Code, Maimonides also sometimes implies that character, good or bad, is inextricably bound up with the opinions a person holds. For instance, he says that "the Torah descends to the extreme point in the *thought* of a man and cuts off his evil impulse, for the nature of man inclines toward increasing his possessions and watching over his money" (H. Temurah, 4.13, emphasis added).

Occasionally *de'ah* refers simply to a passion; in HD anger, for example, is called a bad *de'ah* (2.3). Passions are not as such singled out in Maimonides' discussion of morality; the word *de'ah* blurs the Greek distinction between *ēthē* (characters) and *pathē* (passions). His treatment of moral phenomena is in this respect faithful to the biblical-rabbinic tradition, which does not have a word designating the passions. Maimonides does not need a word for "passion" to deal with the subject of ethics. In the whole of *EC* he does not use the Arabic word for

4. The Stoics might have exercised an influence upon Maimonides in his choice of a term that generally means "opinion" to encompass the passions. Galen's writings are one source through which Maimonides could have known this Stoic view. For example, in *De Placitis Hippocratis et Platonis*, Galen cites the Greek Stoic, Chrysippus, as viewing the passions as kinds of judgments (ed. Phillip De Lacy, part 1, p. 292.17–18, and passim). Maimonides was familiar with this work by Galen; it is referred to in *Pirqei Mosheh* (*Fuṣūl Mūsā fi'l-Ṭibb*), chap. 25, ed. Schacht and Meyerhof, pp. 67 (Eng.) and 80 (Arabic). Cf. Cicero, *De Finibus*, 3.35.

"passion" but refers simply to "states of the soul" and "moral habits."[5]

It should be noted, finally, that "philosophic ethics" is not as such referred to in HD, nor is there a term for "virtue" or for such virtues as "moderation." Terms that derive from the philosophic tradition will not, however, be set off with quotation marks.

5. My discussion of the term *de'ah* is partly drawn from my article, "Language and Ethics: Reflections on Maimonides' 'Ethics'," which contains a fuller examination of the transmission of Greek moral terminology into the Hebrew language than I have given above.

FIVE

The "Laws Concerning Character Traits" (Hilkhot De'ot): Philosophic Ethics and Piety

THE WAY OF THE WISE MEN

HD is positioned between H. Yesodei ha-Torah ("Laws Concerning the Foundations of the Torah") and H. Talmud Torah ("Laws Concerning the Study of Torah"). Since the prophets are responsible for the foundations, they are dominant in H. Yesodei ha-Torah; the wise man has a special place in the discussion of philosophic ethics (HD); the rabbi (*rav*) takes on importance in the "Laws Concerning the Study of Torah" (H. Talmud Torah). The rabbi is hardly mentioned in the text of the Code proper until H. Talmud Torah. There is, I believe, only one reference to "the *rav*" in HD itself, in a passage where he is presumed to be a teacher in a quite general sense, giving instruction in the Torah or a craft (e.g., teaching a trade to an orphan; 6.10). In H. Talmud Torah the rabbi is understood to teach Torah to advanced but still young students. Since the term *rav* can be used in the general sense of teacher, there is sometimes an overlap between the rabbi and sage. But the *rav* in an emphatic sense is a teacher of the Torah and, as such, he need not possess wisdom in a comprehensive sense. The rabbi is not the same as a *ḥakham* (wise man).

In his explanation of the Oral Law, Maimonides repeatedly refers to what the "wise men" said or commanded. He does not have recourse to the Hebrew equivalent of the familiar talmudic expression, *tannu rabbanan*, "our rabbis taught." The wise men, as it were, take the place of the rabbis as the interpreters of the Torah in what has come to be called the rabbinic period. Through his ubiquitous reference to "wise men," Maimonides can on occasion quietly allude to the philosophers or to sages with philosophic knowledge without arousing suspicion. In some contexts the wise man is assumed to have only knowledge of Jewish law, but in others he is understood to have philosophic knowledge as well. Maimonides takes advantage of the ambiguity of the term *ḥakham* to establish the possible presence of a philosopher-sage within the Jewish community.

The different locutions used to describe the sages can be revealing. Maimonides occasionally refers to the "wise men of Israel," who are thus tacitly contrasted with the "wise men of Greece." The latter have a comprehensive knowledge of the heavens (H. Qiddush ha-Ḥodesh, 17.24). The "wise men of Israel" are concerned not with the heavens (except in connection with matters of calendation) but with carrying on a tradition that has its origin in the distant past; Maimonides does not refer to the "wise men of Israel" when speaking of the Account of the Beginning, but he does refer to the "wise men of Greece."[1] The "wise men of Israel" are characterized as having "received [lit., heard] the tradition [*qabbalah*] regarding the roots of the entire Torah, going back in unbroken succession to Moses."[2] There is no indication that they are capable of demonstrating those roots (nor indeed that the roots are demonstrable). The "wise men of Israel" master them through having listened carefully and learning what has been orally transmitted. But they *are* concerned with the "roots" of the Torah and not solely with the practices prescribed by the Law.

In the first chapter of H. Talmud Torah, Maimonides refers pointedly to the "wise men of Israel," reiterating that they are among the "transmitters of the tradition [*shemuʿah*] going back in unbroken succession to Moses our teacher" (1.9; cf. 1.2). It is necessary to stress that the sages spoken about in H. Talmud Torah are indeed Jewish sages because in the previous section, in HD, there is some ambiguity about who exactly the "wise men" are. The "way of the wise men," which is the middle way, is delineated in HD, and there is no reason to suppose that Maimonides refers here simply to Jews. To the con-

1. H. Yesodei ha-Torah, 3.6; cf. the reference to the "ancient wise men," *ha-ḥakhamim ha-qadmonim*, i.e., the philosophers, in 3.7.
2. *Sefer ha-Maddaʿ*, p. 4a.

trary, evidence abounds that the expression is intended to encompass or allude to the philosophers, who are not as such Jews. Maimonides never refers expressly to the "wise men of Israel" in his discussion of "ethics" in HD, a subject with an emphatically non-Jewish provenance.

He does refer there to the "wise men of old," the *ḥakhamim ha-riʾshonim* (lit., first wise men), who are indeed Jews, but who also possess knowledge of philosophic ethics: they know that the middle way is the correct standard in ethics (HD, 1.4). Who are these wise men? The *ḥakhamim ha-riʾshonim* might seem to be "first" in the sense that they are the earliest of the rabbinic sages, but this impression, conveyed by the Hebrew locution, is a kind of *trompe l'oeil* perpetrated by language. At least that is so in the key example from HD, in which the "wise men of old" are said to have set forth the rectitude of the mean. In Maimonides' talmudic source (which does not refer literally to the middle way) the statement is ascribed to R. Joshua ben Levi, who lived in the period after the completion of the *Mishnah*, a time that is by no means early in the transmission of the Oral Law. When referring to *ḥakhamim ha-riʾshonim*, Maimonides perhaps relies upon a secondary meaning of *riʾshon*, one with no temporal implication; the sages in question would then be the "primary" or "main" ones—those who are "first" in rank.[3]

The *ḥakhamim ha-riʾshonim* play a seminal role in the Maimonidean recapitulation of the halakhah insofar as it is guided by philosophy. They mediate between philosophy and the Law or, if you wish, they enable Maimonides himself to effect a mediation. At any rate, they are presented as knowing how to accommodate philosophic teachings to the Law, and vice versa. They may be said to be experts in practical philosophy insofar as it is used to interpret the Law.

In H. Yesodei ha-Torah Maimonides implies that they have knowledge of physics (Account of the Beginning) and meta-

3. There are relatively few references to the *ḥakhamim ha-riʾshonim* in the Code, about twenty in all; "wise men" without any qualifying adjective occurs over three hundred times (ʾ*Otsar Leshon ha-Rambam* [*Concordance to the Mishneh Torah*], ed. David Assaf, vol. 6).

physics (Account of the Chariot). But their particular concern is with the potential danger that the study of philosophy poses to a more conventional view of the Law: they forbid anyone to speak of physics to more than one person, and of metaphysics even to a single person except through veiled allusions (2.12, 4.10–11). According to H. Tefillah (14.10), they had knowledge of the secret Name of God, the Tetragrammaton, and they zealously guarded this knowledge: "The wise men of old used to teach this name to their worthy students and sons only once every seven years." (Cf. *Guide*, 1.62; they would teach not only the mode of pronouncing the Tetragrammaton but also its meaning.)

The "wise men of old" understood that in the Messianic era the world would not change its course (lit., custom, *minhag*). Hence they said that "there is no difference between this world and the Days of the Messiah except for [the elimination of] the subjugation to the [other] kingdoms" (H. Teshuvah, 9.10). They also explained the true character of the world-to-come to the multitude (ibid., 8.3–4; cf. 8.12).

The "wise men of old" knew that under extreme circumstances a prophet is permitted temporarily to abrogate any law of the Torah, except the prohibition against idolatry (H. Yesodei ha-Torah, 9.3). This knowledge is at the very least consonant with, if it does not draw upon, a philosophic understanding of the need for some latitude in the way the Law is conceived. The restriction upon such flexibility is, of course, determined by the Torah.

In H. Mamrim (2.4) Maimonides again indicates that these sages recognized that the Law might have to be transgressed under extreme circumstances. The "wise men of old" said that one Sabbath should be desecrated to save a grievously ill man so that he will be able to observe many Sabbaths. Drawing upon this judgment, Maimonides generalizes about what a court may do in extremis. To bring many people back to religion or to prevent them from stumbling, a court has the power temporarily to abrogate certain commandments. Maimonides gives the following analogy: Just as a physician might have to cut off a man's hand or foot to save his life, a court might have to permit the temporary transgression of some commandments so that the rest of the Law will be fulfilled. This analogy is redolent of what Alfarabi says about the ruler being a physician of the soul who must act in a manner comparable to that of a physician of the body.[4] The Maimonidean comparison of a law court to a physician is not found in the *Talmud*, but it does draw a certain support from the rabbinic judgment that the Sabbath can be broken for the sake of bodily health.

The "wise men of old" would go to great lengths to avoid being appointed as judges (they would "flee" from being appointed). Even if the need was great, much pressure would have to be placed upon them before they would agree to serve (H. Sanhedrin, 3.10). This is in accord with the view that the Account of the Chariot (metaphysics) is a great thing, and the "discussion of Abbaye and Rava" regarding the halakhah a small thing (H. Yesodei ha-Torah, 4.13). For the "wise men of old," as for the Platonic philosophers, the attraction of a life devoted to theoretical knowledge greatly diminishes the appeal of the practical life.

Since the "wise men of old" are *Jewish* sages, there is sometimes no palpable connection between their practice and philosophy. For example, in honor of the Sabbath, they would do things for its preparation that they would not normally do, such as split wood for the stove, prepare wicks for candles, and shop for food for the Sabbath.[5] The Law does not treat such work as beneath the dignity of the sage; the honor of the Sabbath takes precedence.

*

Maimonides defines the wise man in HD not as someone who has mastered Jewish law but as someone who has ordered his character traits in accordance with the mean. This extraordinary definition, without precedent in the biblical-rabbinic tradition, points toward the philosophic basis of the sage's way of

4. Alfarabi, *Selected Chapters*, ed. Najjar, nos. 3–4 (Dunlop, no. 3). In the Introduction to *CM*, Maimonides compares a judge to a physician (pp. 30–31).

5. H. Shabbat, 30.5. For further illuminating references to the *ḥakhamim ha-ri'shonim*, see H. Temurah, 4.13; H. Tefillin Umezuzah, 6.13; H. Terumot, 1.1. See also below, pp. 145 and 155.

life. The middle way in ethics is the "measure of wisdom," which, Maimonides implies, is distinguishable from the Torah. If the validity of the mean were based upon the Torah, it would not have been necessary for the "wise men of old" to issue a command to follow the middle way. But Maimonides says, "[t]he wise men of old commanded that a man continuously appraise [*sam*] his character traits and evaluate them and direct them in the middle way so that he becomes perfect [*shalem*]."[6] By stating, moreover, that "the right way is the mean . . . *therefore* the wise men of old" commanded that the middle way be followed, Maimonides indicates, albeit covertly, that the rectitude of the mean is independent of the Torah (1.4, emphasis added).[7] The Torah and "wisdom" are presumed to be different sources for determining the right conduct. Only after having described the "way of the wise men" (in 1.4) does Maimonides give the biblical support for the mean, "And you shall walk in His ways" (1.5; Deut. 28.9).

The distinction between Torah and wisdom is potentially disruptive of received opinion, and Maimonides is circumspect in his treatment of this issue. The distinction is, however, occasionally found in places other than the account of the mean proper. Later in HD, for instance, when referring to the sage's speech, Maimonides says: "Concerning matters of Torah and matters of wisdom, the words of the wise man shall be few but full of content" (2.4). It is noteworthy that despite their being different sources of knowledge, the Torah and philosophy call for a similar mode of instruction: both require that substantial content be concentrated into few words; the teacher must get to the heart of the matter, and the student is encouraged to think for himself. To take another example, in H. Teshuvah Maimonides distinguishes the "paths of wisdom" from studying

6. The original talmudic statement reads: "Everyone who appraises (sam) his paths in this world merits and sees the salvation of the Holy One, blessed be He" (Soṭah, 5b; Moʿed Qatan, 5a).

7. See also the explanation of the commandment to imitate God's ways in the *Book of the Commandments*, where Maimonides limits himself to giving the traditional Jewish view of imitatio Dei; there is no mention of the doctrine of the mean (positive precept no. 8).

the Torah and observing the *mitsvot*. A person who loves God properly has no ulterior motive when he "labors in the Torah and in the commandments and walks in the paths of wisdom" (10.3).

Since the middle way is determined by "wisdom" as distinct from Torah, it is in principle separable from the halakhah. Hence there is occasional repetition between the "way of the wise men," set forth in HD, and the halakhah described elsewhere in the Code. For example, a wise man "gives charity according to his means and lends a fitting amount to the needy" (HD, 1.4). This duty is repeated almost verbatim by two separate *mitsvot* recorded later in the Code: "To give charity according to [one's] means" and "To lend to the poor and the indigent" (H. Mattenot 'Aniyyim and H. Malveh Veloveh). The repetition indicates that a wise man has a separate way of life, quite apart from the obligations incumbent upon the community as a whole. Maimonides prescribes a self-sufficient code of conduct for the sage in HD.

The importance of calling the man who adheres to the mean in ethics a *ḥakham* deserves to be underscored. One might have thought that he would be called a *tsaddiq* (just man) rather than a *ḥakham*. The only two biblical verses cited in support of the virtues refer to the conduct of a "just man" (HD, 1.4). And in H. Teshuvah (5.2) the "just man" is characterized by moral goodness; he is juxtaposed to the "wicked man," the "wise man" being contrasted with the "fool." By calling the middle way the "way of the wise men," Maimonides alludes to the overriding importance of *theoria* for determining the moral qualities lying in the mean. The "measure of wisdom" governing the mean is the goal of attaining theoretical wisdom, which, as in *EC*, is understood to be knowledge of God.[8]

The wise men of HD are not "political men," not even in the

8. "A man needs to direct every single one of his deeds solely toward attaining knowledge of the Name, blessed be He" (HD, 3.2). This statement is in the central paragraph of the central chapter of the five chapters in HD devoted to a discussion of the commandment that requires an adherence to the mean. I follow the numbering of paragraphs in the Hyamson edition, which contains an autograph of Maimonides.

restricted sense of being judges. Their knowledge (or quest for knowledge) of metaphysics does not equip them to settle matters of the halakhah. Later in the Code, Maimonides says that judges must be experts in the "wisdom of the Torah," and in addition they must have a little knowledge of such "wisdoms" as medicine, arithmetic, astronomy, and the like; knowledge of physics and metaphysics is not required of them.[9] To be a judge and to be a ḥakham in the emphatic sense are not the same things. Assuming that the sages of HD follow the advice of the "wise men of old," we may infer that they avoid the time-consuming task of settling disputes by being members of a court.

According to HD, the wise men are "physicians of the soul," and people with sick souls are urged to go to them for help (2.1). Because the wise men take the place of the prophets as having the power to admonish the community when it has gone astray, a sage might also act as a "corrector" or "reprover" (mokhiaḥ) for the community (qahal) (H. Teshuvah, 4.4). Now, the "reprover" may rely on a philosophic conception of psycho-therapy when correcting the community, but we should note that Maimonides refers to the sage qua "reprover" not in HD but in H. Teshuvah; he says nothing in HD of the sage's taking the place of the prophets. It would be stretching matters to insist that Maimonides proposes to substitute philosophers for the prophets as the men who are concerned with remedying the moral defects of the community—although he does not exclude that possibility. Perhaps he thought that it was extremely unlikely that such an eventuality would come to pass. In any event, in H. Teshuvah he gives a somewhat conventional description of the sage who will act as "reprover" of the community: "It is necessary to establish in every single community of Israel a great wise man, an elder who is God-fearing from his youth and beloved by them [the people], to admonish the multi-

9. H. Sanhedrin, 1.3, 2.1. We may further note that the community (tsibbur) is required to give honor to a judge (ibid., 25.3). It would not have been necessary for Maimonides to specify this obligation if a judge were assumed to be a ḥakham; there is a separate mitsvah "to honor the wise men" (Sefer ha-Maddaʿ, p. 9a.16), which is discussed in H. Talmud Torah.

tude and make them return in repentance" (H. Teshuvah, 4.4).
Maimonides goes on to describe the person who is in need of
correction but refuses to listen to a sage as follows: "He [the sin-
ner] persists in his sins, which are good in his eyes." This echoes
the description of sick souls in HD, 2.1. In HD itself, Maimonides indicates that the ḥakham treats sick souls through prescribing a suitable course of conduct on an individual basis (cf.
the parallel account of the physicians of the soul in EC, chap. 3).

   In diverse parts of the Code the wise man is assumed to have
various functions. An ambiguity regarding the meaning of the
ḥakham pervades the Code; he is not simply the philosopher-
sage depicted in HD. In some contexts he is presumed to be
simply an expert on the halakhah and strictly ritual matters.[10]
A sage might also have a certain role in the economic affairs of
the city. Thus, artisans are permitted to fix among themselves
the days on which they sell their products and they may punish
any offender, but if the city has a "respected wise man" (ḥakham ḥashuv), he must approve the agreement. Maimonides
refers here, albeit in passing, to the general task of the sage "to
improve" (letaqqen) the community (H. Mekhirah, 14.10–11).

   It is the wise man depicted in HD that most concerns us
here. The objection might be made that there is only one ḥakham in the Code, which is in a sense true. The ḥakham is
nonetheless described differently in diverse parts of the Code,
so that one wonders what the account of philosophic ethics has
to do with the various activities of the ḥakham that are specifically concerned with the halakhah. The problem is comparable
to that regarding the relationship between the brief sketch of
physics and metaphysics in the opening chapters of the Code
(H. Yesodei ha-Torah, chaps. 1–4) and the halakhah proper.
The enlightenment that Maimonides proposes to effect does
not have consistency as its first priority. This will also be evident in the next section, where we shall consider the relationship of piety to wisdom.

   10. To be certified for ritual slaughter (shehitah), for example, a man must
perform the acts of ritual slaughter correctly a number of times in the presence
of a ḥakham (H. Shehitah, 4.3; cf. H. Talmud Torah, 6.14).

THE CONFLICT BETWEEN PIETY AND THE MIDDLE WAY:
HUMILITY AND ANGER

Both wise men and pious men are models of conduct in the biblical-rabbinic tradition, and in the Maimonidean recapitulation of the Oral Law they remain paradigms of excellence. But through his account of piety, Maimonides also differentiates the specifically Jewish morality from philosophic ethics. Whereas a wise man follows the middle way, a pious man inclines toward one or another of the two extremes (HD, 1.4–5).

The explicit distinction between the wise and the pious has precedent in a talmudic passage which, however, does not concern ethics. According to the *Talmud*, Rabba bar Rav Huna maintained that pious men do not kill snakes and spiders on the Sabbath, but he was told: "The spirit of wise men does not guide these pious men."[11] Somewhat closer to what we find in HD is a distinction made by the early eleventh-century Jewish thinker, Abraham bar Ḥiyya, in his *Hegyon ha-Nefesh*. A wise man, he says, has a theoretical kind of wisdom; a pious man is characterized by the "fear of his Creator and good deeds." Piety leads a man to despise the things of this world so that his soul will be fit to ascend from the "lower world" to the "upper world."[12] Thus bar Ḥiyya interprets the pious man's conduct from a neo-Platonic perspective; piety, when conjoined with wisdom, directly contributes to the soul's ascent to the higher regions. Although piety for bar Ḥiyya is, broadly speaking, concerned with moral virtue and hence has a certain kinship with the account of piety in HD, the latter work contains no neo-Platonic overtones; no particular power is ascribed to piety for preparing the soul's ascent along the lines envisaged by bar Ḥiyya.

The discussion of piety in HD differs somewhat from that in *Eight Chapters*, where piety is unqualifiedly instrumental to the mean. In HD *ḥasidut* is at least provisionally the standard for a separate way of life. One of the consequences of this dif-

11. Shabbat, 121b. I am grateful to Rabbi David Shapiro for having originally called my attention to this passage. See also Berakhot, 57b.

12. Abraham bar Ḥiyya, *Hegyon ha-Nefesh*, p. 5.

ference between the two works is that the extremes are defined somewhat differently in HD than in *EC*. In HD one of the two extremes with respect to a given virtue is usually so delineated that it is a suitable guidepost for someone who simply follows the way of piety. Thus, the absence of anger is regarded there as tranquility of the mind. The two extremes regarding anger are described as follows in HD: "There is a man who is irascible, perpetually angry, and another man who has a tranquil mind [*da'ato meyushevet 'alav*] and does not become angry at all" or is rarely so (1.1). According to *EC*, however, the deficient extreme is servility, which is a vice, and it is therefore a dubious guideline for piety as interpreted in HD.[13] To take another example, in *EC* the deficient extreme connected with earning a livelihood is laziness; in HD, at the comparable extreme, a man is satisfied with very little and does not "chase" to fulfill his needs, but he is not regarded as lazy. Through his account of the extremes in HD, Maimonides moves toward resolving the problem that piety, by requiring conduct that inclines toward an extreme, encourages a person to acquire a vice.

In most instances, a pious man departs only a little from the mean, but he goes all the way to the extremes of self-abasement and the absence of anger, respectively; the Law itself requires going to these two extremes (HD, 2.3). Piety conflicts with the sage's morality, for Maimonides expressly says that a wise man is humble (1.5), that is, he follows the middle way. And there is a definition of the middle way regarding anger in the "way of the wise men" (1.4). The contradictory requirements of wisdom and piety are indicative of the difference between philosophic ethics and the Jewish tradition. Through his account of piety, Maimonides takes into consideration the Law's propensity to go toward the extreme with respect to humility and anger.

The need to differentiate Jewish morality from the doctrine of the mean is evident from various rabbinic precepts cited in HD, such as the following: "Anyone who is angry—it is as if he worships idols" (2.3). The blanket rabbinic disapproval of anger is at odds with the teaching of a middle way. So too, the ex-

---

13. The account of the extremes in *EC* is in chap. 4, pp. 379–80.

treme of self-abasement, which is required by a number of Jewish precepts (2.3), conflicts with the mean. Let us note that the Jewish quotations supporting an outright condemnation of anger are all taken from the rabbinic tradition: the *Talmud* appears to be stricter in this matter than Scripture. In the Bible, there is the example of Moses—to say nothing of other prophets—who sometimes vented his anger upon the Israelites.[14] If Moses is not the model for pious conduct in connection with anger, he does set an example regarding extreme humility; he is called by Scripture itself "extremely humble" (Num. 12.3). The biblical basis for the Law's teaching regarding humility is also manifest in the Deuteronomic warning against a man's having a haughty heart lest he forget the Lord his God (Deut. 8.14; cited in a rabbinic quotation in HD, 2.3). Whereas the standard set by piety with respect to humility is clearly rooted in the Bible, pious conduct regarding anger is based upon the *Talmud*. There is no commandment, however, in the Torah to be extremely humble;[15] it was the rabbinic sages who commanded that a man go to the extreme opposed to arrogance (HD, 2.3).

Because Maimonides faithfully presents the Jewish teachings, a conflict with the doctrine of the mean is unavoidable. He does not attempt to form a synthesis between the conflicting requirements. The middle way between opposing extremes is the right standard for the regulation of all character traits (1.4); and yet, the Law in certain instances requires conduct that goes to the extreme. Maimonides does, however, artfully show how the conflict can be mitigated. He does so through his explanation of how to cure the diseases of the soul.

The account of therapy is in the paragraph that immediately precedes the Law's teaching regarding anger and humility, and to illustrate how to heal sickness of the soul, Maimonides

---

14. According to *EC*, Moses did not go to the deficient extreme but followed the middle way in anger. He departed from the mean in the direction of irascibility once and consequently was forbidden to enter the promised land (chap. 4, near end).

15. Maimonides thus differs from *Halakhot Gedolot*, which includes the command to be lowly of spirit among the 613 commandments (p. 14).

chooses, not accidentally, to explain the remedies for irascibility and arrogance. The antidote for irascibility is to allow oneself to be struck and cursed, but not to respond (2.2). The Law calls for training oneself "not to feel anything, even in response to things that [usually] provoke anger" (2.3). The Law, then, is salutary for those who need to chasten irascibility. As for haughtiness, the therapy requires a man to "endure much degradation and sit lower than anyone else and wear worn-out, shabby garments which make the wearer despised, and do similar things until his haughty heart is uprooted" (2.2). The Law requires that a man have an exceedingly lowly spirit (*shefal ruaḥ*) (2.3). We shall see that in other parts of the Code "lowliness of the spirit" implies that a person is (or has been) in a degraded condition. Further, in 2.3, Maimonides cites the command of R. Levitas, "Be extremely lowly of spirit," which is interpreted in the "Commentary on Avot" (4.4) from a therapeutic viewpoint. This is the very dictum that elicited the ship anecdote about the "virtuous man" (*fāḍil*), whose comportment (wearing tattered clothes, etc.) is redolent of the description in HD of what is needed for therapy. In short, the Law's requirements regarding anger and humility are expeditious for the cure of the soul's diseases.

This conception of piety does not completely eliminate the conflict between philosophic ethics and the Law. Psychotherapy is only a temporary measure, but the Law's position, as stated in 2.3, does not have a provisional character: "A man is forbidden to accustom himself to the mean"—he is commanded to go the extremes opposed to arrogance and rage. The goal of psychotherapy, as specified in 2.2, is to attain the middle way. After a man has been cured of his vices, he should follow the standard of the mean "all his days" (2.2). Furthermore, the therapeutic justification of piety presupposes that all Jews require such treatment. But it cannot be assumed that all Jews have the vices of irascibility and arrogance (the character traits found among people vary greatly and are found at *both* extremes [1.1]).

Should an irascible person aim at completely eliminating any disposition toward anger? Joseph ben Judah, the favorite disciple of Maimonides, argues that a person must first train himself to achieve the middle way; only then would he be in a position to go further and discipline himself to reach the level of piety.[16] It is surely correct that the goal of the cure for sick souls is to attain the mean (HD, 2.2). If we limit ourselves to what Maimonides says when he speaks about therapy, it appears that a man should be satisfied if, having been irascible, he can discipline himself to attain the mildness of the middle way. This point is somewhat obscured because, in accordance with the Jewish tradition, Maimonides also says that it is forbidden to follow the middle way in connection with anger (2.3).

Piety with respect to anger is not only a training for healing a disease of the soul; it can also represent a higher moral achievement than following the path ordained by "wisdom," for greater serenity is attained through the complete absence of anger than through following the mean. The practical difference between piety and the middle way is not very great, because someone who follows the mean would only be occasionally angry. It is nonetheless important to note that ḥasidut is in this instance superior to the middle way. Someone might gainsay such superiority, alleging that the pious man's lack of anger betrays a slavish disposition.[17] But, to repeat, whereas EC depicts the deficient extreme as "servility," in HD the extreme opposed to irascibility is tranquility of the mind (1.1).

On the basis of HD itself, there are grounds for wondering whether the pious absence of anger is truly meritorious. In the account of the mean, the extremes are described as follows: "A man shall not be irascible and easily angered, nor be like a corpse that feels nothing" (1.4). To be like a corpse is hardly a desirable condition; it is clearly a vice, and is understood to be such from the standpoint of the middle way. This description of the deficient extreme in 1.4 differs from that in 1.1, where it is depicted as tranquility of the mind. To be corpselike is akin to the remedy for irascibility, which requires not responding when provoked. But at a higher stage, if a man goes beyond the middle way, the "deficient extreme" can be understood as se-

16. *Sefer Musar*, Commentary on Avot, 2.20. He does not limit this generalization to pious conduct regarding anger.
17. Cf. Aristotle, *Nic. Eth.* 1126a6–8.

renity. If a person has reached this stage, he is not corpselike but tranquil in circumstances when anger might be thought to be suitable.[18]

If piety in the case of anger can be superior to the mean, a further difficulty becomes evident owing to the occasional usefulness of anger. A wise man becomes angry solely to prevent the recurrence of a serious misdeed (a "large matter," *davar gadol*; Maimonides does not speak here of a sin). Justifiable anger is purely pragmatic.[19] The question therefore arises: If anger sometimes serves a useful purpose, does a pious man relinquish his responsibility to administer a reproof when such is necessary? Maimonides resolves this problem by commending a show of anger when it would be useful for correcting members of his household or community; a pious man should feign anger while keeping "his mind tranquil within himself" (*da'ato meyushevet beino levein 'atsmo*) (2.3).

Although piety regarding anger can be superior to the middle way, that is not the case with self-abasement.[20] The difficulty of regarding the latter as simply good is evident from an examination of the meaning of "lowliness of the spirit" (*shiflut ha-ruah*) in other parts of the Code. Penitents are described as

18. David Rosin notes that the Maimonidean teaching regarding anger and pride is indicative of the difference between the Jewish tradition and the Aristotelian mean (*Die Ethik des Maimonides*, pp. 86–87). But according to Rosin, Maimonides unconditionally condemns the deficient extreme for anger (p. 86 and n. 6). Rosin does not take into consideration that this extreme is described differently in 1.1 than in 1.4—nor that tranquility of the mind (1.1) is a suitable guideline for piety.

19. No reference is made in HD, 1.4, to anger at the maligning of one's honor; the mean is defined there in such a manner as to be compatible with the sage's humility. The pragmatic character of the Maimonidean account may be contrasted with what Aristotle says about the virtue of "gentleness" in the *Nicomachean Ethics*. The gentleman's nobility might rouse him to anger to defend his honor or that of his household and close friends (1126a6–8).

20. Regarding the difference between humility and anger, cf. the selectivity exercised by Maimonides in his use of the *Talmud* in HD, 2.3. He quotes the rabbinic sages when they say about an angry person: "If he is a wise man, his wisdom departs from him; and if he is a prophet, his prophecy departs from him." The *Talmud* makes a comparable statement about the proud man (*ha-mityaher*) but it is omitted from HD (*BT*, Pesahim, 66b; see the commentary of R. Elazar Roqeah on HD, 2.3.) It appears that pride, unlike anger, does not imperil the presence of wisdom.

"lowly [shefelim] and exceedingly humble" (H. Teshuvah, 7.10); a slave's soul is "lowly" (shefelah) (H. ʿAvadim, 1.7); the souls of widows and orphans are described in the same manner (HD, 6.10). Shiflut sometimes refers to the degradation resulting from the Exile. Thus an apostate who abandons his Jewish heritage during a time of persecution in effect says, "What advantage is there for me to cleave to Israel, who are lowly and persecuted [shefelim venirdafim]?" (H. Teshuvah, 3.18). Maimonides juxtaposes malkhut (political independence, lit., kingdom) to shiflut, thus underscoring the lowly condition of Jews in the Exile (ibid., 9.1). The precept that requires self-abasement suits the circumstances of the Exile, but this very suitability casts doubt upon whether it is simply good.

Self-abasement is instrumental for achieving serenity in the face of insult, that is, for attaining perfect humility. This is implied by the statement that summarizes the discussion of piety: "The way of the just men is to be insulted but not to insult [in return]; they hear themselves reviled but do not reply; they act out of love and rejoice in affliction. Scripture says about them: 'And those who love Him are like the sun rising in its power' (Judges 5.31)."[21] Maimonides refers here not to ḥasidim but to tsaddiqim (just men), which suggests an agreement with the standard of the mean (cf. the reference to the "just man" in the only two biblical verses cited in support of the mean in HD, 1.4). There is, moreover, no reference in the above statement to suffering degradation (bizayon), which is required of a person with a sick soul (2.2). We may also note that according to Joseph ben Judah, a person who is insulted but does not respond in kind follows the middle way.[22]

It is inappropriate for people with responsible positions in the community to abase themselves habitually. A parnas (com-

21. HD, 2.3. The quotation is found in a number of places in the Talmud, though without such conduct being identified as the way of the "just men," tsaddiqim (Yomaʾ, 23a; Gittin, 36b; Shabbat 58b). In Derekh ʾErets Rabbah (chap. 2), the passage is followed by a statement that praises "those who are despised in their eyes." Maimonides never speaks of the pious or just men in this fashion.

22. Sefer Musar, Commentary on Avot, 3.13. See also Maimonides' account of the virtuous man in the ship anecdote (CM, Avot, 4.4; above, pp. 40–41).

munity leader), for instance, should practice humility rather than self-abasement. "It is forbidden for a man to rule over the community with arrogance; rather [he shall rule] with humility [*anavah*] and fear [*yir'ah*]" (H. Sanhedrin, 25.1). The middle way of *anavah* is also appropriate for a judge. Referring to the model of Moses that a judge should emulate, Maimonides says, "Just as Moses our master was humble, so too, every judge needs to be humble" (ibid., 2.7)—in this context Moses himself is referred to as "humble" rather than "very humble." It is hardly suitable for a judge to abase himself before people who must recognize his authority when he settles a dispute.

The potential conflict between self-abasement and what is needed for the public good is acute in the case of a king. Maimonides deals with this problem by making an exception for a king: the latter should not conduct himself "with arrogance [*gasut lev*] more than is sufficient" (H. Melakhim, 2.6). A king, then, may occasionally display hauteur for the community's well-being. Still, Maimonides stresses that Moses is the model for a king, who must accordingly be "exceedingly humble." The exemplary conduct of Moses does not, however, imply that Moses abased himself in his dealings with the Israelites. "He [Moses] bore their troubles and their burden and their complaints and their anger like a nursing father bears the infant; Scripture called him a shepherd" (ibid.). No more than a nursing-father or male nurse (*'omen*) abases himself before an infant did Moses abase himself before the Israelites. It is thus dubious not only whether the king should repeatedly abase himself, but also whether the command in HD to imitate the extreme humility of Moses requires a continuous abasing of oneself.

If the king is forebearing with people when they abuse him with unjustified complaints, he emulates the conduct of Moses. Maimonides commends the same conduct to the judge and the *parnas*; they, too, must emulate Moses by behaving like a "nursing-father" in their dealings with the people. But, as we have seen, they are only required to be humble. It turns out that extreme humility (specified for a king) and humility (specified for a judge and a *parnas*) require essentially the same behavior: indifference to insult, made possible by the absence of haughtiness. The difference between piety and the middle way tends to collapse at this point. Since self-abasement is only a temporary strategy for attaining the mean, the discussion of humility has a malleability that permits diverse descriptions in different contexts.

The way that Maimonides makes use of the Torah's reference to Moses as a "nursing-father" is worth pausing over; it is a striking instance of the freedom Maimonides assumes for himself in interpreting the biblical text. And yet his interpretation is not alien to the spirit of the biblical teaching. As described in the Torah, Moses is far from being a model of forbearance: he complains to God about the difficult burden that was placed upon him, his bitter words having been aroused by the cries of the Israelites to return to the fleshpots of Egypt.

> And Moses said to the Lord: "Wherefore have You dealt ill
> with Your servant; and wherefore have I not found favor in
> Your sight, that You lay the burden of all this people upon me?
> Have I conceived all this people? Have I brought them forth,
> that You should say to me: Carry them in your bosom, as a
> nursing-father (ʾomen) carries the sucking child, to the land
> which You did swear to their fathers? Whence should I have
> meat to give to all this people? for they trouble me with their
> weeping, saying: 'Give us meat, that we may eat.' I am not able
> to bear all this people myself alone, because it is too heavy for
> me." (Num. 11.11–14)

Even if Moses does not behave here like a "nursing-father" with an infant, the Torah implies that he should have done so; the Maimonidean interpretation of the metaphor is authentically biblical.

How is the subject of honor treated in HD? In his initial account of the mean, Maimonides says nothing about the right attitude toward honor; we are merely told that a wise man is humble (1.5). Later in HD, however, we learn that "pursuing" or "chasing after" honor (rodef ʾaḥer ha-kavod) is bad (2.7); Maimonides implies that a sensible concern with honor is compatible with the way a sage comports himself. A man should not go to the extreme of shunning all honor (3.1)—except, of course, for therapeutic purposes.

From the explanation of the commandment to love your neighbor as yourself, it is clear that people in general want to be honored: A person should treat his neighbor with honor, *just as he wants honor for himself* (6.3). In the *Commentary on the Mishnah*, Maimonides says that most, if not all, people are willing to endure great hardship to have the pleasure of being honored. He proposes in *CM* to take advantage of the strength of the desire for honor—not, however, as a stimulus to encourage men to act nobly when engaging in politics (as in Aristotle), but to motivate students to be diligent in their study of the Torah. Before they have reached the stage in which they recognize that knowledge should be sought for its own sake alone, students should be motivated by appealing to their desire for honor (*CM*, Sanhedrin, 10.1, pp. 198, 204). It is noteworthy that this sort of motivation is assumed in the Code to be efficacious not only for novices but also for men who are quite advanced in their studies. Although the love of God, which is the highest motivation for the study of the Torah, excludes the desire for any reward, including that of honor, it is rare for anyone to reach this stage of perfection; not even every wise man attains it (H. Teshuvah, 10.2–4).

To want to be honored as a reward for ruling the community is condemned in the Code. A ruler should be concerned with guarding the honor of Heaven rather than with receiving honor for himself (H. Teshuvah, 3.23). Fear of Heaven is a prerequisite for all offices, including that of kingship; wisdom is desirable but not indispensable for a future monarch (H. Melakhim, 1.7). Not *ḥasidut* but *yirʾat shamayim*, a conventional sort of piety attuned to the observance of the Law, is a prerequisite for office; fear of Heaven, as it were, replaces the desire for honor as the proper motivation for a ruler. The desire to receive honor for ruling is, of course, contrary to the model set by Moses, whose extreme humility enabled him to bear so well his ill-usage by the Israelites.

A person can receive the honor that is due him, and yet

be extremely humble. The tokens of honor can be accepted without any inner exaltation. The combination of external honor and a lowly heart is evident from the description of the king. "Just as Scripture apportioned great honor to him, and everyone is obliged to honor him, so too, it commanded that his heart within him be lowly [*shafel*] and contrite. As it is said, 'And my heart is contrite within me'" (Ps. 109.22; H. Melakhim, 2.6). Maimonides thereby preserves the Deuteronomic teaching that warns the king against "exalting his heart [*lev*] above his brothers" (Deut. 17.20; cited in the Code ad loc.). It is questionable, though, whether the king can follow this dictum on the occasions when he must display hauteur (*gasut lev*) for the common good.

It is a commandment to honor those who are learned in the Torah, but neither the "great wise men" nor the "pious men of old" were jealous of their honor. Although the Law allows them to excommunicate anyone who has insulted them in private, they would refrain from doing so (H. Talmud Torah, 7.12). They followed the advice that Solomon "in his wisdom" had given: "Pay no heed to all the words which they speak" (Eccles. 7.21). This precept, according to Maimonides, requires "closing one's ears" to the insults of fools. In a now-familiar formula, he observes that the early pious men would "hear themselves reviled and not reply," but "not only that"—he stresses the addition—"they would forgive the person who reviles them and pardon him."[23] As for the "great wise men," there is no indication that they would forgive someone who insulted them— they are simply oblivious to insult. They lack the concern for the other person that is implicit in forgiveness.[24] Furthermore, and this is most surprising, there is an element of pride in the way that the "great wise men" view themselves. They "re-

23. According to HD, 6.9, it is the measure of piety to forgive the offence of a simpleton or a confused person. See also below, p. 143.

24. It is possible that the early pious men would forgive the other person because of his ignorance and that no concern for him is implied. Cf. what Maimonides says about the contentious Master Zechariah, the Av Bet Din of the Yeshivah in Baghdad: "He is forgiven due to his ignorance" (*Iggrot ha-Rambam*, p. 57; *Ethical Writings*, pp. 117–118).

garded themselves worthy of praise [mishtabḥin] for their fine deeds [maʿasim naʾim], and they used to say that they never excommunicated anyone or placed anyone under a ban for the sake of their own honor."[25] This remarkable statement contains language that is suggestive of Aristotelian "greatness of soul," though without the gentleman's singular concern with honor.

In his account of ḥasidut in HD Maimonides places humility and anger at the forefront of the discussion. Why does he single out these two qualities for special treatment? I have suggested that piety in these instances differentiates Jewish morality from the doctrine of the mean. While correct, this does not suffice to explain his procedure: there are moral qualities that are an integral part of the Jewish tradition but are neglected in his account of piety. For example, to foster compassion is a major purpose of the Law according to Maimonides' own *Book of the Commandments* (Root 9, pp. 32–33), and yet his discussion of piety in HD scants any reference to mercy. Maimonides takes his bearings, insofar as possible, from man's final end. The disciplining of rage and arrogance is the focal point of his discussion of piety because such a training is salutary for the contemplative life. The philosophic standpoint supplies the guiding principle for his reconstitution of Jewish morality.

I want to make it clear again that although philosophy makes possible a lucid, well-grounded ordering of Jewish law, its presence in the Code precludes perfect consistency. The description of King David dancing before the ark is a further case in point; it shows that the biblical-rabbinic tradition is not in

25. Regarding the distinction between what is naʾeh and what is permitted by the halakhah, cf. the discussion of the scholar's eligibility to receive boshet, i.e., money given as recompense for an affront. Maimonides notes that the custom of giving such compensation was followed in Spain, but he adds that there were scholars (talmidei ḥakhamim) who would forgive the insult, which is the fine, or suitable (naʾeh), way to behave. To do what is "fine" involves giving up a considerable sum of money, for the boshet is quite substantial (H. Ḥovel Umazziq, 3.5–6). The difference between what is fine (naʾeh) and what is permitted by the Law is redolent of the philosophic distinction between the fine or noble (to kalon) and what is specified by the law (nomos).

every respect amenable to the (philosophic) defense of self-abasement as a means for attaining the middle way. David was viewed with contempt by the queen, who rebuked him for having debased himself before the handmaids of his servants. Maimonides quotes what David said in response to her: "I shall be yet more abased than this and be lowly [*shafel*] in my own eyes" (2 Sam. 6.22). Maimonides, of course, speaks approvingly of David's conduct. Through a restatement of the extremes, he also, as it were, alludes to a certain difference between Aristotelian magnanimity and the Jewish teaching of self-abasement: the haughty man "allots honor to himself and is honored in his eyes"; at the other extreme is the man who "lowers himself [*mashpil ʿatsmo*] and treats his body lightly" (H. Lulav, 8.15). There is no indication that King David's "lowering" himself and neglecting his dignity had a therapeutic function.

To explain the manifest contradictions in HD, I have concentrated upon the consequences of the Maimonidean introduction of philosophic ethics into the Law. For purposes of clarity, I have omitted some further qualifications that must now be made. There is evidence in the Code that the rabbinic tradition, multifaceted as it is, does not speak with a single voice upon all ethical matters. Thus, the Oral Law does not unambiguously condemn all expressions of anger; Maimonides refers, for instance, to the propriety of a teacher's occasionally becoming angry to shake indifferent students out of their lethargy (H. Talmud Torah, 4.5). It can, however, be argued that in his treatment of piety, Maimonides takes into consideration the dominant stratum of the Oral Law.

The problem of how to characterize Maimonides' view of piety is further complicated by his observation in *CM* that the rabbinic sages sometimes exaggerated for a pedagogic purpose. Maimonides indicates in the "Commentary on Avot" that such was their intent when they said that a haughty person should be excommunicated (see above, p. 56). This statement is reproduced in HD without any indication that it is an exaggeration (2.3). Maimonides also says in the "Commentary on Avot" (2.13)—but, again, not in HD—that the sages exaggerated when they declared that an angry person is like an idolator. To understand the contradictions in the Code, we cannot ignore the use of hyperbole for persuading people to conduct themselves properly. However, it is doubtful that the rabbinic sages regarded all their strictures upon pride and anger as rhetorical excess; at any rate, their overt position is in accord with our understanding of piety as exemplifying a basically Jewish teaching.

The overall movement of our analysis has been from the point at which we recognized a sharp difference between the standards of wisdom and piety to a stage in which the distinction loses some of its force. The difference between the doctrine of the mean and the Law remains intact. But piety is not implacably opposed to the standard of wisdom because inclining toward an extreme can be instrumental to the mean. The question of whether philosophic ethics is superior to religious morality, or vice versa, tends to lose its significance: both are a moral preparation for attaining knowledge of God. The more pressing problem that Maimonides had to confront—and which he resolves—is how to adapt *both* the philosophic and the Jewish precepts to the specific needs of jurisprudence required by a code of Jewish law.

A Further Exploration of the Mean

Besides the right disposition regarding anger, Maimonides defines the mean with respect to the following four qualities: bodily desire, acquiring money for oneself, giving money to others, and joy (HD, 1.4). By expressly defining the middle way in these instances, Maimonides underscores the importance of the sage's having the virtues related to each of these *de'ot.* There are conflicting requirements in HD concerning only humility and anger; Maimonides implies that a basic affinity exists between philosophic ethics and the Jewish tradition in connection with the above four qualities.

Moderation

A wise man "shall only desire the things which the body needs and without which it is impossible to live" (1.4). This remarkably strict definition sounds more like an extreme than the middle way. But at the deficient extreme a person has an "exceedingly pure body," so that "he does not even desire the few things the body needs" (1.1). It is clear from what is said later in HD that Maimonides regards the sage's guideline to be bodily health rather than bare survival (see 4.1). What is suitable for health is, however, viewed in quite a stringent manner. For example, a person should eat not to satiety but to the point of being about three-quarters full (4.2; concerning what is best for bodily health in sexual matters, see 4.19).

The strict definition of the mean is in accord with the rigorous regimen required by the study of the Torah. Thus, the following conduct is called the "way of Torah": "You shall eat a morsel of bread with salt, you shall sleep on the ground, you shall live a life of pain, and in the Torah shall you labor" (H. Talmud Torah, 3.6). Still, we should note that in HD itself Maimonides emphatically opposes asceticism. The standard of the mean does not conflict with having an attractive (na'eh) home and wearing attractive, or "suitable" (na'eh) clothes (3.1). It is when he speaks about the goal of man's life being to attain knowlege of God that the apparent severity of the mean is relaxed; from the viewpoint of the goal of *theoria*, there is no need to eschew an attractive home, attractive clothes, and so on. The middle way in fact does not preclude having considerable possessions. The sage's morality only restricts *desire* to what it is impossible to live without; it is designed to make him as self-sufficient as possible.

Maimonides devotes almost an entire chapter, the fourth of the seven chapters in HD, to enumerating foods that are harmful to the body's health; it forms a kind of supplement to the account of moderation in 1.4. Not a single one of the "forbidden foods" (pork, etc.) is among the foods listed as detrimental to health in chapter 4! The laws concerning "forbidden foods" as well as "forbidden sexual acts" are in the Book of Holiness, whose purpose according to the Code is to effect a separation between the Jewish nation and the rest of the nations. This form of holiness does not appear to be in accord with the doctrine of the mean (see above, pp. 65 and 76).

Broadly speaking, philosophy and the Law agree in commending the virtue of moderation. This can be substantiated by what Maimonides says in the Introduction to *CM*, where he expressly refers to the harmony that exists between the Jewish tradition and philosophy regarding this matter. He declares that it is the beginning of wisdom (lit., knowledge, *ʿilm*) not to partake of bodily pleasure except for what is necessary to sustain the body. This standard is followed not only by "the philosophers" but also by the abstemious *ʿabid*, a term connoting, roughly, "pious man," who is said to follow the mean in "natural matters." Maimonides also uses the religious conception of *zuhd* (abstinence, abstemiousness) to describe a man having both moral and intellectual virtue: such a person is called an "abstemious [*zāhid*] knower."[26]

Earning a Livelihood

A wise man limits his work to what he needs "for the present" (HD, 1.4). The right standard is again defined in such a manner as to be at the far edge of what is conceivably a middle way. This severe restriction upon work is dependent upon the aforementioned limitation on the pleasures of the body; the sage can keep his work to a minimum because of the strict constraint upon bodily desire.

It is striking that although Maimonides defines the middle way with respect to only five moral qualities, he includes the right attitude toward earning a living among the five. HD contains what might be called an artisan morality, designed in part to meet the exigencies of the Exile. Needless to say, Maimonides does not address a landed gentry which can be assumed as a matter of course to have the leisure needed to pursue wisdom. Nor does he think it appropriate for a sage to be dependent upon the community for his livelihood. The stringency of the mean takes into consideration a sage's need to earn his own livelihood under the difficult circumstances of the Exile; he

26. *CM*, Introd., pp. 42–43. Maimonides also says there, hyperbolically, that "the well-being [or, with the Hamburger ed., improvement, *iṣlāh*] of the soul comes about through the destruction of the body" (p. 42). From the context, it appears that he means that every form of self-indulgence should be rigorously avoided.

must train himself to be content if he can meet his present needs.

The middle way also takes into consideration certain restrictions upon one's work that are recommended in the rabbinic tradition. It is in accord, for example, with the rabbinic precept that one should labor only a little in one's livelihood and much in the Torah. Linking this precept to the rabbinic dictum that a man should rejoice in his lot, Maimonides notes that a person should be content with whatever *little* is his portion (HD, 2.7; the original rabbinic statement reads, "Who is the rich man? He who rejoices in his lot" [Avot, 4.1]).

In H. Talmud Torah we are told that an artisan (*ba'al 'omanut*) should work for three hours and study nine hours. The nine hours devoted to study should be divided into time spent upon (1) the Written Law, (2) the Oral Law, and (3) inferring one thing from another, that is, *talmud*. What Maimonides calls *talmud* includes *pardes*, the Accounts of the Chariot and of the Beginning (metaphysics and physics), and he says that once a man has developed in wisdom, he should spend his time primarily upon these subjects (H. Talmud Torah, 1.11–12). Thus, the limitation upon time spent in earning a livelihood is appropriate for the study of both Torah and philosophy. (One might wonder whether it is possible for a man to meet his needs by working only three hours a day. The above division of the day appears to be more of a desideratum than something that is likely to be followed. Later in H. Talmud Torah, Maimonides in fact remarks that a man acquires most of his wisdom at night [3.13].)

It is dubious whether so strict a regulation of work is in keeping with the counsel concerning marriage in chapter 5 of HD, where the interests of the community and hence the family come into consideration. Maimonides says that a "sensible man" (*ba'al de'ah*) follows this order: first he acquires a trade, then he buys a home, and only afterward does he marry (5.11). But how, we may wonder, could a man save up money to buy a home if he works only enough to meet his present needs? It is from the perspective of the human form and its matter that Maimonides says that a man should be content if he can meet his immediate needs (1.4). Ethical conduct governed by a devotion to *theoria* abstracts from the family.

Although the middle way adumbrated in HD does not specify how a man should earn his living, Maimonides speaks highly of manual labor elsewhere in the Code. According to H. Talmud Torah, it is a sign of the "great merit" (*ma'alah gedolah*) of the "pious men of old" that they would labor with their hands to make a living (3.11). The "great wise men" also made their living through manual labor: they were "hewers of wood, drawers of water for [the irrigation of] gardens, ironsmiths," and so on (H. Mattenot 'Aniyyim, 10.18). When speaking about the great wise men, Maimonides stresses the importance of being as self-sufficient as possible: "A man should always push himself and suffer hardship but not be dependent upon [or, stand in need of] his fellow creatures" (ibid.). When speaking about the early pious men, Maimonides stresses that someone who allows himself to be supported by the community "degrades the Torah and extinguishes the light of religion [*dat*]"; further, the early pious men were scrupulous to avoid any behavior that might be suggestive of profaning God's Name (H. Talmud Torah, 3.11).

The Maimonidean evaluation of manual labor differs sharply from a common Greek view that disparages such labor. For Maimonides, the nature of man, that is, the theoretical character of man's rational nature, does not imply any disparagement of manual labor. Hence it is not beneath the dignity of a sage to engage in such work. There are, moreover, the examples of Hillel and other rabbinic sages who supported themselves by the labor of their hands. Scripture itself looks favorably upon this sort of work. Maimonides cites the following biblical verse to show that manual labor is meritorious: "When you eat of the labor of your hands you shall be praised [*'ashrekha*] and it will go well with you" (ibid.; Ps. 128.2).

Generosity

A sage "shall give charity [*tsedaqah*] and lend a fitting amount to the needy" (HD, 1.4). This position, which is dictated by "wisdom," is broadly the same as that taken by the Torah; as we have already noted, two *mitsvot* discussed independently of the middle way require giving charity and lending money to the poor. The reference to lending money to the poor is itself indicative of the Jewish setting of the discussion—the Torah requires that assistance be given to the needy through non-interest-bearing loans (Exod. 22.24; Deut. 15.8 [*Sefer ha-Madda'*, p. 9a.5–7]; no mention is made of lending money to the poor in Aristotle's description of liberality in the *Nic. Eth.*).

The middle way is compatible with what Maimonides says later in the Code about the highest kind of *tsedaqah*, whose aim is to make a man self-supporting. The acme of *tsedaqah* is to give a poor man "a gift or a loan or set up a partnership with him or establish him in a trade" (H. Mattenot 'Aniyyim, 10.7). The sage's morality does not, however, place the same stress upon generosity as that found in the halakhah proper. According to the "Laws of Gifts for the Poor," the giving of charity (*tsedaqah*) is one of the characteristics of the seed of Abraham, and the commandment to give charity is the greatest of all the positive commandments (10.1). We should also note that *tsedaqah* has a broader denotation than the word "charity." Besides including help given to the poor to become self-sufficient, *tsedaqah* encompasses supporting elderly parents and also children after they have reached maturity—sons so that they can study Torah, and daughters so that they can avoid any indignity connected with the lack of the means of support (ibid., 10.16).

The Middle Way Regarding Joyfulness

It is part of the "way of the wise men" to have a constantly joyful disposition. A sage "shall not be frivolous and buffoonish [*soheq*] nor sad and mournful, but rejoice all his days, calmly, with a pleasant countenance [or cheerful demeanor]" (1.4). By treating a cheerful disposition as a virtue in HD, Maimonides corrects a shortcoming of *EC*, where melancholia is regarded as harmful to the contemplative life but is not among the moral vices included in the formal account of the mean (chap. 4). To be "sad and mournful" in HD is clearly an extreme that is opposed to the mean. As in *EC*, however, by commending a joyful disposition, Maimonides takes account of what is needed to combat the melancholia induced by the Exile.

The definition of the mean comports with the above-cited rabbinic precept that a man should rejoice in his portion. As for the denigration of buffoonery, later in HD (2.7) Maimonides quotes the rabbinic sages as saying that "laughter [seḥoq] and levity bring about illicit sexual conduct." Jesting is itself a kind of sexual transgression (H. ʾIssurei Biʾah, 22.21; cf. 21.2). This might explain why Maimonides does not refer to wit in the Code as a virtue, though it is treated as such in EC.

The description of the middle way in HD draws upon what Shammai had said in an apothegm recorded in Avot (1.14): "Greet every man with a pleasant countenance." It is noteworthy that Avot contains a saying by R. Ishmael in a rather similar vein, "Greet every man with joy"; as Maimonides observes in his "Commentary on Avot" (3.15), this duty is more extreme than what Shammai's saying calls for. And in his account of the mean in HD, Maimonides does not specify that every single person be greeted joyfully, but only that a sage have a "pleasant countenance." The "disciple of wise men," though, is supposed to "greet every man first, so that they will be pleasantly disposed to him" (HD, 5.7). While not incompatible with the mean, this precept goes beyond what is strictly required by philosophic ethics (as specified in HD, 1.4).

*

Although no definitions are given for the mean with respect to compassion and courage, the extremes are set forth in 1.1, where Maimonides juxtaposes cruelty to mercy, and being soft-hearted to being strong-hearted (ʾamits lev). By omitting a definition of the mean in these instances, Maimonides detracts from the significance of compassion and courage for the sage's way of life. But he makes it clear that the middle way is the correct standard with respect to these qualities, too.

The philosophers do not regard compassion as a virtue. Since the Jewish tradition places considerable emphasis upon this quality, however, Maimonides can hardly avoid giving some attention to it in his treatment of "ethics" in a comprehensive code of Jewish law. What is extraordinary is not so much that compassion is included in HD, but that it is not more central. By indicating that a middle way is required and that to be *raḥman*, "compassionate," is an extreme, Maimonides administers a corrective to any misunderstanding that might arise regarding this quality. Still, compassion, precisely as a kind of extreme, has a place within the Jewish community, above all, during the Exile. In "Laws of Gifts for the Poor" (10.2), after referring to all Jews as brothers because they are descendants of Abraham, Maimonides continues: "And if brother will not have mercy upon brother, who will have mercy upon them and to whom shall the poor of Israel raise their eyes? To the Gentiles who hate them and persecute them? No, their eyes look only to [lit., hang upon] their brothers."[27]

By teaching that a middle way between compassion and cruelty is the "right way," Maimonides indicates that in some circumstances mercy is called for, and in others not. Besides exercising compassion with regard to the poor, one should have "great mercy" for widows and orphans (HD, 6.10). On some occasions compassion is interdicted; for instance, no pity should be shown when attempting to stop a murder or rape (*Sefer ha-Madda'*, p. 16a.1–2). Nor should a court be merciful in dealing with such a transgression (H. Sanhedrin, 20.4). To take another example, a judge is forbidden to be partial and to have pity upon a poor man who has been charged with an offense (*Sefer ha-Madda'*, p. 15b.8–9). It is very rare for the extreme opposed to compassion (i.e., cruelty) to be commended in the Code. In one place, though, Maimonides says that "cruelty against those who lead the people astray after vanities [*hevel*, insubstantial things] is compassion toward the world" (H. Sanhedrin, 11.5).

To grasp the objection to the view that compassion is simply good, it is instructive to consider what Maimonides' son says in his own magnum opus. R. Abraham ben Maimon condemns

27. According to Aristotle, mercy is "a feeling of pain, caused by the sight of some evil, destructive or painful, which befalls one who does not deserve it" (*Rhetoric* 1385b13–14). The question of whether a person deserves mercy does not have the same import in the Code. For example, mercy should be shown to all poor Jews, irrespective of whether they deserve their misfortune.

the extreme of mercy because it makes a man's soul "tender and excessively impressionable" (i.e., subject to passion, *infiʿāl*).[28] This remark is redolent of *Guide*, 2.40, where the following individuals are said to be at opposite extremes: (1) a man who is so cruel that he kills his son in a fit of anger, and (2) a man so compassionate that his soul is too "tender" to kill an insect. (In describing the latter extreme, Abraham ben Maimon uses the example of a man too tender to kill a chicken.) Maimonides views the extreme of compassion as a kind of weakness of the soul which is manifest in the inability to inflict harm (or apparent harm) in the unusual circumstance when doing so is appropriate.[29]

In the final pair of extremes listed in HD, 1.1, being soft-hearted is opposed to being strong-hearted. The latter expression, *'amits lev*, can refer to the hardening of the heart against giving charity or redeeming captives (H. Mattenot ʿAniyyim, 7.2, 8.10). But when it has this meaning, the opposite extreme is compassion. By juxtaposing "strong-hearted" to "soft-hearted" in HD, Maimonides shows that the middle way in this instance is, roughly, courage. Judges might have to be strong in heart to save the oppressed from an oppressor; the example the Code holds up to them is the action of Moses in coming to the aid of a group of young women who were prevented from watering their flock by some evil shepherds (H. Sanhedrin, 2.7). As for the opposite extreme, a warrior is called "soft-hearted" if his heart lacks the strength that would enable him to hold his ground in battle (H. Melakhim, 7.15). To be soft-hearted—which differs from being compassionate—is never commended in the Code.

THE "DISCIPLE OF WISE MEN"; THE ROLE OF EXEMPLARY CONDUCT

In the philosophic tradition, a distinction is made between the wise man and the philosopher; the latter does not possess

28. *The High Ways to Perfection of Abraham Maimonides*, vol. 1, p. 162.
29. Cf. the following statement by Shlomo Pines about the prophetic law-givers and statesmen: they "must not be deterred from following a politically

wisdom but his quest for it is all-consuming. There is no exact parallel in the Jewish tradition, but if we may be allowed a bit of license, we can detect a rough similarity in a distinction highlighted by Maimonides in HD, namely, that between the wise man and the student of the wise men: If a man is not wise, he can at least be devoted to learning from the wise men. Chapter 5 is addressed mainly to such a student.

Maimonides begins the chapter by indicating that it will contain an account of the wise man's deeds as distinct from his character traits. But after referring to what is suitable for the wise man in two early subsections of the chapter, Maimonides directs almost all the remaining parts of chapter 5 to the *talmid hakhamim*. The "disciple of wise men" is not yet "wise"; he does not follow the middle way. Maimonides therefore sometimes addresses him with a vigorous rhetorical flourish; for example, when a "disciple of wise men" speaks, he should not shout and scream like cattle and wild beasts, but converse calmly and gently (5.7). No such language is found in the account of a wise man's speech (2.4–5). (See also, e.g., 5.4: in his sexual conduct the "student" should not behave like a rooster.) Chapter 5 also contains some counsels of piety, which have a corrective force; there are in fact overlapping directives concerning "wisdom" and "piety" in this chapter. The moral requirements of the "student" consist of a mixture of "piety" and "wisdom."

The "disciple of wise men" is a mature man who earns a livelihood and supports a family, but whose mode of existence is basically that of a student. In speaking of him Maimonides does not use the more familiar rabbinic expression, *talmid hakham*; he refers to a single individual (*talmid*) who is, however, a student of various "wise men" (*hakhamim*). Through the plural ("wise men"), Maimonides alludes to the student's need to master the teachings not only of the Jewish sages but also the philosophers. This is a further reason for a special regimen being laid down for the student: he requires a moral

correct course of action by the fact that it hurts individuals" ("Maimonides," in *The Encyclopaedia of Philosophy*, vol. 5, p. 133).

preparation for investigating the full range of theoretical wisdom, including the Account of Chariot. This regimen does not, however, isolate him from society and the responsibilities connected with life in the community.

An unavoidable ambiguity runs through chapter 5 because, on the one hand, it is addressed primarily to the "disciple of wise men," and on the other, it specifies actions that are for the sage as well. The sage's actions can be treated together with those of the "student" because both are required to act in an exemplary fashion. Chapter 5 closes with the following biblical verse: "You are My servant, Israel, in whom I will be glorified" (Isa. 49.3). This verse alludes to the sanctification of God's Name, which denotes, inter alia, being a model for the people at large. The same verse concludes chapter 5 of H. Yesodei ha-Torah, which is devoted to an explanation of *qiddush ha-shem*. People in general are obliged to imitate the conduct of the sages and their disciples (HD, 6.2).

As described in this context, the deeds associated with the virtue of moderation take into consideration the need to uphold one's dignity in the presence of others. Besides indicating that a sage eats only enough to keep him alive, which follows the strict definition of the mean in 1.4, Maimonides adds here that he should not eat in the marketplace or in a store except because of great need "so that he is not degraded before his fellow creatures" (5.1–2). A wise man, moreover, must be careful to avoid becoming drunk, not only because self-indulgence is a disease of the soul, but because if he is drunk before the general run of people, he profanes the Name of God (5.3).[30]

A warning against the extreme of *gasut ha-ruah* (arrogance) recurs a number of times in chapter 5. The student should speak softly and be careful in his speech, lest his words appear like those of the arrogant (5.7); he should not walk in the manner of the arrogant (5.8); his garb should not be that of arrogant men (5.9). Presumably as a corrective discipline that aims at

30. Aristotle, in his much fuller discussion of the virtue of moderation in the *Nicomachean Ethics*, says nothing about the gentleman's having to be careful not to disgrace himself before the multitude; the noble-and-good man is not presented as a model for other people to imitate.

eliminating any haughtiness, the scholar looks down when walking, as though he were praying (5.8). He is, moreover, particularly concerned with removing enmity and establishing peace among people. He himself speaks "in praise of his fellow-man, never disparagingly" (5.7), which, by giving people more than their due, is a form of "loving-kindness" (hesed). (Cf. Nic. Eth. 1125a7–8: The Aristotelian great-souled man refrains from either praising or blaming others. Nor is there any indication that he modestly casts his gaze downward when walking.)

The scholar's mode of sexual conduct, also called the "path of holiness," is in part guided by the needs of moral training. Through the strictness of his sexual practice, "he makes his soul holy, he purifies himself, and he improves [or corrects] his character traits" (5.5) The therapeutic purpose of "holiness" explains why Maimonides says that the scholar should have relations with "modesty/sense of shame" (bushah); there is no implication that sexual relations are inherently shameful. To have a sense of shame (bushah) is distinguishable from being na'eh, "fine," "attractive." The former is associated with piety, the latter with wisdom. Thus, as a rhetorical device to encourage the "disciple" to have sexual relations in the right manner, Maimonides says that if he does so his sons will be (1) "fine" (na'im) and (2) "have a sense of shame" (bayyshanim), and they will be fit for (3) wisdom and (4) piety; (1) and (3) are correlated, as are (2) and (4). In the account of the mean, there is no indication that a "sense of shame" is necessary for a sage (1.4).

Maimonides summarizes the business conduct of a "disciple of wise men" as follows: "he is among the oppressed and not the oppressors, among the insulted and not those who insult" (5.13). This statement is similar to the summary of pious conduct with respect to humility and anger (2.3), but Maimonides adds here what is particularly germane to business dealings, namely, that a man should prefer to be oppressed rather than be the agent of oppression. Among the dictates of piety given in this context are the following: A man should be scrupulous (medaqdeq) with himself but lax toward others; if others unfairly take him to litigation he should be forgiving of them; he should willingly lend money and be gracious (*honen*) in dealing with a debtor; he should not take away the business of his fellowman or "straiten" anyone in his business dealings. Maimonides in effect prescribes that the "disciple" conduct himself with *hesed* (loving-kindness), whereby the other person is given more than his due.

A number of reasons can be given for the scholar's business conduct. By curbing any tendency that he might have toward greed, piety in the marketplace is efficacious for acquiring the virtue of contentment. Such piety also sets an example for the rest of the community, mitigating the potential harshness of the day-to-day activity of earning a living. The pious men, moreover, tend to be indifferent to the things of this world, which is justifiable ultimately by the supremacy of *theoria*; conduct ruled by man's contemplative end is conducive to a gentle sort of competition in the marketplace.

The business conduct of the "disciple of wise men" goes beyond the letter of the law. Maimonides refers explicitly to this aspect of piety in the following statement: "He [the disciple] obligates himself in matters of buying and selling where the Torah does not obligate him." According to Jewish law, words do not suffice to consummate a business deal; a contract must be signed, money exchanged, or some other arrangement sanctioned by the halakhah be made before the agreement is binding (H. Mekhirah, 1.1–3). But the scholar always keeps his word; his no is no, and his yes is yes (HD, 5.13). This is called negotiating in "faithfulness" (*'emunah*), which Maimonides commends not only in HD but also in H. Mekhirah, where he adds that someone who goes back on his word is not guided by the "spirit of the wise men" (7.8). Wisdom as well as piety call for "faithfulness" in business conduct.

To illustrate Maimonides' procedure throughout chapter 5 of HD, we might note some of the Jewish sources of the scholar's business conduct (5.13). The statement that "he lends money and is gracious [toward the debtor]" is taken from the Psalms (112.5). Since Maimonides regards the Book of Psalms as part of the Oral Law, he can readily incorporate verses from this book into his articulation of the halakhah. He also draws, of course, upon the *Talmud*; for example, the statement that "he [the disciple] gives in and yields [*mevatter*] to others when he buys from them, and he is not exacting of them" echoes what two elderly sages said when asked what was meritorious in their lives. Both of their replies included the remark, "I have been yielding [*vattran*] in connection with my possessions" (Megillah, 28a). The statement in HD that "he shall not take away business from his fellowman," is also taken from the *Talmud* (it is grounded there, remarkably, upon Ezekiel's statement that a man "shall not defile his neighbor's wife" [Ezek. 18.6; *BT*, Sanhedrin, 81a]). It is of course Maimonides who, on the basis of a comprehensive conception of a good human life, produces the ensemble. And it is he who, out of the richness of the diversified material in the Jewish sources, fashions a separate code of conduct for the "disciple of wise men."

A Note on the Wise Man's Speech; The Problem of Truthfulness

Maimonides lays down the following rule in HD delimiting speech: "He [a man] shall speak only about a matter concerned with wisdom or matters that are necessary to keep his body alive" (2.4). Speech for any other purpose is "idle conversation"; the needs of man's rational and bodily nature govern what constitutes idle talk. Although Maimonides implies at first that the above rule is for everyone, he proceeds to indicate that it is in fact directed to the wise man. ("Likewise, concerning words of Torah and words of wisdom, the words of the wise man shall be few, but full of content." Cf. also the saying of Solomon, quoted in 2.5, "Words of wise men, spoken calmly, are listened to" [Eccles. 9.17].)

There is a difference between the wise man's rule of speech and that designed for the "disciple of wise men." In chapter 5 of HD, Maimonides indicates that the "student" should "speak only when performing deeds of loving-kindness [*gemilut ḥasadim*] or about matters of wisdom and the like" (5.7). Because loving-kindness is not essential for satisfying the needs of man's bodily and rational nature, there is no reference to *ḥesed* in the account of the wise man's speech (2.4–5). The "disciple of wise men" is more clearly part of the community; Maimonides therefore incorporates the directive concerning *hesed* into the general regimen of the scholar. This is not to say that the rule for the "student" is exclusively for him. Maimonides does, however, indicate that different points of view lead to diverse rules for the regulation of speech.

An act of beneficence might require telling a lie on occasion. Maimonides refers here specifically to altering one's words "in matters concerning peace and the like."[31] A lie for the sake of peace can be exemplified by a letter from Maimonides to Samuel ben Ali, as reported in the correspondence of Maimonides with his disciple, Joseph. The latter, who was in Baghdad at the time, had quarreled bitterly with Samuel ben Ali over, among other things, who should be appointed to the office of Exilarchate. Maimonides wrote a long letter to Joseph urging him to show respect for Samuel, who was after all an elder in the community holding a position deserving respect. Samuel ben Ali had written to Maimonides, charging that Joseph had called him a "foolish old man." Maimonides responded with a conciliatory letter, which is not extant; as reported to Joseph, he said: "In his [Joseph's] letter which is in my hand he praises you and says that there is no one like you in Iraq." By declaring that Joseph "praised" Samuel when saying that there was no one like him in the whole of Iraq, Maimonides undoubtedly made a small emendation for the sake of peace.[32]

The question arises whether irony conflicts with the Jewish teaching regarding purity of the heart. Directly after the formal account of the wise man's speech (in HD, 2.4–5), Maimonides speaks about the need for being upright in the sense of having a pure heart in dealing with other people. "There shall not be

31. HD, 5.7. In "Laws Concerning Robbery and Lost Objects" (14.13), Maimonides also speaks of the propriety of shading the truth on occasion. He refers again to a lie connected with "matters of peace" but he adds examples that are specifically rooted in the Jewish tradition; e.g., denying (out of modesty) that one has been studying the talmudic tractate dealing with menstruation. The statement in HD, 5.7, is more generalized, suitable for Jew and non-Jew alike. It is indicative of the quasi-universal character of the work.

32. *'Iggrot ha-Rambam*, p. 61; *Ethical Writings*, p. 119.

one thing in his mouth and another in his heart, but what is within shall be like what is without" (2.6). In selling meat to a Gentile, for instance, it is forbidden to pretend that an animal that died a natural death had been killed by ritual slaughter. So too, a host should not feign generosity and offer refreshment to a guest when he knows that it will be refused. It is significant that Maimonides limits his examples to those concerned with material gain or enhancing one's reputation. Not a single example forbidding deception concerning wisdom is given in 2.6; Maimonides quietly alludes to the possibility of deception in connection with esoteric teachings.[33]

The rule regulating the wise man's speech (2.4) does not preclude dissembling one's words through the judicious use of contradictions, such as one finds in the *Guide*.[34] Whereas a pure heart requires that "what is within" be in harmony with the spoken word, irony depends upon the ability to dissemble one's words. An author's use of irony for the public good or for his own protection would conflict with the biblical requirement of purity of the heart.

According to the *Guide*, belief is the affirmation that what exists outside the intellect is the same as what the intellect apprehends (1.50). Maimonides emphasizes the difference between what is affirmed by the intellect and what is uttered in speech: "Belief is not the meaning that is uttered, but the meaning that is formed [or conceived] in the soul." This difference between belief and the spoken word has a bearing upon how a philosophic man should conduct himself within the

33. Cf. H. Yesodei ha-Torah, 2.12, 4.11. There is no absolute prohibition in the Torah against telling a lie. The prohibition in the Torah, "You shall not tell a lie," *loʾ teshaqqru* (Lev. 19.11), forbids lying about another person's goods or money that you have in your possession because, e.g., they have been deposited with you for safekeeping (*Sefer ha-Maddaʿ*, p. 15a; negative precept no. 249; H. Shevuʿot, 1.8).

A change in one's words might on occasion be justified by fairness. For example, if a man's pitcher of honey breaks and someone with empty jars offers to save the honey but demands an exorbitant fee, it is permitted to agree to pay whatever he asks but later to give him only what is a fair price (H. Gezelah Veʾavedah, 12.6; see also 12.7).

34. *Guide*, Introd. [10a–b, 11b]; Leo Strauss, *Persecution and the Art of Writing*, pp. 60–94.

confines of the Jewish community. The Code delimits heresy in terms of what a man says as distinct from what he thinks. Thus, "he who *says* that there is no God, the world has no ruler, etc." is classed as a *min* (heretic), and "he who *says* that prophecy does not exist . . . [or] who denies the prophecy of Moses, etc." is an Epicurean. To be classified among "those who deny the Torah," a man must *say* that the Torah does not stem from the Lord (H. Teshuvah, 3.15–17, emphases added).

The distinction between belief and utterance is also important for Jews in the Exile. According to the *Letter on Apostasy*, if a man is forced to profess belief in the prophecy of Muhammad and is unable to travel to a place where he can live openly as a Jew, he should say that he accepts Muhammad as a prophet. Maimonides stresses that only a profession "in speech" was required by the forced conversion of his day, which was a relatively minor concession. In his practice, a Jew could continue to follow the Law.[35]

35. '*Iggarot le-Rabbenu Mosheh ben Maimon*, p. 118.

SIX

The Commandments
in the "Laws Concerning
Character Traits"

In the *Guide* Maimonides describes the general usefulness of the commandments in HD as follows: "All concern moral qualities in virtue of which the association among people is in good condition" (3.38). Largely illustrative of the biblical-rabbinic tendency to go toward the extreme, they are justifiable both for the moral training of the individual and for the community's well-being. They do not deal with the family, except tangentially (cf. 5.10–11). Given his broad understanding of the term *deʿah*, Maimonides could easily have included the commandments to honor one's father and mother and to be fearful (or very reverent) of them in HD; they are found in other parts of the Code. The omission of such commandments is indicative of the significance of man's nature for determining the content of the work. For Maimonides in effect denies that marriage, and hence the family, exist by nature: the human form and its matter do not as such dispose human beings to establish families. Man is by nature a political (or social), as distinct from a familial, being.

Despite the broad usefulness of the commandments in HD, if a man transgresses one of them, he cannot be punished by a law court. Wrong actions, not faulty character traits, are subject to human punishment. Since, for example, hatred of a fellow Jew has its locus in the heart, it is not a punishable offense (HD, 6.5). Even slander, which is interpreted as a *deʿah*, is not punishable by man (cf. H. Sanhedrin, 18.1; *CM*, Makkot, 3.1, p. 236.)

The bulk of HD is comprised of a discussion of the first commandment, which is directed primarily to the wise men and their students. The remaining ten commandments, found in the final two chapters, are addressed more emphatically to the people as a whole. As set forth in its heading, HD contains the following *mitsvot:* "To imitate His ways; to cleave to those who know Him; to love neighbors; to love the converts; not to hate brothers; to rebuke [your neighbor when he has done wrong]; not to put [anyone] to shame; not to afflict the distressed; not to go about as a talebearer; not to take revenge; not to bear a grudge." These precepts are mainly based upon the nineteenth chapter of Leviticus, which may be said to be the chief locus of "biblical ethics."

In the following discussion I follow the order of the commandments in HD, beginning with a few additional comments concerning the first commandment, which has already received some attention.

To Imitate His Ways

Since Maimonides bases the doctrine of the mean upon the biblical verse, "And you shall walk in His ways," the question arises as to how the biblical view of God's ways is related to the philosophic conception of nature. Although this question is not addressed in HD, Maimonides does refer to "nature" in connection with what is given by man's bodily make-up. From birth, a man has certain character traits owing to the "nature of his body"; he also more easily acquires certain traits because of his "nature" (1.2). Nature comes to light in HD as something that has to be dealt with by the right moral training. (See also 1.3: If a person finds his "nature" inclining toward one or another extreme character trait, he must bring it back to the mean.) Maimonides does not say whether the body's nature in some instances imposes an unalterable obstacle to human freedom.[1] In any event, the "ways of God" provide a model for human conduct; according to the explicit teaching of HD, nature does not.

The obligation to imitate the ways of God is not part of the

1. See above, p. 13; below, pp. 166–67.

Account of the Chariot (metaphysics) adumbrated in the "Laws of the Foundations of the Torah" (chaps. 1–2).[2] This commandment is independent of a philosophic conception of the deity and His relation to the world; it is not part of philosophy proper. Rather, it takes its place in the Maimonidean adaptation of the Law to the ethical teachings of the philosophers; as already noted, God's ways are said to be "middle ways" (HD, 1.5).

Maimonides first singles out three qualities to be imitated. Because God is *called* gracious, merciful, and holy, a Jew is obliged to acquire these characteristics (1.6). It is questionable whether such qualities are strictly in accordance with the middle way. The qualities of holiness and mercy certainly do not lie in the mean (to be *raḥman* is depicted as an extreme in 1.1). As for being gracious (*ḥannun*), it too goes to the extreme: according to the *Guide* (1.54), to be gracious is to give something to beings that they cannot claim as their due; the paradigm for man is God's graciousness in bringing the beings into existence and governing them. Being gracious, like being abundant in loving-kindness, which is also among the ways of God that a Jew must imitate, supplements the essentially self-centered orientation of philosophic ethics. Whereas the middle way aims at a man's own perfection (HD, 1.4), Jewish law directs the sage to act graciously and with *ḥesed* in his conduct with other people.

In 1.6 Maimonides proceeds to list the following attributes of God as a model for human conduct: A Jew must be "slow to anger and abundant in loving-kindness, just and righteous, perfect, powerful and strong." This description is redolent of the Mosaic theophany that refers to God as "slow to anger and abundant in loving-kindness and truth . . ." (Exod. 34.6). Maimonides, however, omits the reference to truth! The omission is pregnant with the hint that it is impossible for a sage always to tell the truth because of his concern with the public good or with his own preservation.

To say that one should imitate God's ways by being "powerful

2. Cf. the observation by Leo Strauss regarding the subjects that are excluded from the Account of the Chariot ("Notes on Maimonides' *Book of Knowledge*," in *Studies in Platonic Political Philosophy*, p. 193).

and strong" might occasion surprise. Samuel David Luzzatto says that it is ridiculous to suppose that man could even begin to attempt to imitate the unfathomable power of the deity; he adds that no Jewish source supports such a view, and contends that the Maimonidean reference to power and strength here is an unabashed concession to the philosophers. Luzzatto, a nineteenth-century opponent of Maimonides, is particularly sensitive to issues connected with Athens and Jerusalem. Luzzatto maintains that whereas the philosophers are concerned solely with the perfection of their own souls, the descendants of Abraham are taught to cultivate compassion and loving-kindness.[3] We should at least note, however, that Maimonides includes these characteristics among the "ways of God" which a Jew must imitate; I have suggested that *hesed* supplements the philosophic teaching. It is true, though, that loving-kindness lacks the centrality in the Maimonidean account that Luzzatto gives it, and HD lays down the mean as the appropriate standard with respect to compassion. As for the "power" and "strength" that a Jew is obliged to cultivate, we may wonder whether Maimonides intended to counteract the abjectness that was produced by the Exile.[4] Did he, perhaps, wish to ameliorate what Spinoza was to call the effeminizing influence of the Law?[5] At any rate, we cannot assume that the medieval Jewish Enlightenment was oblivious to certain problems that were addressed by political Zionism during the modern Enlightenment.

Maimonides is, of course, selective in his account of God's attributes in HD. Elsewhere in the Code, when specifying which names of God it is forbidden and which it is permitted to erase, he gives a somewhat different list. Among the names that are used to praise God and that it is permitted to erase are the following: "gracious and merciful, great, powerful, and awesome, faithful, jealous, and strong" (H. Yesodei ha-Torah, 6.5).

3. Samuel David Luzzatto, *Yesodei ha-Torah* [*Foundations of the Torah*], chap. 1, n. 1.

4. See above, p. 67. The Jewish tendency to confuse servility with gentleness can be understood as due to the Exile as well as the Law.

5. Spinoza, *Theological-Political Treatise*, chap. 3 (near end); English trans. by R. H. M. Elwes, p. 56.

Clearly, not all of these qualities are suitable for man to follow. Maimonides, for example, does not say in HD that man should attempt to imitate God's greatness. Earlier, he indicates that God "recognizes His greatness and His splendor" (ibid., 2.9); there is no Jewish precedent that would justify man's comparing himself with the deity and thinking of himself in this manner.[6] And Maimonides does not teach that it is appropriate to regard oneself in this way.

It is evident once again that his procedure in HD does not lend itself to a tidy analysis. We cannot give an unambiguous description of the imitation of God's ways and identify it as the Jewish account *simpliciter* in contradistinction to the philosophic account of the mean in HD, 1.1–4. To flesh out what is undoubtedly a biblical teaching (to walk in God's ways), Maimonides interjects a content that draws not only upon the rabbinic tradition but also upon a philosophic, or in any case ambiguously Jewish, teaching. Such a dovetailing of Jewish and non-Jewish elements is the inevitable result of his approaching the legal material as a philosophic codifier.

To Cleave to Those Who Know Him

Following rabbinic tradition, Maimonides interprets the biblical verse, "And to Him shall you cleave" (Deut. 10.20), as requiring that a man attach himself to the wise men and their disciples (6.2). In his explanation, he singles out the "disciples of the wise" as the individuals with whom people should associate by engaging in business with them, eating and drinking with them, and so on. The scholars who serve as such models presumably do not practice the way of "separation"; they are not Pharisees, who would avoid having meals with the common people.

There is some tension between this commandment and the contemplative life, at least as the latter is depicted in the *Guide*, where Maimonides says: "Every excellent man stays frequently

6. David Shapiro has noted that imitating God's wisdom is lauded in the philosophic tradition, but not in the Torah. See his "Wisdom and Knowledge of God in Biblical and Talmudic Thought," in *Studies in Jewish Thought*, vol. 1, pp. 44–62.

in solitude and does not meet anyone unless it is necessary" (3.51 [125a]). Perhaps for this reason, in the course of articulating the precept in HD, Maimonides pointedly refers to the "disciples of the wise" as those with whom people should associate. It is questionable whether, or to what extent, "those who know Him" will be available as models for the community's well-being. There is an ambiguity inherent in this commandment, owing to the asymmetry that exists between the needs of man's rational nature and his political nature.

The conception of moral education presupposed by this precept differs from that found in Plato's *Republic* and Aristotle's *Nicomachean Ethics*. The philosophers of the *Republic* and the political men of the *Nicomachean Ethics* are distant from the people; they do not have an appreciable effect, as models, upon the behavior of the multitude. Moral education takes place in other ways.[7] Because the Jewish sages are supposed to be models for the conduct of the people, they are cautioned against being aloof (H. Yesodei ha-Torah, 5.11). Their exemplary behavior is a form of *qiddush ha-shem* (sanctification of God's Name), which is indicative of the Jewish setting of the imitation of the wise men and their disciples.

To Love One's Neighbors

The commandment concerning love of one's neighbor stands in apparent contrast to the doctrine of the mean, which contains no reference to one's neighbor, much less to loving him "as yourself." The commandment almost constitutes a challenge to the philosophic conception of the mean as the correct standard in moral matters. Through his interpretation of the precept, Maimonides mitigates the antagonism with the mean and, indeed, makes the Jewish precept compatible with the contemplative life.

The precept, as interpreted by Maimonides, takes its bearings from two fundamental human concerns, those regarding one's honor and one's possessions. A person should be solicitous of the honor and possessions of his fellowman, just as he is so-

7. In the *Laws*, however, Plato refers to the importance of the example set by the elders for the education of the young (729B–C).

licitous of his own (HD, 6.3). The commandment abstracts
from any inequality with respect either to moral and intellectual qualities or to wealth. Indeed, a kind of equality underlies
this precept: the desire for honor and the desire to have one's
property respected are assumed to be the same for all. Since
love of neighbor, so interpreted, would eliminate two potent
causes of strife among all human beings, it would of course facilitate decent relations among people.

Love of neighbor is not based upon the deserts of the other
person. Maimonides does not say that the other person should
be honored because of his moral qualities or his wisdom, nor is
there any reason to suppose that the neighbor's material goods
merit special consideration. To love your neighbor is to act
with *ḥesed*, loving-kindness, as distinct from justice; according to the *Guide*, *ḥesed* (or beneficence) calls for giving a person more than he can justly claim (3.53). The Law can obligate
a person to give others more than is their due: *ḥesed* in this
instance is the subject of a command.

Because the neighbor wants to be honored, one "needs to
speak in praise of him" (again, *ḥesed* is called for). Maimonides
does not go so far as to say that the other person should be
praised when he deserves blame, but a disposition to praise
rather than to speak ill of the neighbor should be cultivated.
This is reminiscent of an observation Maimonides makes when
speaking of the love of God in the *Book of the Commandments*. He says that a love of God leads to praising Him, which
Maimonides infers from love among human beings: "[I]f you
love an individual, you praise him . . ." (positive precept no. 3).

He gives no rabbinic support in HD for interpreting love of
neighbor in terms of honor and possessions. Nor is any support
to be found in the standard medieval commentaries on the
Code. Maimonides does cite a rabbinic precept to show the
peril of disobeying the commandment under discussion: "Whoever glorifies himself through debasing his fellowman has no
portion in the world-to-come." The same rabbinic dictum is
cited in H. Teshuvah (4.6), where Maimonides amplifies upon
its meaning. To give honor to oneself (*mitkabed*) by debasing
another person refers to an attitude toward others whereby a

man compares his good deeds and his wisdom with those of someone else in order to regard himself as honorable (mekhubad) and the other person as contemptible. (In other words, Maimonides tacitly opposes a corrupted form of Aristotelian greatness of soul in which a man thinks himself superior through making an invidious comparison with others rather than simply recognizing his own excellence.)

The obligation to love your neighbor as yourself is elaborated in H. ʾEvel (14.1), which in fact contains a fuller discussion of this precept than is found in HD. The following duties are subsumed under love of neighbor in H. ʾEvel ("Laws of Mourning"): (1) to visit the sick; (2) to comfort the mourners; (3) to participate in removing the dead; (4) to arrange a wedding for the bride; (5) to accompany guests who are leaving the city; (6) to take care of all the needs of the burial, to lift up the casket, to walk before it, to lament, to dig the grave, and bury the body; (7) to cause the bride and the groom to rejoice, and to furnish them with their needs. (I follow Maimonides' order, but the numbers are mine.) These precepts are instances of gemilut ḥasadim (deeds of kindness), which essentially (begufo) have no prescribed limit upon their observance. Hence, we may add, they are not readily compatible with the contemplative life; they require time and effort that would encroach upon the demands of study and intellectual apprehension. For this reason, I suggest, they are excluded from the discussion of love of one's neighbor in HD.

To justify the precepts listed in H. ʾEvel, Maimonides gives his own formulation of the golden rule. The negative wording of Hillel ("What is hateful to you, do not do to your fellowman") would not be appropriate for these precepts: they all require positive action of one kind or another. Maimonides articulates the rule as follows: "All the things that you want others to do for you, do for those who are your brothers in the Torah and in [performing] the commandments." The requisite actions are not left to the individual to determine; Maimonides removes the potentially subjective element in the golden rule by setting it firmly within the context of the Jewish law. The application of the rule is determined by the halakhah: a person is obligated to visit the sick, to comfort the mourners, and so forth. The golden rule would then take the form: Just as you would want to be visited when you are sick, you should visit the sick, and so forth.

Although Maimonides does not cite the golden rule in HD, in his discussion of love of one's neighbor in the *Book of the Commandments* he gives the following formulation of the rule: Everything that I want for myself, I want "something like it" for my neighbor (positive precept no. 206). The problematic character of the golden rule is evident if we ask whether everything that a wise man wants for himself he can reasonably want for others; what is of greatest moment to him, namely, the attainment of knowledge, may be a matter of complete indifference to the neighbor. If the neighbor is unwilling or unable to acquire theoretical knowledge, it would of course be foolish for a sage to want it for him. The equality presupposed by a strict formulation of the golden rule (everything I want for myself, I want for the neighbor) conflicts with the inequality of man. It is this difficulty, I suggest, that led Maimonides to omit the rule from HD. The equality that *is* introduced (namely, that connected with honor and possessions) has in view the well-being of the community.

The precept to love your neighbor is restricted in its applicability to members of a particular nation who are associated with one another through a religious bond. It is incumbent upon Jews to love "every single individual of Israel" (HD) or, alternatively, all "members of the covenant" (Introduction to *MT*, List of Commandments, positive precept no. 206). The particularity inherent in neighborly love is also evident from what Maimonides says in the *Commentary on the Mishnah* after having discussed the thirteen foundations of the Law: If someone accepts these foundations, it is obligatory "to love him and have compassion on him" (Commentary on Sanhedrin, 10.1, p. 217). The obligation to love and hence to honor all Jews has important implications for matters of jurisprudence. Thus, under extreme circumstances, a judge is permitted, if necessary, to mete out punishment that is harsher than the law prescribes. But despite the leeway given to a judge in extremis, Maimonides cautions that "in everything his [the judge's] actions shall be for the sake of Heaven, and the honor of the creatures shall not be slight in his eyes . . . and *a fortiori* the honor of the descendants of Abraham, Isaac, and Jacob, who hold fast to the Torah of truth" (*MT*, H. Sanhedrin, 24.8).

In sum, the needs of man's political nature guide the explanation of the duty to love one's neighbor. The other person's desire for honor is to be respected not because he is a rational being, but because the concern with honor found among people in general ought to be respected in order to have a well-ordered community. From the standpoint of man's rational nature, the neighbor may deserve little honor, but the teaching of *hesed* supersedes any judgment concerning his deserts. The Jewish precept with respect to neighborly love disregards the order of rank based upon the philosophic conception of the human soul.

To Love the Converts (*Gerim*)

Following the rabbinic tradition, Maimonides interprets the word *ger* (lit., stranger) in this law as meaning "convert" (HD, 6.4). The duty to love the *ger*, then, does not obligate Jews who have been persecuted to love their oppressors. It should be noted, though, that in the *Guide* Maimonides says that Jews should remember any benefit that was given to them by non-Jews in the past. Referring primarily to one's relatives but also to other people, including non-Jews, Maimonides says: "Everyone who was useful to you . . . in a time of distress, even if afterwards he treated you ill, ought necessarily to have merit attached to him because of the past." In support of this teaching, Maimonides cites a biblical verse that warns against having animosity toward an Edomite, which is a rabbinic appellation for a Christian. He also quotes a verse in this context referring to Egyptians: "You shall not abhor an Egyptian because you were a stranger in his land" (Deut. 23.8). The hospitality accorded to Jacob and his sons in Egypt should be remembered, even though, as Maimonides says, the Egyptians treated us badly at a later time (*Guide*, 3.42 [95a–b]). In other words, resentment ought to be overcome through a generous memory, recollecting the earlier beneficence wherever feasible.

Not to Hate One's Brothers

Although it is generally preferable to refrain from harboring resentment, the Law does not forbid the hatred of the oppressors of Jews in the Exile. The prohibition against "hating your brother in your heart" applies only to the hatred of fellow-Jews. Anyone who hates "one Israelite" in his heart transgresses this law (HD, 6.5).

Is it ever permissible to hate another Jew? The religious basis of the duty to love one's neighbor also establishes the possibility of the hatred of a transgressor of the Law. This is evident in the context in which Maimonides says (as we noted earlier) that if a person sees a friend and an enemy (lit., one whom he hates), both of whom need assistance with a beast of burden, the enemy should be helped first. Maimonides then poses the question: how could there properly be someone who is the object of hatred—since the Torah prohibits the hatred of fellow Jews? The answer is that if there is a sinner who has been rebuked but refuses to mend his ways, it is obligatory to hate him until he repents (H. Rotseaḥ Ushemirat Nafesh, 13.14).

To Rebuke

The commandment to rebuke is divided into two parts. (1) A man is obligated to rebuke a person who has sinned against him so that hatred does not arise in his heart; in this instance the law aims at the well-being of the person who has been sinned against (HD, 6.6). (2) A man is obligated to admonish a transgressor for the latter's own good. Thus, if a person is seen "who follows a way that is not good, it is a commandment to make him return to the good and to make known to him that he sins against himself by his evil actions" (6.7). The first part of this commandment echoes the middle way concerning anger, which calls for an expression of anger to prevent the recurrence of a "large matter." But when the admonition is solely for the benefit of the other person, one must speak "calmly and gently," not with anger. As Maimonides proceeds to explicate what a fraternal admonition requires, the departure from philosophic ethics becomes evident, for, he says, a Jew has a duty to admonish the sinner until being struck by him. The scope of the obligation also goes beyond what philosophy by itself would call for: a Jew is responsible for the sin of all those whose transgression he could have prevented through an admonition (6.7).

The first part of the commandment requiring that a sinner be rebuked is on the face of it contrary to what piety dictates. Maimonides therefore goes on to say that if the other person is very simple or his mind is confused and he is forgiven and no hatred is felt in one's heart, it is the "measure of piety" to refrain from admonishing him (6.9; cf. 2.3). The famous letter to the Jews of Yemen contains a memorable example of the application of this dictum in a political context. A false Messiah had arisen whose preposterous claims had placed the Jewish community of Yemen in peril. Maimonides recommends that he be put temporarily in chains until the Gentiles realize that he is demented, but there is no need to rebuke him. "I have no doubt that he is mad, and a sick person should not be rebuked or reproved for an illness brought on through no fault of his own."[8]

Earlier, in the discussion of neighborly love, we noted that Maimonides uses the literary device of omission to accommodate his account of the halakhah to what is suitable for a sage. The same method is to be found in his discussion of the commandment to rebuke. In the *Book of the Commandments*, Maimonides stresses that even a lesser man should censure a superior man when it is deemed appropriate (positive precept no. 205). This statement about what a "lesser man" should do is omitted from HD; it is not relevant to what is appropriate for a sage's code of conduct. Maimonides fashions the ethics of HD, wherever possible, to what is suitable for a wise man; HD as a whole (and not only chapters 1 through 5) takes into consideration a philosopher-sage who is a member of the Jewish community.

Not to Put Anyone to Shame

The command not to put anyone to shame is, as it were, a corollary to love of one's neighbor because putting a person to

8. *Epistle to Yemen*, p. 84 (Judeo-Arabic); p. xvi (English trans.). See also chap. 5, n. 24.

shame implies that his desire for honor has not been respected.
The prohibition against shaming another person also acts as a
brake against abusing the duty to rebuke another person when
he has committed a sin. If an admonition is necessary, Maimonides says that it should be administered in private. But in
"matters of Heaven" as distinct from those "between man and
his fellowman," it is permitted to humiliate a person in public
if he does not repent in private. The prophets were therefore
justified in putting people to shame in public: they limited
themselves to "matters of Heaven" (HD, 6.8).

The reference to the prophets here throws light upon a vex-
ing problem. Does the Torah itself sanction their admonitions
of the people of Israel? Maimonides regards the verse, "You
shall surely rebuke your neighbor" (Lev. 19.17) as giving them
such authority. This justification depends upon the validity of
the Oral Law, for the Pentateuch refers only to reproving another person to remove hatred from one's own heart. The more
comprehensive Maimonidean account, which includes the
duty to admonish others for their sake, is part of his "explanation" of the Written Law. The "explanation," as it were, retro-
actively justifies prophetic admonition.

What Maimonides says about the prophets in HD, however, poses the following difficulty: How are we to understand
his statement that they restricted themselves to "matters of
Heaven"? Did not Maimonides know what every fifth-grader in
Sunday school knows, that the prophets were concerned to a
large extent with justice and hence, presumably, with matters
"between man and his fellowman"? However this conundrum
must finally be resolved, let us note that the "Laws Concerning Repentance" (4.4) contains a passage that might prove
helpful. When speaking of Isaiah's castigation of Israel there,
Maimonides again makes no mention of justice. He cites three
verses from Isaiah, the central one of which alludes to the need
for knowledge: "The ox knows his master . . . [but Israel does
not know, My people does not understand]" (Isa. 1.3). In the
same context, two of the three admonitory verses cited from
the Torah also refer to the need for knowledge; for example,

Israel is censured in Deuteronomy as a "foolish and unwise people" (32.6). Maimonides alludes to the importance of imparting knowledge along with a suitable admonition when a rebuke is called for.

Apart from the question of how to understand the prophets, the Code contains occasional examples that show that even in matters "between man and his fellowman," the prohibition against putting a person to shame is not absolute. For instance, a man is obligated by a special "decree of the wise men" to feed his children until they are old enough to take care of themselves. If he refuses, he should be scolded, humiliated, and remonstrated with. If he persists in his dereliction, his behavior should be publicized in a proclamation that derides him for being more contemptible than a bird that is ritually unclean but which, after all, feeds its young. A derelict father cannot be strictly "compelled" to feed his children after they are six years old, but the suasion of shame should be exploited to the fullest (H. ʾIshut, 12.14).

A prohibition against ever putting a man to shame would presumably be contrary to philosophic ethics. Maimonides observes that the "wise men of old" (ḥakhamim ha-riʾshonim), who propounded the doctrine of the mean within the Jewish community, said, "Anyone who puts a decent man [ʾadam kasher] of Israel to shame has no portion in the world-to-come" (H. Ḥovel Umazziq, 3.7). They imply that it might occasionally be necessary to put a man who is not decent (kasher) to shame.

Not to Afflict the Distressed

Although the commandment, as stated in the heading of HD, refers to the "distressed" in general, Maimonides confines his discussion of it in the body of HD to the treatment of widows and orphans. The Jewish teaching goes beyond the middle way; philosophic ethics does not as such require that special consideration be given to widows and orphans. The same objects of concern spoken about in the articulation of love of one's neighbor recur here: one should be solicitous of their honor and possessions; in fact, greater solicitude for their possessions than

for one's own is called for. In addition, one should be careful
not grieve them "with words."

Wherever appropriate in the Code, Maimonides states an exception to the rule, and in this instance he indicates that a
teacher (*rav*) is permitted to treat widows and orphans sternly
if it is necessary for their own good. Even so, he should "guide
them calmly, with great mercy, and honor." This is the only
place in HD where Maimonides refers to the need for "great
mercy."

Not to Go About as a Talebearer

The biblical verse upon which the commandment "You shall
not go about as a talebearer among My people" is based is immediately followed in the Torah by the statement, "You shall
not stand idly by the blood of your neighbor" (both are in Lev.
19.16). According to Maimonides, the proximity of these two
apparently disparate statements calls attention to the mortal
danger to which innocent people might be exposed by a bearer
of tales (HD, 7.1–2). He refers in particular to the peril faced by
Jews in the Exile: talebearing "is a great sin and causes many
people of Israel to be killed." Even truthful reports can provoke
untold harm, be it during the Exile or at other times. To show
the general danger of talebearing, Maimonides cites the truthful report of Doeg the Edomite to Saul about the assistance
rendered by the priests of Nob to David when the latter was
fleeing from Saul. This report caused the death of countless
people in Nob (1 Sam. 22.6–19). (David himself had prudently
dissembled when he stopped at Nob during his flight from
Saul; he told the priest there that he was on a mission from the
king and needed supplies for his men [1 Sam. 21.2–3].)

A "tale-bearer" (*rakhil*) is someone who simply gossips about
another person. It is also forbidden to speak ill of anyone, that
is, to engage in "evil speech" (*leshon ha-ra*). Maimonides
evaluates the danger of "evil speech" primarily, though not exclusively, from the standpoint of basic human needs, that is,
those of the body. "Whoever relates things which, if repeated,
would harm the body or possessions of his fellowman or would

only distress or frighten him—this is evil speech [*harei zeh leshon ha-ra*]!" (7.5).

The prohibition against "evil speech" requires an extreme form of conduct that is consonant with man's contemplative end: the quest for knowledge so elevates a man that he has no desire to engage in such speech. But the prohibition is not altogether compatible with the requirements of man's political nature, for the difficulty that we encountered in our discussion of the "Commentary on Avot" is germane here as well. Let us recall that according to *EC*, it is "virtuous" to vilify the wicked so that innocent people are not victimized (chap. 5)—despite the Law's condemnation of speaking ill of other people.[9]

Not to Take Revenge; Not to Bear a Grudge

Maimonides brings reason to bear in different ways in different parts of HD. One way can be illustrated by the following rule, which lends support to the prohibitions against grudge-bearing and vengefulness. "It is proper for a man to overlook all the things of the world, for according to those who understand, everything is vain and empty and not worth taking vegeance for" (7.7). The supremacy of *theoria* renders all other things insignificant. Put differently, the philosophic conception of the soul's intellectual form undergirds the Jewish prohibitions against vengefulness and grudge-bearing (cf. H. Teshuvah, 8.6–10). This might seem to be puzzling because the philosophic perspective of *EC* treats these very precepts as part of a discipline for curing the soul's diseases: they go towards an extreme for the sake of counteracting the vice of rage. But the soul can be viewed from somewhat different vantage points. On the one hand, its appetitive part must be brought into a state of equilibrium; on the other hand, the soul's intellectual end tends to make the things of this world a matter of indifference.

*

Maimonides in a sense lowers the status of the Decalogue, at least concerning its place in "Jewish ethics": none of the Ten

9. See above, p. 54.

Commandments is included in HD. Since they are largely concerned with beliefs and actions, they are not part of ethics
proper. It is astonishing, however, that Maimonides does not
include the prohibition, "You shall not covet . . . ," in his discussion of ethics. He places it in "Laws Concerning Robbery
and Lost Objects" (1.9). Maimonides divides the Tenth Commandment into two *mitsvot*, "You shall not covet" and "You
shall not desire," the latter being found in the Deuteronomic
version of the Ten Commandments ("You shall not covet your
neighbor's wife and you shall not desire your neighbor's house,
etc." [Deut. 5.21]). There is some question about whether the
prohibition against wanting a neighbor's possessions is practicable because it is dubious whether a passion can be proscribed.
Maimonides in effect deals with this problem by the way that
he interprets these two *mitsvot*. "You shall not covet" pro-
scribes hectoring the neighbor to induce him to sell one of his
possessions; a transgression occurs only if a purchase has been
made. (Given the way that "coveting" is interpreted, the neighbor's wife is excluded from being a coveted object—she is not
mentioned when Maimonides explains the meaning of "You
shall not covet.") "You shall not desire" forbids a man to scheme
in his heart about how to acquire something belonging to the
neighbor, but without putting the plan into action (the wife
inter alia is mentioned here). The passion by itself does not
suffice to constitute a sin.[10]

In HD the desire to obtain a neighbor's possessions is largely
restricted by the doctrine of the mean, which limits a man's de-

10. See the commentary of Abraham ibn Ezra on Exod. 20.14, which shows
that the question of whether a passion can be the subject of a command was a
live issue for Spanish Jewry. Regarding the Tenth Commandment, he says:
"Many people are amazed at this commandment: How will a man be able not
to covet a beautiful thing in his heart to the extent that it is coveted [*nehmad*]
by his eyes?" Ibn Ezra gives the following answer. Once a villager with common sense (or correct judgment, *da'at nekhonah*) saw the beautiful daughter of
a king. He did not desire in his heart to lie with her because he knew that that
would be impossible. So too, a man does not desire to lie with his mother even
though she is beautiful, for he has been habituated to know that she is forbidden to him. Similarly, every intelligent person knows not to desire his neighbor's beautiful wife or possessions.

sire to what he truly needs. The middle way does, however, leave open the possibility for a poor man to desire an object belonging to a neighbor that he himself needs. Nor does the Tenth Commandment as interpreted in the Code proscribe such a desire—he is only forbidden to devise a plan for obtaining the object.

SEVEN

Additional Moral and Religious Teachings in the Code

THE SANCTIFICATION OF GOD'S NAME (*QIDDUSH HA-SHEM*)

Because of the courage required to fulfill the commandment to sanctify God's Name, one might think that it belongs in the section of the Code dealing with ethics. It is not in HD, however, but in the "Laws Concerning the Foundations of the Torah" (chap. 5); it is fundamental to the preservation of the Law and hence of the Jewish people. To understand its position in the Code, we should also observe that it has a different character from the bulk of the commandments in HD. Whereas those laws are consonant with the goal of *theoria*, this is not the case with *qiddush ha-shem*. It is dubious whether the ultimate sacrifice of martyrdom, as understood by Jewish law, is compatible with the philosophic life.

It is noteworthy that Maimonides does not say that *qiddush ha-shem* in the sense of martyrdom is the "measure of piety," whose articulation in HD stands in agreement with philosophic ethics. In the course of discussing *qiddush ha-shem*, Maimonides does, however, cite a biblical verse that refers to martyrs as *ḥasidim*, thereby alluding to the emphatically Jewish character of *qiddush ha-shem*. The following verse is applied to individuals who sanctify God's Name in public: "Gather unto Me My pious men, who make a covenant with Me through a sacrifice [of their lives]" (Ps. 50.5; H. Yesodei ha-Torah, 5.4).

The general obligation concerning *qiddush ha-shem* is enjoined by the biblical verse, "I shall be sanctified among the people of Israel" (Lev. 22.32). This verse does not suffice to require the surrender of one's life; the duty of martyrdom is

150

based, in addition, upon the command, "You shall love the Lord your God with all your heart, with all your soul, and with all your might" (Deut. 6.5; H. Yesodei ha-Torah, 5.7). A Jew is required to give up his life rather than transgress three laws: the prohibitions against idolatry, murder, and sexual sins (i.e., the "illicit sexual unions," 'arayot).[1] Only one of these three prohibitions is found among the "generally accepted opinions" set forth in EC, namely, that proscribing murder. There is, however, no indication in the Code or EC that a non-Jew is obligated to refuse to commit murder if he has to pay for his refusal with his life. Qiddush ha-shem is not among the seven Noahidic commandments. (From the viewpoint of the Torah, it would be incorrect to say that a Gentile should risk his life to save a Jew.)

Can reason be employed in any manner to justify laws that fall under qiddush ha-shem? Maimonides says that the "mind inclines" toward the rule that "one life should not be destroyed [to save] another life." He applies this rule to the following two instances. If Gentiles demand that a certain individual be turned over to them to be slain or they will kill another man in his stead, the first man should not be surrendered. And if, for medical reasons, the substitution of one life for another is requested, it is forbidden to accede to the request (H. Yesodei ha-Torah, 5.7). Since the mind only inclines toward the rule in question, it does not controvert the Maimonidean denial of the existence of "rational laws." (Would the mind incline toward refusing to substitute a habitual drunkard for a sage held captive and threatened with death if the drunkard is not surrendered?)

Qiddush ha-shem manifests a form of courage rooted in the beliefs of the Jewish community. It is tempting to compare the man who acts to sanctify God's Name with the Aristotelian gentleman who willingly gives up his life for the sake of "the noble" (to kalon). However, according to Aristotle, the desire to do what is noble in the face of danger follows as a matter of

1. Even these prohibitions may be violated under certain circumstances; see H. Yesodei ha-Torah, 5.2

course if a man has the virtue of courage. The basis of *qiddush ha-shem* is not a particular state of character, but the desire to profess publicly a belief in God and to preserve the Jewish religion against those who threaten it. A courageous man, according to Aristotle, acts "for the sake of the noble" above all as a free man when facing the danger of death in battle. *Qiddush ha-shem* comes to light under very different circumstances: it determines how a Jew should behave under compulsion; in its emphatic sense, it is inseparable from the vulnerability of the Jew in the Exile. Once the Messianic kingdom is established, however, and Jewish warriors come into existence, the situation is of course different, though the duty to sanctify God's Name remains in force. "He [a Jewish warrior] fights with all his heart, without fear, and his intention shall be solely to sanctify [God's] Name . . ." (H. Melakhim, 7.15).

In H. Yesodei ha-Torah, Maimonides elaborates upon the meaning of *qiddush ha-shem* as follows: If a man refrains from a transgression not because of fear or a desire for honor but solely "because of the Creator, blessed be He," he sanctifies the Name of God (5.10). Such laudable conduct is illustrated by the refusal of the Patriarch Joseph to go to bed with Potiphar's wife. As interpreted by Maimonides, there was no reason for Joseph's refusal except the command of God; he acted solely "because of the Creator." (Nothing is said here about any ingratitude that would have been displayed toward his benefactor, Potiphar, by an adulterous liaison.) This interpretation of Joseph's behavior is consonant with the way adultery is understood in *EC*, where, as we have seen, the "illicit sexual unions" are classified among the "traditional laws," which lack a reason.[2] They are illustrative of specifically Jewish conduct.

Qiddush ha-shem does not necessarily require the risk of one's life. We have already noted that by acting as a model for the behavior of other people, a man sanctifies God's Name. This is germane to the question of how sharply the wise man's conduct is set off from that of the pious man. From the discussion of *qiddush ha-shem*, it is clear that because the wise man

2. See above, pp. 75–76.

must be particularly careful in his conduct, his mode of life tends to be assimilated to the way of piety. Thus, a sage must be "scrupulous" (*medaqdeq*) with himself so that others will "praise" and "love" him, and hence want to be like him. The greater the wise man, the more particular he is obliged to be; he accordingly approaches the standard of piety.[3] It is indeed meet for a sage to be insulted and not insult in return; he should go so far as to honor "even those who disparage him." If people who are contemptuous of him are treated with respect, they might come under his salutary influence in the future.

Thus the discussion of the sage in this context tends to corroborate our interpretion of HD: whatever the theoretical implications of the standard of "wisdom," the practical ramifications of "piety" on the one hand and "wisdom" on the other are not, finally, so different. The present context shows that because a wise man must live in an exemplary fashion, he is inclined to be "pious."

HOLINESS AND "SEPARATION" (*PERISHUT*)

The subject of holiness is prominent in the discussion of the prophet's mode of life in H. Yesodei ha-Torah. To determine whether a man is indeed a prophet, one must consider whether he has been following the way of "holiness" (*qedushah*) and "separation" (*perishut*). A prophet separates himself from the vanities and the intrigues of the times and "from the general ways of the people, who walk in the darkness of the time." The path of holiness, like the "way of the wise men," is a preparation for *theoria*. The prophet trains himself to keep his mind completely clear of vain and empty matters, so that he may apprehend the holy and pure spheres, which are indicative of the wisdom of the Holy One, blessed be He (H. Yesodei ha-Torah, 7.1, 7). Although the regimen of the prophets is more stringent than that of the wise men, it is not fundamentally different; the sages, too, separate themselves from the follies of the day.

3. Maimonides therefore sometimes refers to the similarity in the conduct of the great wise men and the "pious men of old" (*hasidim ha-ri'shonim*). See above, pp. 112, 119; cf. below, p. 155.

The Pharisees, who are among the "pious men of old" (ḥasidim ha-riʾshonim), are similar to the prophets in that they, too, follow the way of "separation." It is clearer in the case of the Pharisees, however, that they do so as a cure for the diseases of the soul. Maimonides gives the following justification for their practice: "Separation brings about purity of the body from evil deeds, and purity of the body brings about holiness [i.e., separation] of the soul from bad character traits [deʿot], and holiness of the soul causes the imitation of the Shekhinah."[4] As in CM, Maimonides interprets the "separation" of the Pharisees not as a preoccupation with ritual matters but as a form of moral self-discipline.

In H. ʾIssurei Biʾah, the way of holiness is interpreted as counteracting the temptation to transgress laws regarding illicit sexual unions (ʿarayot): "It is proper for a man to subdue his [evil] impulse in this matter [the illicit sexual unions] and to accustom himself to practice exceeding holiness and to have pure thoughts and an upright character so that he will be saved from them" (22.20). Because the laws regarding ʿarayot go beyond the middle way, the stringent measure of "exceeding holiness" is needed to check the desire to transgress them. Maimonides mentions a number of steps that should be taken, and proceeds to lay particular stress upon the pursuit of wisdom. More precisely, he says that a man should "empty himself and his thought [of everything except] words of Torah and [should] expand his mind with wisdom." Since Torah and wisdom are understood here to be two different subjects, the latter presumably refers to philosophy. Maimonides goes on to refer just to wisdom, that is, philosophy: "For the thought of illicit sexual acts [ʿarayot] prevails only in a heart devoid of wisdom" (ibid. 22.21).

The example that we encountered in CM regarding the sexual conduct of one of the "pure virtuous men" recurs in the

4. H. Ṭumʾat ʾOkhlin, 16.12. According to HD, 5.2, the "pious, just men of old" carefully avoided occasions on which people indulge themselves in food and drink; they never went to a public celebration unless it concerned their own families. The wise men, however, would sometimes attend a public feast when it was connected with the performance of a mitsvah.

Code. Among the great wise men and pious men of old was a man who never noticed his wife's figure "because his heart had turned from vain things to matters of truth, which take hold of the hearts of holy men [qedoshim]" (ibid., 21.24). Wherever possible, Maimonides forms a nexus between holiness and the love of the truth.[5]

OTHER EXAMPLES OF PIETY IN THE CODE

The examples of piety found outside of HD refer, most clearly, to conduct "inside the line of the law"; they exhibit in one manner or another conduct that inclines toward an extreme. They are sometimes suggestive of a Jewish viewpoint as distinct from a philosophic one—though it is admittedly risky to make such a judgment except where Maimonides expressly compares piety with wisdom. Most are illustrative of a form of beneficence, that is, *hesed* (loving-kindness). It will be convenient simply to list such instances of piety.

1. The first example refers to an unambiguous agreement between Jewish morality and philosophic ethics; in this instance, which concerns the treatment of slaves, Maimonides speaks of the conduct that is called for by both "piety" and "wisdom."

Both require that slaves be treated with kindness. Although the Law permits working a non-Jewish slave harshly, it is not the "measure of piety" to do so. "The measure of piety and the ways of wisdom are that a man shall be merciful [*rahman*] and pursue justice, and that he not make his [the slave's] yoke burdensome . . ." (H. 'Avadim, 9.8). In this instance justice is conjoined with compassion (which is an extreme). Maimonides cites the example set by the *hakhamim ha-ri'shonim* (wise men of old), who would give the slave the same food that they themselves ate, and would see to it that the slave ate first.

---

5. Cf. the epigraph to the *Guide*. Concerning the *Guide*'s path, Maimonides says: "The unclean and the fool shall not pass over it; it shall be called the way of holiness" (adapted from Isa. 35.8). Maimonides occasionally uses the language of purification to explain his purpose in the *Guide*; see, for example, his reference to *takhlīs*, to the "purification" of the virtuous one from the false opinions that had become attached to him (Introd. [9b]).

He proceeds to marshal a number of arguments from the Jewish tradition to show that slaves should not be treated with severity. (a) It is characteristic of the "seed of our father Abraham" to be compassionate, in contrast to the idolators, who are characterized by cruelty. (b) Job set an example for later generations by heeding the complaints of slaves. In addition, Job intimates that slavery exists by what we may call convention: "Did not He that made me in the womb make him? And did not One fashion us in the womb?" (31.15). (c) It is incumbent upon Jews to imitate God's ways and, according to Scripture, "His mercy extends over all His works." (d) Whoever treats others with compassion will himself be treated with compassion, a dictum that is based upon Scripture.

Elsewhere in the Code, Maimonides condemns slavery through an explanation of the rabbinic dictum, "Let the poor be members of your household" (Avot, 1.5), which, he says, means that it is preferable that the work of the household be done by the poor rather than by slaves (H. Mattenot ʿAniyyim, 10.17).

2. The Law places an obligation upon a man to assist his fellowman when the latter's beast of burden is lying down because of the weight of its load, and also to help him load the animal if necessary. If, however, a person is an elder and is not accustomed to do such work because it is contrary to his dignity, he is exempt from having to help someone else. The rule is that "if it were his [animal] and he would load and unload [it], then he is obliged to load and unload that of his fellowman. [Nevertheless] if he is a pious man and acts inside the line of the law, he shall load and unload with [his fellowman] even if he is a great prince . . ." (H. Rotseaḥ Ushemirat Nafesh, 13.4). Although a communal leader would normally have a certain concern with preserving his dignity, piety requires that a man be indifferent to honor when it would interfere with helping someone in need. And again, we see that Jewish morality exhibits no disdain for physical labor.

3. The Law requires a farmer to leave the gleanings from his crops for the poor. If he has to irrigate the land, it is the measure of piety for him to collect the gleanings and place them on

a wall (H. Mattenot ʿAniyyim, 4.8). Since to leave the gleanings is itself a departure from the mean (*EC*, chap. 4), we may infer that the extra effort entailed by this practice is a further "excess" with respect to generosity.

4. "If a person buys an article from one of five people, and each one of them makes a claim, saying, 'I am the vendor of the article,' and the vendee does not know from whom he bought, then he must leave the purchase price among them and depart. . . . If the vendee is a pious man he will pay each one in order to discharge his duty in the sight of Heaven" (H. Mekhirah, 20.2, trans. of Yale ed.). In this instance the pious man ensures that justice is done to the person who deserves the money. But his largesse presumably goes beyond the dictates of strict justice.

5. The beneficence in the following instance also shows a pious man's wanting to make certain that no one is aggrieved on his account. "If one gives another a defective selaʿ [a valuable coin] and the aggrieved party becomes aware of the defect even as long as 12 months later he may return it. If it is possible, however, to spend the money, though with some effort, he may not return it after a lapse of time, unless the first party accepts it as an act of piety" (H. Mekhirah, 12.12). The pious man in this instance is "inside the line of the law" regulating fraud.

6. If a man leaves his produce in another man's quarters through some form of deceit, the Law allows the second party simply to put the produce onto the street. But the measure of piety is to inform the court so that they may rent a proper place for the goods. The pious man is scrupulous, that is, he is "inside the line of the law" to make certain that he does not transgress the commandment to return a lost article to its owner (H. Sekhirut, 7.7).

7. According to the Law, a man who invests money in another man's business must share equally in the loss and the profit. If, however, someone has an agreement to suffer more of the loss and take less of the profit, he is a pious man; he acts "inside the line of the law" that forbids the taking of interest (H. Malveh Veloveh, 5.8). At the other extreme is the man who

takes a disproportionate amount of the profit, a practice that is forbidden because it smacks of taking interest.

8. It is the measure of piety to collect the monetary equivalent of the second tithe even after the destruction of the Second Temple. In his own name Maimonides adds that after the money is collected in Babylonia and Egypt, it should be sent to the land of Israel to help the poor (H. Maʿaser Sheini, 1.14–2.2; cf. H. Terumot, 1.1).

9. If a man wills his possessions to people other than the rightful heirs, even if they have not behaved properly, he lacks the spirit of the wise men. Maimonides goes on to say that a pious man (ʾadam ḥasid) would refrain from testifying in court against the dispossessed heirs. Even if the latter appear to deserve to be cut out of the will because of their conduct, ḥasidut specifies that they be treated with kindness (H. Naḥalot, 6.11). But more than kindness is involved here: the pious men attempt to prevent strife within the family and the community. In the Guide, when delivering a warning against begrudging a rightful heir his property, Maimonides says: "This most just Law safeguards and fortifies this moral quality—I refer to taking care of relatives and protecting them" (3.42 [94b]).

10. Pious men go out of their way to prevent harm through some accident. "The pious men of old would bury thorns and glass in their fields at a depth of three hand-breadths . . . and others would burn them with fire and others cast them into the sea or river so that no one be hurt by them" (H. Nizqei Mamon, 13.22).

The following are instances of piety that go beyond the letter of the law, but they do not concern beneficence.

1. The "pious men of old" have greater powers of endurance than most people, as is evident from their conduct on the eve of the fast of the Ninth of Av. They used to eat a dry crust of bread with water, and sit sad and desolate, like someone whose deceased lies before him. Maimonides adds that "it is proper for wise men to do likewise or close to it"; a small difference between the pious and the wise is preserved here (H. Taʿaniyyot, 5.9).

2. A distinctive form of Jewish excellence is found among those who choose to remain in the land of Israel even under harsh economic conditions. Although the Law forbids someone who dwells there to leave, it allows emigration if a famine has struck the land; however, the "measure of piety" is to remain (H. Melakhim, 5.9). We may infer that this goes beyond what would be dictated by the way of "wisdom."

3. The "early pious men" spent considerable time in prayer: they "used to tarry one hour before prayer and one hour after prayer and lengthen their prayer by one hour" (H. Tefillah, 4.16). This would require the strict limitation upon the desire for money dictated by the way of piety.

4. Although a Jew is not obligated to buy a *talit* (fringed garment), a man who is pious (*'adam ḥasid*) will have his own *talit*, thus going beyond what is required by the law (H. Tsitsit, 3.11).

5. The holiday of Sukkot is a particularly joyful occasion, and Maimonides refers to excesses to which the pious men would go in their celebration of Sukkot when the Temple was in existence. Along with the "great wise men of Israel," the heads of the Yeshivot, and so on, the pious men would dance, sing, and clap their hands in the Temple (H. Lulav, 8.14); the holiday impels them to go beyond the middle way concerning joyfulness.

If we consider the large picture, Maimonides mainly selects instances of piety that can be accommodated to the framework of ethics sketched in HD. He excludes from the Code some talmudic examples of piety that do not fit his (largely) moral interpretation of *ḥasidut*. For example, the *Talmud* states that because the "pious men of old" liked to bring a sin offering as a sacrifice to the Temple, they would go to ingenious lengths so that they would be obliged to do so.[6] Maimonides does not cite this example in the Code. The only instance of piety mentioned in connection with the Temple refers to the exuberance of the

6. Nedarim, 10a. Cf. Adolph Büchler, *Types of Jewish-Palestinian Piety from 70 B.C.E. to 70 C.E.*, pp. 76–78.

ḥasidim on the festival of Sukkot. He also omits a rabbinic reference to the "pious men of old" according to which they gave precedence to visiting a house of mourning over going to a house of feasting (Semaḥot, 12). This preference for sadness rather than joy is contrary to the stress that Maimonides places upon the need for cheerfulness in HD.

In EC Maimonides refers to certain pious Jews ("virtuous men") who, as a cure for the soul's diseases, used to engage in such ascetic practices as fasting, rising at night, wearing garments of wool and hair, and so on. In keeping with the warning in EC against behaving in this manner (chap. 4), he excludes such examples of pious conduct from the Code. It is nonetheless true that if a person inclines toward self-indulgence, the cure for such an illness is to go toward the opposing extreme. In the Guide Maimonides refers to the therapeutic value of ascetic practice: "If the act of disobedience [of the Law] consists in corporeal pleasures, [a man] must weary and afflict his body by means of fasting and awakening at night" (3.46 [106a]). It is the more remarkable that the Code does not contain any commendation of ascetic behavior. Again, as in EC, Maimonides does not want the therapeutic departure from the mean to be misunderstood; his interpretation of piety is not intended to encourage any tendency toward the ascetic affliction of the body.

III

The Guide of
the Perplexed

EIGHT

Some Ethical Issues in the *Guide*

For Maimonides, an elucidation of the Law is impossible without recourse to concepts that stem from philosophy. Now, one might attempt to understand Scripture completely in its own terms, and such an approach may be of great value for certain purposes, but it would not be an elucidation that is at the same time a defense of the Law. For the latter, one must refer now and again to the "being" of things and, concerning matters of human conduct, reference to man's nature is necessary. Philosophy is therefore indispensable to the sort of biblical exegesis found in the *Guide*.

Although it is not among the purposes of the *Guide* to deal with ethics, (3.8, end), Maimonides does sometimes discuss ethical matters in the course of explicating the Law. I shall limit myself to commenting on a few salient features of that discussion.

MORAL PREREQUISITES OF THE PROPHETS (*GUIDE*, 2.38 AND 2.36)

To give an account of such biblical verses as, "I have made you this day a fortified city" (Jer. 1.18), Maimonides introduces the Platonic notion of *thumos* (spiritedness, boldness) into his discussion of the Law (*Guide*, 2.38). But as he himself indicates, he interprets "boldness" (*iqdām: thumos*) in his own manner. "This power [of boldness], which is among the soul's powers, is according to me ['*indī*] like the power of expulsion among the natural powers." Unlike Plato, Maimonides regards "boldness" as analogous to a bodily power whose purpose is to repel what is contrary to the body's health: "boldness" is a power within the soul that enables a person to protect himself from injury. If man did not have such a power, "he would not be moved in his thought to ward off that which would harm him." Although *iqdām* is a power of the soul, it has a basis in the natural disposition of the body. The power of *iqdām* is part of nature's stewardship of man that enables him to survive, and hence is integral to what we are tempted to call, using modern terminology, the drive for self-preservation.

The power of *iqdām* does not have only a defensive purpose, for it also makes possible advancing against an enemy; at this point the similarity to Platonic *thumos* is quite evident. Moses had to be powerfully endowed with "boldness" to "go forward" and confront Pharaoh in order to free the Hebrew slaves. How, then, are we to understand the biblical phrase, "I shall be with you," which in the Book of Exodus points toward a divine source of the prophet's strength? Referring to this verse among others, Maimonides says that the power of *iqdām* is greatly strengthened when the intellect "overflows" toward it. In other words, the "boldness" of the prophets was informed by intelligence; Maimonides seems to mean inter alia that a clear intellectual assessment of potentially dangerous circumstances increases a man's confidence. (Maimonides' interpretation of the verse, "I shall be with you," also alludes to God's providence, or the "divine overflow," which is manifest in the power of the human intellect; see *Guide*, 3.17 [35b–37b].)

An individual's "boldness" is determined partly by his natural disposition. Maimonides refers here also to the effect that a person's opinions have upon his courage: his natural disposition may be either strengthened or weakened by the convictions that he holds. There is accordingly a connection between faith and fortitude, as is evident from the letter to Yemen. Maimonides says that the faith (*īmān*) stemming from the Sinaitic revelation makes our fortitude (*iqdām*) steadfast during "these difficult times" of persecution.[1]

Since "boldness," according to Maimonides, is comparable

---

1. *Epistle to Yemen*, p. 30 (Judeo-Arabic). Cf. above, pp. 151–52.

to the natural power of expulsion, it is basically concerned with avoiding harm. It is—contrary to Platonic *thumos* (*Repub.* 581A–B)—not as such concerned with honor. The exercise of "boldness" is therefore consonant with the Code's teaching concerning humility, and even with the "pious" absence of anger (that is, with tranquility of the mind as distinct from being corpselike). The *Guide's* discussion of "boldness," moreover, comports with the requirements of man's contemplative end. Since the intellect (*'aql: nous*) is the form of the human soul, the various powers of the soul must be so understood that they are subordinated to the theoretical life (*EC*, chap. 1, end). For this reason, I suggest, Maimonides interprets "boldness" or *thumos* as having fundamentally a defensive function, comparable to the natural power of expulsion.[2] This is, of course, not to deny that it can also move a person to engage in political action, as is evident from the lives of the prophets.

To turn now to the question of whether a prophet is desirous of honor, this issue is in a way dealt with in *Guide*, 2.36, where Maimonides refers, more specifically, to the prophet's attitude toward the multitude. To want honor from the multitude or to want to dominate them would be unworthy of a prophet. Maimonides argues the point by speaking in especially demeaning terms of most people: they are like domesticated cattle or wild beasts. This anti-egalitarian statement is designed to turn one away from wanting the adulation of the multitude (2.36 [79b]); it is by no means indicative of how people in general should be treated. It is compatible with piety and love of one's neighbor—with being lowly before people and treating them with honor. The regimen of *ḥasidut*, which trains a person to be indifferent to praise, is in fact buttressed by the judgment that the opinion of the multitude is not worth caring about.

Because a prophet's desire should be channeled toward attaining theoretical knowledge, he must also hold a tight rein upon bodily desire. This teaching receives unusual support

2. Cf. *Guide*, 2.36 [79b]. A perfect man living in solitude has to be able to ward off harm from those among the multitude who might attempt to harm him.

from Aristotle's *Nicomachean Ethics*, which, according to Maimonides, regards the sense of touch as a "disgrace to us" because we share this sense with the animals. I note first that despite the low view of the body that is occasionally expressed in the *Guide* and is reinforced in a number of places by this quotation, such a view is not derived from neo-Platonism; Maimonides ascribes it to Aristotle and, presumably, to "the philosophers." Second, it follows from the Maimonidean view of man's rational nature that whatever concerns bodily pleasure is foreign to his "humanity" and hence is something that man shares with the other animals; in comparison with the actualization of the intellect, which makes man human, the sense of touch is seen as a disgrace. Further, Maimonides underscores what would be salutary for the *Guide*'s addressee, Joseph ben Judah, who needed to have his attention drawn to this matter. (Maimonides addresses him directly at one point in the *Guide* as follows: "O you who neglect your own soul so that its whiteness has turned into blackness through the corporeal faculties having gained dominion over it" [3.54, 134a].) Finally, the *Guide* expressly states that if a man's matter does not dominate or corrupt him, "that matter is a divine gift" [3.8 [13a]].

THE VICES AND MATTER (*GUIDE*, 3.8)

In the course of discussing God's providence, Maimonides ascribes the existence of evil to matter, and hence denies that God is responsible for the presence of evil in the world. The problem of the relationship between the vices and matter is taken up in this context.

All evils, Maimonides argues, are privations because they arise from matter as distinct from form. "The nature and the true reality of matter are such that it never ceases to be joined to privation." The matter constituting the human body proves to be unstable or intractable; Maimonides says that it continually attempts to throw off the form that it has. Insofar as nature is identified with matter as such, it cannot be said to be good. True, every material thing has a form, which is the source of good, but the discussion of matter in *Guide*, 3.8 indicates the difficulty of speaking of nature as unqualifiedly the guide for a good human life. (In the *Treatise on Asthma*, Maimonides says that it is necessary for a good man to "conquer" or "subdue" nature [chap. 8].)

Maimonides does not go so far as to say that the body as such is evil; he says that insofar as there are evils in the world, their source is matter. Still, even the desire for food is assumed to manifest a privation, that is, the absence of form or intellect; the desire for food is from one viewpoint an evil—though from the standpoint of the human being as a whole it is, of course, a good. So far as ethics is concerned, the body in general tends to be opposed to the working of reason. To bring the matter constituting the body under control, man's form must "subjugate it, quell its impulses, and bring it back to the best and most harmonious state that is possible" (3.8). Once again, a middle way (a "harmonious state") is the desideratum, but this time its suitability is arrived at through a reflection upon the nature of matter.

Since Maimonides indicates in this context that anger is rooted in matter, the above account of the "privation" inherent in matter is capable of justifying the Code's dictum regarding piety, according to which all anger is simply bad (HD, 2.3). We are again struck by the diversity of perspectives that can be brought to bear upon ethical questions.

COMPASSION (*GUIDE*, 3.39)

One might wonder how Maimonides, a master of classical political philosophy, deals with the biblical concern with the poor and downtrodden. In *Guide*, 3.39, he discusses the commandments germane to this topic. His interpretation of the biblical position is not incompatible with the (philosophic) emphasis upon intellectual perfection as adumbrated in other parts of the *Guide*.

Maimonides refers first in 3.39 to the duty to give material assistance to the poor and to strengthen them in various ways. In addition, we are urged "not to press hard upon those in straits and not to afflict the hearts of individuals in a weak position" [84b]. No biblical support is given for the dictum that we should not "afflict [their] hearts," although it is arguably implied by the verse, "You shall not afflict [*lo' tonu*] one another" (Lev. 25.17). According to the Code, this verse prohibits a man from afflicting another person "with words." (The prohibition is interpreted there in a quite general sense, though, and while it might be understood as encompassing an admonition concerning the poor and downtrodden, no particular mention is made of them. Thus, a penitent should not be reminded of his previous sins; a person who is ignorant of a certain "wisdom" [*ḥokhmah*] should not be asked for his opinion about the matter; and so on [H. Mekhirah, 14.12–14].) The *Guide* explains the biblical law, "You shall not afflict him [*lo' tonennu*]," that is, a runaway slave, as forbidding us to "pain his heart with speech" (3.39 [86a]; Deut. 23.17).

The Torah contains the extraordinary injunction that a runaway slave must not be returned to his master. This law, according to the *Guide*, requires helping not only runaway slaves but all Jews who seek refuge: it "makes us acquire this noble moral quality [i.e., the right disposition toward compassion], I mean, that we protect and defend those who seek our protection and not deliver them over to those from whom they have fled." Because the *Guide* gives the Torah's meaning as distinct from the legalistic explanation of the Law (*fiqh*), Maimonides had a certain latitude in his interpretation of Scripture (3.41). In this instance, he goes much beyond the strict rabbinic view of the law in question. According to the Code (which gives the rabbinic position), the biblical prohibition, "You shall not deliver a slave to his master," forbids compelling a slave who has fled to the land of Israel to be returned to his master (H. ʿAvadim, 8.10–11). The broad extension that Maimonides gives to the meaning of a "runaway slave" is patently useful for the conditions of the Exile.[3]

3. Maimonides himself took the lead in collecting funds in 1169 to ransom

Compassion, as we know from the Code, is by its very nature an excess. Because in some circumstances it is appropriate and in others it is not, one can speak of the need to strike a middle way regarding mercy. On the one hand, it is obligatory to protect the innocent in need of help, but on the other "the wrongdoer who acts unjustly should not be protected when he seeks our protection and should not be pitied . . . for pity for wrongdoers and evil men is tantamount to cruelty with regard to all the creatures" (*Guide*, 3.39 [86a–b]).

Nothing that Maimonides says about compassion in 3.39 implies that philosophy is opposed to the biblical concern with the weak and the oppressed. It is apposite to recall that according to the Code, the Jewish tradition and philosophy are in agreement regarding how slaves should be treated. According to both the "ways of wisdom" and the "measure of piety," a slave should be treated with mercy (H. ʿAvadim, 9.8). This statement has all the more force when we realize that it is the sole instance in the Code in which "wisdom" and "piety" are expressly said to be in agreement with one another.

GOD'S ACTIONS AND HUMAN CONDUCT (*GUIDE*, 3.53–54)

The *Guide* closes with an explanation of a verse from Jeremiah, "I am the Lord who exercises loving-kindness [*ḥesed*], judgment [*mishpat*], and justice [*tsedaqah*] in the earth, for in these things do I delight says the Lord" (9.23). As interpreted by Maimonides, this statement obligates a Jew to imitate God's beneficence, judgment, and justice as they are manifest in His governance of the world. This account of God's attributes of action is oriented toward the right conduct of life; it is not part of metaphysics or physics, knowledge of which is purely theoretical, choiceworthy for its own sake alone. The Maimonidean discussion of these attributes takes the form of biblical exe-

Jewish captives in desperate straits who had been victims of a Crusader attack upon an Egyptian community. See S. D. Goitein, "Moses Maimonides, Man of Action: A Revision of the Master's Biography in Light of Geniza Documents," pp. 155–67.

gesis. It is not part of philosophy proper, but rather "the science of the Law in its true sense" (*Guide,* Introd. [3a]).

The attribute of justice is most specifically related to ethics: a man does justice to the rational part of his soul by acquiring the moral virtues (3.53). Through possessing the moral virtues, a person is also just in the secondary sense of being impelled to give others their due. Such justice is exemplified by binding up the wounds of an injured person and by returning a pledge to the poor; Maimonides indicates that the latter is an instance of "justice" (*tsedaqah*) according to the Torah. It is striking that he selects examples that involve helping people in dire straits. Would the moral virtues by themselves guide a person to act in such a manner? The Maimonidean interpretation of justice here is a preparation for understanding the biblical view of God's attribute of justice, and God's justice is manifest in compassion toward the weak: He endows the living with faculties that enable them to survive [131b]. We have to keep continually in mind that this discussion is not part of ethics proper but part of the true science of the Law. The Law is a sine qua non for directing a virtuous individual to perform the aforementioned acts of compassion. (The *endoxa* listed in chapter 6 of *EC* remain the examples par excellence of rules of justice that are coordinated with the moral virtues; they all, let us recall, refer to constraints upon conduct. See above, p. 71.)

God's actions are regarded here as the model for human conduct. Is this a completely fanciful view? Does it have any basis whatsoever in the "being" of things? An appeal to God's actions as operating in the domain of nature is one way of resolving the problem posed by the presence of purpose in natural things. Matter cannot move itself; nature qua matter is, so to speak, dumb. The purposive order of nature is indicative of the action of an intellectual source upon matter. As Maimonides puts it in *Guide,* 3.19: "According to the general consensus of the philosophers, nature is not endowed with intellect and the capacity for governance. Rather does this craftsmanlike governance proceed, according to the opinion of the philosophers, from an intellectual principle [or source]; and, according to our opinion, it is the act of an intelligent being who impressed all the faculties in question into all the things in which a natural faculty exists" [40b].[4] Since nature, that is, matter, cannot by itself achieve the "thoughtlike" activity found in natural things, one must appeal to a transcendent source—either to an intellectual principle or to God's actions—to explain the purposiveness of natural entities. Maimonides also sometimes speaks of a "divine art" operative in natural entities.[5]

In the above-cited passage he indicates that "our opinion" is similar, though not identical, to that of "the philosophers." The latter do not refer to God's actions; they limit themselves to speaking of an "intellectual principle" that has causal agency. But elsewhere Maimonides indicates that certain post-Aristotelian philosophers go so far as to refer to God's actions where Aristotle himself speaks only of the wisdom of nature. Those philosophers maintain that "His actions, may He be exalted, are most perfect; there is nothing in them that is defective . . . ." Maimonides treats this view as equivalent to Aristotle's opinion that nature "does everything in the most perfect way possible" and is accordingly wise (2.14 [31a]).

A reference to God's actions, then, is not without any foundation in a rational or philosophic account of the world; even some of the philosophers speak in this manner. This is not yet to specify those actions in the particular manner of Jeremiah, nor in the way that they are set forth in the Mosaic theophany of the thirteen attributes, which refers mainly to actions of compassion. (In 3.54, when interpreting the passage from Jeremiah, Maimonides refers the reader back to his discussion of the Mosaic theophany in 1.54.) However, the intelligence manifest in nature helps to justify the reference to various of God's actions spoken of in Scripture; God's compassion, for instance, is

4. Cf. Aristotle, *Metaphysics* 1072b14: the prime mover is the principle or source, *archē*, upon which not only the heavens but also nature depend.

5. In *CM*, Introd. (p. 39), Maimonides refers to "the divine art and natural wisdom" through which the various species come into existence. See also *Guide*, 3.32 (beg.). Cf. Alexander of Aphrodisias, commentary on the *Prior Analytics*, *Commentaria in Aristotelem graeca*, vol. 2, pt. 1, p. 3.24–25; idem, *On Aristotle's Metaphysics 1*, p. 13, n. 8.

manifest in the forces that preserve the embryo and then the infant, so that human life is sustained (1.54).

The attributes of actions nonetheless have a metaphorical character. For example, God is called merciful because His actions resemble actions that, if performed by human beings, would be called merciful; God does not strictly possess the quality of mercy. The same holds for God's beneficence, justice, and judgment; we can ascribe such actions to the deity because they have a likeness to human actions. Now, according to the *Logic*, premises that make use of comparison and analogy are poetic. The biblical account of God's "attributes of action" has the form of a poetical argument. That account, as interpreted by Maimonides, can also be designated as rhetorical; analogy is utilized in a rhetorical argument, which, moreover, relies upon one or more premises that derive from a properly constituted authority or tradition (*Logic*, chap. 8).

It should be noted that Maimonides does not regard the account of God's actions to be imitated by man as mythical. In fact, he does not speak of "myths" at all, and accordingly does not differentiate between *mythos* and *logos*. Poetic premises are part of "reasoned discourse"; they are a particular kind of *logos*. A poetic "speech" or *logos* is not a mere invention. As students of medieval logic will know, Maimonides (following Alfarabi) classifies the art of poetics under logic. It is, I believe, important to keep this in mind when attempting to understand the "speech" of Jeremiah regarding God's attributes.

A poetic argument contains premises with at least *some* plausibility. Besides our observation that there are (post-Aristotelian) philosophers who refer to the actions of God, consider the following. (1) The question arises: Why does the deity bring the world into existence? It could not be for the sake of God Himself because He is completely self-sufficient and derives no benefit from the beings. Nor do the beings have any claim in justice to be brought into existence. Maimonides accordingly says that it is through His overflowing beneficence, that is, God's ḥesed, that the world exists. The model for man's acting with loving-kindness is God's ḥesed in bringing the whole into existence. (There is no implication here about *creatio ex nihilo*; Maimonides refers to the ordering of things such that they possess existence as discrete parts of an ordered whole.) Nevertheless, it is only by an analogy to human beneficence that the action of *ḥesed* can be ascribed to God. (2) Maimonides draws upon natural science to give an account of God's justice. The natural things have powers that preserve them in existence (nutritive powers, etc.), and God is called just (*tsaddiq*) "because of His mercy toward the weak—I refer to the governance of the living being by means of its powers [or faculties]" (3.53). (3) The meaning of God's "judgment" (*mishpaṭ*) is more difficult to fathom. By "judgment" in this context Maimonides refers to meting out rewards and punishments in accordance with one's deserts. A comprehensive discussion of God's "judgment" would require examining Maimonides' conception of providence, a subject that extends beyond the boundaries of this book.

Since it is tempting to give a skeptical portrayal of the attributes of action referred to by Jeremiah, I have tended to stress the "reasoned" element in this poetic discourse. But knowledge of those attributes, I reiterate, is not part of metaphysics. Maimonides says that *after* a man has engaged in *theoria* he should conduct himself in accordance with the aforementioned attributes of God (3.54 [135a]).

Is there a nonbiblical basis for acting with beneficence, as this term is interpreted in 3.53? Maimonides answers this question, in passing, in another part of the *Guide*, where he compares the governance exercised by the heavenly bodies with the beneficence of a superior human being. When an "overflow" from those celestial entities imparts a benefaction to an inferior entity, they themselves receive no benefit. Their bestowing of "gifts" is "like the giving of gifts by a generous and superior man who does it because of the nobility of his nature and the excellence of his disposition, not because of the hope for any reward" (1.72 [104a]). Thus, the "nature" and the "disposition" of such a man cause him to act with beneficence; he expects nothing for himself. (Maimonides adds that to act in this manner is to become like the deity, but he does not say that the duty to imitate God is the basis of that superior man's beneficence.)

THE QUESTION OF ASCETICISM

It is sometimes alleged that the *Guide* contains a more ascetic account of the requirements of moral conduct than do the legalistic works. But the same practical ramifications of the soul's intellectual form, conjoined as it is with matter, inform them all. For example, in the Introduction to *CM*, in a passage redolent of some parts of the *Guide*, Maimonides likens a hedonist to a man whose "matter is separated [from his intellect] and is floating in a primordial [*hiyūlī*] sea."[6] As for the Code, one could hardly imagine a stricter view of the mean than that which restricts bodily desire to what it is impossible to live without (HD, 1.4). And a pious man is supposed to incline a little toward the deficient extreme! (See also our discussion of the "disciple's" sexual conduct; above, p. 126).

In *Guide*, 3.8, Maimonides refers to the defectiveness and shamefulness of the body's impulses, which appear in this light not only because of the "privation" inherent in matter but also because of the nobility of man's intellectual form. The Code contains a comparable statement: If man compares himself with the "pure forms that are separate from matter," he will recognize that he is a lowly being, "like a vessel filled with shame" (H. Yesodei ha-Torah, 4.12). In *Guide*, 3.8, Maimonides invents an anecdote about a man who is ordered by a king to transfer dung from one place to another; the fulfillment of bodily desire is likened to such activity, the point being merely that a man should diminish his desires as much as possible. The story is a piece of rhetoric and, when understood as having a pedagogic intent, it is perfectly compatible with the statement in the same context that if a man's body is composed of

6. *CM*, Introd., p. 42. See also the hyperbolic statement in the same context: "the well-being [or, with Hamburger, improvement] of the soul comes about through the destruction of the body."

suitable matter, it is a "divine gift." Rhetoric, let us recall, can employ the device of exaggeration to achieve its goal. To reinforce the rhetorical point, Maimonides proceeds to cite a number of biblical verses that are critical of self-indulgence, such as Isaiah's censure of the wicked: "For all [their] tables are full of vomit, dung is in every place" (Isa. 28.7–8). The identical passage is quoted in the Code, in HD (5.1), as part of a condemnation of gluttony.

H. Davidson contends that the *Guide*, as distinct from *CM* and *MT*, advocates a "total renunciation of physical desire" ("The Middle Way in Maimonides' Ethics," p. 51 and passim). But the "extirpation" of physical desire, which is recommended by the *Guide* according to Davidson (pp. 58 and 65), is impossible for a human being. Maimonides never indicates that the desire for such things as food, drink, sexual intercourse, and shelter can or should be eliminated. The Law indeed opposes the burdens of asceticism, such as a monastic life (*Guide*, 2.39). What the *Guide* does teach is that a person should extinguish the desire for things engendered by the imagination (e.g., 1.5). The passages cited by Davidson do not support his position. In 2.36, for example, when indicating that to be a prophet a man must abolish his desire for "bestial things," Maimonides refers specifically to a preference for bodily pleasure as distinct from what is useful for the body [78b]; he does not refer to the elimination of desire *tout court*. According to 3.33, one purpose of the Law is to bring about the "abandonment of the desires and depreciating them and restraining them *insofar as possible*" ([73a], emphasis added).

Towards an Overview:
Theoria and *Praxis*

From a contemporary viewpoint Maimonides appears to be somewhat eclectic, but this "eclecticism" is only the flexibility implicit in the way that he uses "the philosophers" to interpret the Law. By stating in *EC* that he draws upon the works of the ancient philosophers, among others, Maimonides makes it clear that he relies upon both Plato and Aristotle in ethical matters. He follows a similar procedure in the *Guide:* not only does he use the Aristotelian conception of "ethics" (states of character) and occasionally cite Aristotle's *Ethics,* he also makes use of Plato, as in the reference to the prophet's need for "boldness" (*iqdām: thumos*).[1] In fact, through the mediation of Alfarabi, Maimonides is indebted to Plato for the view that the purification of one's character is a prerequisite for the contemplative life. Alfarabi traces this view to Plato's statement in the *Phaedo* that "whoever is not completely pure is unable to approach that which is completely pure."[2]

Alfarabi had himself paved the way for a somewhat "eclectic" approach to *praxis.* Wedded to neither Plato or Aristotle, he makes a judicious use of both.[3] Maimonides, then, had a

1. *Guide,* 2.38. See also *Guide,* 3.11, where Maimonides refers simply to the "privation of knowledge," whose consequence is that people harm themselves and others; no mention is made there of habits (*hexeis*) or character traits.

2. *Fīmā Yanbaghī an Yuqaddam qabl Taʿallum al-Falsafa* [*Introduction to Aristotle*], p. 52.19–22; *Phaedo* 67B.

3. For example, when Alfarabi sets forth the attributes of the Imam or philosopher-statesman in the *Virtuous City* (p. 248), he makes free use of book 6 of Plato's *Republic.* But even here, where he most evidently relies upon Plato, he commends the "love of honor" in a manner redolent of Aristotelian magnanimity: it will induce a man to shun doing anything that is beneath his dignity. And while there is no mention of the standard of the mean in the ac-

notable precedent for his conception of Greek philosophy as containing a rich storehouse of materials that, in matters of *praxis*, could be used as he saw fit. If we were to assume that one must be either a "Platonist" or an "Aristotelian," his treatment of the classical tradition would represent a disgraceful mixture of incompatible elements. As it is, we have to understand Maimonides' procedure in the light of how he (and Alfarabi) regard the relationship between *theoria* and *praxis*. There is even a prima facie basis for recognizing a fundamental agreement between Plato and Aristotle that is relevant to this issue. Both Plato and Aristotle regard *theoria* as the highest human endeavor, and they agree that man is by nature a political being. Hence they may be said to agree regarding the principles for the framework within which *praxis* must be understood. This agreement underlies the latitude exercised by Maimonides in his use of materials from what we might call the Platonic-Aristotelian tradition. This is not to say that Maimonides appropriates, without further ado, the above principles. I have already indicated that his view of man's political nature differs to some extent from that of Aristotle.

*

The theoretical sciences, for Maimonides, lay the foundation for ethics. In taking this approach to *praxis*, Maimonides follows the lead of Alfarabi. In the *Enumeration of the Sciences*, Alfarabi prescribes the following sequence of study: language, logic, mathematics, physics, metaphysics—and, finally, political science (including ethics). In a similar enumeration, though with a minimum of explication, Maimonides in his *Logic* specifies essentially the same order; the study of political science, which includes ethics, follows the study of physics and metaphysics (chap. 14). And in the *Guide* he recommends the following course of inquiry for an adherent of the Law: first the Torah should be studied; then wisdom in an absolute sense, which uses demonstration; and finally "the actions

count of the moral requirements for a ruler in the *Virtuous City*, in other works, such as the *Tanbīh* and the *Fuṣūl*, Alfarabi regards the middle way as the correct standard in ethics.

through which one's way of life may be ennobled should be precisely defined" (3.54). The theoretical sciences thus make possible the proper determination of precepts regarding conduct.

In *Guide*, 3.27, when Maimonides sets forth the ends of the Law, he says that "it has been demonstrated" that man has two perfections, that of the soul and that of the body. It is a demonstrative premise that bodily health is a natural end of human life; even though it is known through common experience, it is demonstrative. According to the *Logic*, a demonstrative premise can be attained through experience; for example, the medicinal property of some nutriments is demonstrative, that is, certain (chap. 8). It is also demonstrative, or self-evident, that man has to live in concert with others to fulfill his need for food, shelter, and so on. Because of the requirements of bodily perfection, man is a political being. As for the soul's perfection, it "consists in his [man's] knowing everything concerning all the beings that is within the capacity of man to know in accordance with his ultimate perfection." The actualization of the intellect (ʿaql: nous), which has a theoretical character, is identified with man's becoming "rational [nāṭiq] in actuality." Maimonides moves in the direction of conflating the distinction between *logos* (nuṭq) and *nous*.

Man's rational nature is thus clearly distinct from his political nature. Basing man's political nature upon the human body, Maimonides strongly tends to disengage man's political make-up from his rational nature. He differs from Thomas Aquinas, who maintains that man's natural inclination toward reason (ratio) leads human beings to live in a community.[4] Far from divorcing man's political nature from his rational nature, Aquinas bases the former upon the latter. And, quite consistently, Aquinas maintains that the intellect by itself is capable of guiding human conduct; the practical intellect contains precepts of the natural law, which direct man in his reasoning when dealing with other people. But according to Maimonides, man's rational nature, understood in the strict sense, has a completely theoretical character. While lacking any sort of

4. *Summa Theologiae*, 1–2, 94.2.

natural guidance for conduct, the intellect does by nature apprehend the validity of the first intelligibles, which are indispensable for the theoretical sciences (*EC*, chap. 2).

When it is directed toward its true end, the human intellect is not concerned with practical matters. Besides what Maimonides says in 3.27, this is evident from the account of Adam in the *Guide*: Adam had attained intellectual perfection but he was unaware of the "generally accepted opinions," which deal with the noble and the base; he did not even know that to go around naked is base (1.2). His rationality, despite its perfection, did not enable him to know anything about the noble and the base; human speech (*logos*) is not as such concerned with the good and the bad but with the true and the false. To be truly human, man can dispense with knowledge of good and evil, but not with truth and falsehood.

How does Maimonides arrive at this conception of man's rational nature? The Introduction to the *Commentary on the Mishnah* contains the fullest account of his procedure, but even there it is extraordinarily compressed. Maimonides says that he follows "the ancients," who established the "universal proposition" that every entity has an end (p. 39). They found, moreover, that every species has only a single end. To determine the end of the human species, Maimonides first considers the variety of human activities, and he argues that all human activities except that of the theoretical intellect are the means to some further end; the attainment of theoretical knowledge is alone choiceworthy for its own sake (p. 41). Now, a demonstrative argument requires showing the impossibility of alternative accounts, and Maimonides proceeds to exclude the possible alternatives to this view of man's end. In a passage that we cited earlier, Maimonides excludes the following as possible ends: a life devoted to pleasure, the activity of an artisan, and the activity of a political man. It will be convenient to quote the passage again. Showing that he regards the argument as demonstrative rather than dialectical, Maimonides says, "It is *impossible* that the end of man be that he eat or drink or engage in sexual intercourse or build a wall or become a king because [1] these activities are accidents in relation to him, they do not add to his substance; [2] moreover, all these activities are performed not only by him but also by some other species of animals" (emphasis added).[5] Only a theoretical kind of knowledge, he adds, can enhance man's substance.

But does not man use reason when he acts as an artisan or a political being? And do not these practical activities also differentiate man from the other animals?[6] In the above passage Maimonides considers human nature from the highest point of view: he identifies man's substance or essence with his final end. The formal cause or "whatness" of a living thing is identical with the final cause;[7] man's essence can, then, be specified in terms of attaining theoretical knowledge. Maimonides describes man's rational nature, that is, the use of "speech" (nuṭq: logos) that renders him human, as the "formation of intelligibles" through which the "true realities" of things are apprehended (CM, Introd., pp. 41–42). Man's rational nature is thus understood on the basis of a premise derived from the theoretical sciences (the formal cause of a living thing is identical with its final cause). It is man's rational nature so understood that forms the guiding principle of Maimonides' ethics.

Aristotle's articulation of man's rational nature in the Politics and the Nicomachean Ethics differs somewhat from the Maimonidean position. According to the Politics, man's speech points toward his political nature; typically human speech is concerned with what is useful and just; it does not indicate that theoria is the end of human life. This practical orientation of logos comports with Aristotle's view in the Nicomachean Ethics regarding the use of logos that is characteristic of man— even if the Nicomachean Ethics leaves room for regarding "speech" as an essential element in theorizing as well (cf. 1098a8). Aristotle's account of logos in book 1 of the Nicomachean Ethics lays the groundwork for the gentleman's use of practical wisdom in political matters; to deliberate and to exercise choice manifest a distinctively human excellence. Aris-

---

5. CM, Introd., p. 41; above, p. 19.
6. Guide, 1.72 [102b–103a]. See also Logic, chap. 14 (beg.).
7. Guide, 3.13; Alfarabi, Book of Letters, sec. 1; Aristotle, Physics 198a24–26. The natural form is the same as the substance of a thing (Guide, 1.1).

totle's position is, however, not so far removed from that of
Maimonides if we ask what the ultimate purpose of all practical activity is, and we recognize that the highest employment
of "speech" is in the service of *nous*.

While some basis exists for thinking that Maimonides interprets "speech" in the manner of Alfarabi, it seems to me that
they differ to some extent in the way that they regard man's political nature. In the *Attainment of Happiness*, Alfarabi says
that every human being has an "inborn disposition" (*fiṭra*) to
join with others "in the labor that he ought [or, it is fitting] to
perform."[8] Alfarabi refers here to a natural inclination in human beings to come together for the cultivation of the intellect
as well as for the body's well-being. The presence of such an
inclination in the human species is explicable by man's "inborn disposition" (*fiṭra*) to attain perfection.[9] Maimonides, on
the other hand, never refers to a natural inclination to combine
with others for a common purpose. Because he views human
nature very strictly in terms of form and matter, he tacitly denies that man has such an inclination.

This is not to say that Maimonides denies the importance of
various kinds of sociability for human life. He recognizes, of
course, that for the attainment of man's final end, it is highly
desirable, if not necessary, to work with and learn from others.
In the "Commentary on Avot" (1.6), he cites the friendship of
the student for his teacher, and vice versa, as the highest kind
of friendship. As for the general need for companionship, his
most striking statement is in a context in which he considers
the reasons for the existence of the nonwise: one purpose is to
provide company for a sage so that the latter may relax and
"joke around" with them. Maimonides, very surprisingly, commends even heretics for this purpose, presumably because they
are less constrained in their speech than people who are devout
(*CM*, Introd., p. 45). The significance of companionship in
human life is also evident from what Maimonides calls the
"friendship of trust." In this kind of friendship, a person does

8. Ed. Al-Yasin, p. 61 (Mahdi, sec. 18).
9. *Virtuous City*, p. 228.

not withhold anything from what he tells his friend: "He discloses all things, whether they are noble or base, without fear that any fault will be attached to him [because of what he says] . . . and if his soul trusts this individual to such an extent, he is very relaxed in his conversation and friendship."[10] This sort of companionship, incidentally, is incompatible with Aristotelian noble pride: the perfect gentleman does not do anything base; he has no faults that would be disclosed to a friend in a frank conversation. The highest kind of friendship—according to both Maimonides and Aristotle—is the "friendship of virtue," which is devoted to a good that friends have in common, namely, knowledge.

A further qualification is already quite apparent. Maimonides does not draw so sharp a distinction between man's rational form and his political nature as to exclude the intellect's practical activity from playing a significant role in the life of the community. If man had only a theoretical intellect along with a body, he would be in a sorry state indeed. He would not survive. Because of the complexity of the needs of the human body, man has to develop a variety of arts for the well-being of the body. And because the body's needs require that he live in society, he must also be capable of deliberating and distinguishing the noble from the base. The goodness of nature, or God's governance, requires that the human intellect possess certain practical functions. But let us note again that man's rational nature does not lead him to live in a community. It is because of his bodily nature that he must be a member of society, and for this reason he is capable of "thought" (fikr), "deliberation" (rawīya), and various kinds of "governance" (tadbīr). Because man is a political being, the human intellect must be capable of diverse practical activities,[11] and the ability to exercise political rule must be found in at least some mem-

10. CM, Avot, 1.6. Regarding the general significance of friendship, see also *Guide*, 3.49 [113a], where Maimonides cites Aristotle's discussion of friendship in the *Nicomachean Ethics*. In CM, Avot, 1.6, Maimonides cites Aristotle as saying that the friend is a second self (cf. *Nic. Eth.* 1166a31–32).

11. *Guide*, 1.72 [102b–103a]. Aquinas as it were reverses the position of Maimonides: Because man is a rational being, he is a political being.

bers of the human species. "It is part of the wisdom of the deity with regard to the permanence of this species . . . that He put into its nature that individuals belonging to it should have the faculty of ruling" (*Guide*, 2.40 [85b]).

Because practical as well as theoretical activities are found in the human intellect, we might wonder how the intellect's unity is to be understood. Maimonides posits the existence of a "hylic," or potential (material), intellect in the human species having the capacity to engage in both practical and theoretical activities.[12] Now, the "essence" and "true reality" of the intellect are apprehension (1.68). Thus—Maimonides implies— even the practical activity of the intellect is constituted by apprehension.[13] This does not mean, however, that the intellect's practical activity is always or usually merely receptive. A philosophic legislator, for instance, might have to fashion conventions in such a manner as to bring them into conformity with a given end. In practical matters, then, the intellect might have to be constructive. The construction is simultaneously an apprehension; it involves apprehending what is fitting to achieve the end that the intellect sets before itself. This activity of the intellect approximates the intellectual work of an artisan. In the *Logic*, for example, Maimonides says that the learned men of past communities used to fashion (*taṣnaʿu*) regimes and laws; the verb translated as "fashion" refers etymologically to the work of an artisan (chap. 14). Even in theorizing, it is necessary to "make" intelligibles: "[T]he intellect

12. *Guide*, 1.72 [102b]. For a comprehensive discussion of Maimonides' view of the intellect, see Alexander Altmann, "Maimonides on the Intellect and the Scope of Metaphysics," in his *Von der mittelalterlichen zur modernen Aufklärung*, pp. 60–129.

13. It is the intellect that apprehends the noble and the base. According to the *Logic* (chap. 8), the "generally accepted opinions" (*mashhūrāt*), which are concerned with the noble and the base, are propositions; hence they must be apprehended by the intellect. In *EC* Maimonides says that the intellect distinguishes between the base and the noble (chap. 1, near end). See also *Guide*, 1.2 (ed. Joel, 16.24–25). The Pines translation of the following passage from *Guide*, 1.2, can be misleading: "Fine and bad, on the other hand, belong to the things generally accepted as known (*al-mashhūrāt*), not to those cognized by the intellect (*al-maʿqūlāt*)" (trans. Pines, p. 24, bot.; ed. Joel, 16.18). Maimonides' intention here is to distinguish what is "generally accepted" from the "intelligibles."

is the agent [or maker, *fāʿil*] of the intelligible with respect to its being an intelligible" (*Guide*, 2.20 [46a]).

Deliberation requires an intellectual perception of what is "fitting," or what ought to be done, in a particular case to achieve a given end (*EC*, chap. 1, near end). In its ability to perceive what is "fitting," the soul's rational faculty differs, for instance, from its nutritive powers. As Maimonides observes in the *Guide*, the latter function during the ingestion of food without any regard to the needs of the body; for example, digestion proceeds apace irrespective of whether the body's health is being served. When the human intellect, however, is not misled by the imagination (and when it is properly informed), it determines what food is "fitting," the time when it is "fitting," and the amount that is "fitting"—all for the health of the body (*Guide*, 1.72, [102a]).

Does this aspect of the intellect's practical activity, namely, its concern with what is "fitting" or useful, comport with the theoretical activity of apprehending "true realities"? The theoretical intellect grasps the causes of things, including final causes; to be capable of apprehending the end of a thing requires being able to distinguish the means from the end. Further, knowledge of a thing qua means is itself necessary for understanding certain things; for example, to know the nature of the human body requires understanding that it is adapted to the intellectual end of man. To apprehend what is "fitting" is thus sometimes essential for theoretical knowledge. The intellect's apprehension of what is "fitting" in practical matters is, then, not altogether foreign to its employment in certain theoretical matters. This, of course, is not to deny that the theoretical, as distinct from the practical, activity of the intellect deals with immutable things.

*

Let us reconsider how ethics is regarded when the goal of *theoria* is decisive for determining man's rational nature. First, we must give closer attention to the body's temperaments (or humors). Maimonides maintains that they, like the soul's moral qualities, have to be in a state of equilibrium if they are to sound. There is in fact an intimate relationship between character and temperament. Although states of character follow upon the temperaments, the reverse is also true: the temperaments themselves are indirectly affected by habitual actions.[14] Some actions even have a direct effect upon the temperaments. For example, through eating more than is needed or eating the wrong food, "the veins become plugged up with this matter, sclerosis and putrefaction occur, and the quality of the humors is corrupted and their quantity changed" (*Guide*, 1.72 [102a]). In short, the right sort of moral training is necessary not only for the soul's appetitive faculty but also to bring the body's temperaments into the proper balance.

Broadly speaking, there is an agreement between what is required for bodily health (health being a state of equilibrium) and the needs of the soul's appetitive faculty. The middle way in ethics has a joint basis in the body and the soul. True, this conception of the mean is rather general, but that very generality facilitates the flexibility that is needed by a philosophic codifier of law so that he can adapt his interpretation of the mean to the requirements of a particular context: the equilibrium that constitutes the mean can be specified in somewhat different ways. Since a harmonious character (or equanimity) can even be understood as a departure from the mean, this conception of the soul's well-being can even be used to justify the Code's teaching of piety with respect to anger.

The temperaments bear upon the intellect in a manner that we have yet to consider. Maimonides goes so far as to maintain that human beings differ in their intellectual capacities because of the differences in their bodily temperaments (*CM,* Introd., p. 36). His discussion of the prerequisites of prophecy in the *Guide* sheds light upon the seminal role of the temperaments. A prophet must have a brain whose original substance is harmonious owing to "the purity of its matter"; the liquid components of the brain must not be adversely affected by temperaments (or humors) that stem from other parts of the body (2.36 [79a]). By establishing a harmony within the bodily temperaments, the moral virtues help to bring about and pre-

14. *Guide*, 3.12 [20b]; *Pirqei Mosheh*, 7.20; *EC*, chap. 8 (beg.).

serve the right mixture of liquid in the material substance of the brain.

However significant ethics is from the standpoint of man's final end, its position is nonetheless ancillary. States of character are not an integral part of the perfection of man as man. "It is clear that to this ultimate perfection [i.e., of the intellect] there do not belong either actions or moral qualities" (*Guide*, 3.27). The moral virtues are accidents with respect to what makes man human (cf. *CM*, Introd., pp. 41, 43–44). The moral virtues are not constituents of happiness; happiness comes from the intellect's theoretical activity alone.[15]

This interpretation can be substantiated by the Maimonidean discussion of the Book of Job in the *Guide*. Job possessed the moral virtues, but this did not prevent him from being plunged into a state of misery. Only after attaining theoretical wisdom, that is, an intellectual apprehension of God, did Job gain happiness. Earlier he suffered greatly *despite* the nobility of his character (3.23 [47b]). Let us be clear that the activity of *theoria* is what prevents a person from being disturbed by misfortune. "When he [Job] knew God with a certain knowledge, he admitted that true happiness, which is knowledge of the deity, is guaranteed to all who know Him and that a human being cannot be troubled *in it* [i.e., when his intellect is engaged in the apprehension of the deity] by any of all the misfortunes in question" ([48b], emphasis added). Earlier Job's knowledge of God had been based upon traditional stories; it had not been attained through "the path of *theoria* [naẓar]."

The story of Job also clarifies why the moral virtues in conjunction with sound deliberation are insufficient as a guide for human conduct. Although Job possessed the moral virtues, he mistakenly thought that happiness is gained through health,

15. Cf. Alfarabi, *The Political Regime* (or *Principles of the Beings*), a work that Maimonides singles out for high praise in a letter to Ibn Tibbon. Alfarabi differentiates the following five faculties of the human soul: the theoretical-rational, the practical-rational, the appetitive, the imaginative, and the sentient. He then says: "Happiness, which only man can know and perceive, comes about through the theoretical-rational faculty and *by none of the remaining faculties*" (p. 43.11–12, emphasis added).

wealth and children. Because he lacked theoretical wisdom, he did not correctly assess the things of this world. The possession of *theoria* as distinct from "practical wisdom" is needed to realize that the things of this world bring an illusory form of happiness. Knowledge of what constitutes true happiness places practical matters into the proper perspective.

This throws further light on what we have already observed, namely, that Maimonides does not treat practical wisdom as a separate virtue in his ethical writings.[16] In the *Guide*, too, he tacitly denies that it is a distinct virtue. Thus, in 3.54 he gives four meanings of the Hebrew word for wisdom (*ḥokhmah*), but does not mention practical wisdom. Given the practical connotation of this term in the Book of Proverbs, along with the almost unlimited ingenuity of Maimonides in interpreting the Bible, he could have easily treated *ḥokhmah* as, in one of its senses, the biblical counterpart of *phronēsis*. As it is, he says that "wisdom" has four meanings: intellectual virtue, understood as "the apprehension of true realities"; moral virtue; skill in a practical art, that is, its use in a craft; and an aptitude for ruses (*talaṭṭuf*) and strategems. The last-mentioned is not limited, however, to mere cunning in achieving an unworthy end; ruses and strategems, Maimonides says, might be used for acquiring either the moral or intellectual virtues, and in such instances, we may add, they would manifest a kind of practical wisdom. God, in His "wily graciousness" (*talaṭṭuf*), manifested such wisdom by leading the Israelites on a circuitous route through the desert so that they would develop courage before attempting to conquer the land of Israel. By taking into consideration the people's habits, and only then specifying a course of conduct, the deity acts a model for a human legislator (*Guide*, 3.32). (We may wonder whether the Maimonidean interpretation of piety is a kind ruse guiding devout Jews to recognize that the goal of moral conduct is the middle way.)

Since Maimonides does not, strictly speaking, treat practical wisdom as a virtue, the problem arises: What happens to choice? For Aristotle, moral virtue is dependent upon practical

16. See above, pp. 30–31.

wisdom, which enables a person to make the right choice in particular circumstances. And choice is fundamental in determining whether a man possesses moral virtue; an action may be good, but if a "choice" has not been made, a man does not act out of moral virtue (e.g., the action might be just, but the man himself is not just unless he acts through choice). Although Maimonides assumes that deliberation is generally necessary for moral conduct, the significance of choice is greatly diminished. A noble action is characterized in *EC* as one that stems from moral virtue, but nothing is said about the need for "choice." From the viewpoint of man's contemplative end, what is crucial is that the soul's appetitive power be well ordered. Even if performing the right action usually requires deliberation, habituation by itself might suffice.

The downplaying of choice in the account of ethics is part of a general depreciation of the practical life. Consider what Maimonides says about the Patriarchs and Moses: Even while they engaged in practical affairs, their main attention was directed toward theoretical matters, so much so that to speak of the exercise of "choice" in connection with their conduct seems completely gratuitous. Even when being "occupied with governing people, increasing their fortune, and endeavoring to acquire property . . . they performed these actions with their limbs only, while their intellects were constantly in His presence, may He be exalted" (*Guide*, 3.51 [126b–127a]). (It goes without saying that such conduct is foreign to the Aristotelian gentleman, for whom deliberation and choice in practical matters are intrinsic to virtue. But then, as we have seen, for Maimonides human excellence is not manifest in practical wisdom.)

The emphatic supremacy of *theoria* also affects how old age is regarded in *Guide*, 3.51. Whereas "the bodily powers impede youth in the attainment of most of the moral virtues," this changes as the years pass. When the flame of youthful passion diminishes, the intellect can acquire a new strength and a clearer apprehension [129a]. In 3.54, when Maimonides wants to prove that one of the meanings of "wisdom" (ḥokhmah) is the possession of moral virtue, he cites two biblical verses that refer to the wisdom of the elderly, adding that "the thing that is acquired through mere old age is a disposition to attain moral virtues" [132a]. It is in old age that man is in the best bodily condition for achieving the serenity that is conducive to contemplation. We cannot help but be struck by how far removed this view of moral excellence is from the noble vigor that is essential to the Aristotelian gentleman's conduct when dealing with political matters. Maimonides' conception of man's rational nature leads in a different direction. We should note, though, that he does not always exalt *theoria* so radically at the expense of *praxis;* moreover, his discussion is often intertwined with biblical exegesis in a manner that has an effect upon how *praxis* is regarded. In his account of Moses' confrontation of Pharaoh, for instance, Maimonides underscores the prophet's boldness and vigor (2.38). A preoccupation with *theoria* is not suitable under all circumstances; as he indicates in 3.27, the higher viewpoint must sometimes give way to a more urgent, but lower, consideration.

*

To understand the domain of *praxis,* the subject of law merits our attention again. The validity of law is not apprehended in the same manner as the truths of the theoretical sciences. Some laws, including "customs" that are regarded as binding by the community, are "generally accepted"; others, called "traditions" (*maqbūlāt: mequbalot*), depend for their validity upon an authoritative individual or assembly. Law in general lacks the self-evident character of propositions directly based upon sense perception as well as propositions that are "intelligibles" (e.g., the whole is greater than the part). The validity of these two kinds of propositions is manifest to anyone with sound senses and a sound "inborn disposition" (*fiṭra*). Generally accepted opinions and "traditions" lack such a basis; man has no "inborn disposition" that would lead him to recognize their validity. This position, set forth in the *Logic* (chap. 8), is consistent with what Maimonides says in the *Guide* about Adam before the fall: Adam was altogether oblivious to generally accepted opinions.

There are nonetheless laws whose usefulness is obvious

within the setting of a given community. This point could be obscured were we to place too much weight upon what Maimonides says about Adam in *Guide*, 1.2. We cannot generalize from Adam's original solitary condition to what is evident to people already living in a community. Further, the need for "generally accepted opinions" became evident to Adam after he succumbed to desires engendered by his imagination. The difference in status between nobility and obligation on the one hand and truth and necessity on the other does not imply that the former—that is, the rules and opinions governing *praxis*—are largely obscure.

For people living within the community governed by the Law, there are a whole host of commandments that, according to the *Guide*, are "manifestly useful." Such precepts are called *mishpaṭim* (judgments), which overlap, but are not idential with, the "generally accepted opinions" whose validity is recognized among the nations. The *mishpaṭim* include not only such commonly accepted prohibitions as those against murder and theft but also the precept to love your neighbor as yourself—a precept recognized by Jews in particular as "manifestly useful" (*Guide*, 3.26 and 28). Maimonides says that it is obvious why "*we* were commanded to love one another" ([61b], emphasis added). This precept has a "self-evident" character despite its being dependent upon the promulgation of the Law.

What is manifestly useful might require argumentation. Consider the fourth class of commandments enumerated in the *Guide*, a class that includes the laws regarding the giving of charity, lending money to the poor, and the treatment of slaves. All such laws are "manifestly useful" for instilling compassion for the weak and strengthening in various ways those who are distressed (3.39 [84a–b]). But someone might ask, Why is it so obvious that assistance should be given to the poor? Maimonides answers this question through an appeal to a version of the golden rule. Such laws, he says, "are equally useful in turn to all men. For one who is rich today will be poor tomorrow, or his descendants will be poor; whereas one who is poor today will be rich tomorrow, or his son will be rich" (3.35 [75b]). Thus, an appeal is made to the self-interest of each individual qua bodily being, with the understanding that prosperity is always subject to change. At the same time, Maimonides takes for granted that man is by nature a political being, whose duties to his fellow-man transcend a narrow construal of individual self-interest.

The following is an example of a law that is perhaps more clearly grounded in the particularity of the Jewish tradition, but the reason for the law is, again, "manifest." According to Jewish law, if a man falsely accuses his wife of adultery, he is forbidden ever to divorce her. Maimonides justifies this law by reference to the therapeutic method of curing bad moral habits by the use of contraries: the man had wanted to divorce her because she had become ugly in his eyes, but now he will never be able to send her away. The justice of such a law, Maimonides says, is "manifestly clear" in that it corrects an excess by requiring conduct that goes to the opposite extreme (*Guide*, 3.49 [115a]). The principle invoked by Maimonides has general applicability, and it is on the basis of this principle that the law's validity is palpable.

Stated very generally, the suitability of a law is obvious when it is clearly beneficial for an end set by nature, or when it is justified through a principle derivable from nature. At the same time, despite the "manifest utility" of the commandments that are so justified, different laws, found in the various nations, have a similarly ostensible usefulness. This is only to reiterate that Maimonides denies that there are "rational [or intellectual] laws."

*

Because the rules guiding human conduct are not demonstrative, they lack the certitude that, for practical purposes, is desirable for the direction of human affairs. Maimonides makes every effort to conceal the uncertainty that lingers beneath the surface of the laws guiding *praxis*. The Code has even become famous for its inflexibility owing to Maimonides' omission of his talmudic sources and, as compared with the *Talmud*, the absence of a "dialectical" quality in the work. Maimonides simply lays down what the law is; there is no room for a pro and con discussion in the study of the *Mishneh Torah*. No other work on the Oral Law, he says, is needed;[17] one must simply learn what the halakhah is from the Code itself. There is room for uncertainty, and hence debate, in connection with some of the theoretical issues explored in the *Guide*. But in the domain of *praxis*, which is governed by the Code, the "explanation" is identical with a command that must be obeyed.[18]

If we limit ourselves to the "Laws Concerning Character Traits," the same inflexibility is evident. HD therefore differs from Aristotle's *Nicomachean Ethics*, which is largely dialectical in character. But this difference mainly concerns the surface of the respective works, and however important the surface is, the procedure of Maimonides bears a greater similarity to that of Aristotle than appears from the strictly legalistic nature of HD. Because Maimonides adapts the biblical-rabbinic tradition to the needs of man's twofold nature, HD has all the earmarks of a construction, of the shaping of means to ends. Such an adaptation of law is no more demonstrative than is much of Aristotle's *Nicomachean Ethics*, but it does reflect a different approach to ethics. Maimonides, at any rate, more patently specifies the means to ends that he regards as demonstrable; practical philosophy, for Maimonides, is dependent upon the truths obtained through the theoretical sciences.

In EC as well as HD, he begins, as it were, where Aristotle ends. Whereas Aristotle largely postpones a discussion of the morality relevant to the wise man (*sophos*) until book 10 of the *Nicomachean Ethics*, the Maimonidean doctrine of the mean takes its bearings specifically from man's final end. There is accordingly no place in Maimonides' account of ethics for the gentleman, the *kaloskagathos*. And if man is understood strictly in terms of form and matter, there is no need for the crowning virtue of the Aristotelian gentleman, namely, magnanimity. We have seen, however, that there is a kind of greatness of soul that is in effect espoused by Maimonides, a conception of magnanimity that comports with humility and even with

17. *Sefer ha-Madda'*, p. 4b.
18. See above, p. 86, and below, appendix 1.

self-abasement, properly understood. Humility can be combined with greatness of soul provided that humility is understood primarily as the absence of hauteur and that magnanimity is essentially thinking oneself capable of doing great things.

Greatness of soul so understood was exemplified by Maimonides himself. His high opinion of what he could accomplish is evident from his astonishing statement that whoever studies the *Mishneh Torah* does not need to read another work dealing with the Oral Law; the Code was intended to take the place of the *Talmud* as well as all other halakhic works. Maimonides' view of his accomplishment led R. Abraham ben David to refer to the presence of an "overweening spirit" in him[19]—a remark that is indicative of the extent to which the Maimonidean interpretation of humility departs from the more conventional Jewish view. In any event, whether or not this characterization of Maimonides is exactly on the mark, his capacious view of himself made possible the daring achievement of the *Mishneh Torah*.

The following objection might be made to the conception of magnanimity, tacitly affirmed by Maimonides, that rejects the propriety of the Aristotelian gentleman's claim to honor. The importance of a concern with honor shows itself above all in political matters; the Maimonidean teaching is therefore either defective or restricted in its applicability to the Exile. Without entering again into all the issues that are relevant to this matter, I would note that according to the *Guide* it is "boldness" (*iqdām*) as distinct from the love of honor that is essential for the prophet in his dealings with other nations as well as his own (the prophet is the model for political behavior). A sound judgment with respect to future events—a prophet must be able to make a rapid estimate regarding what will take place in the future—in conjunction with "boldness" is required for dealing with political matters (see 2.38, where "divination" and "boldness" are discussed in tandem). Further, the very flexibility inherent in the Maimonidean approach to

19. Commentary on *MT*, Introduction, near end.

ethics legitimates the use of a "vice" under extreme circumstances for the public good: we have seen that impudence and haughtiness in particular are justifiable when they serve a useful purpose.[20] Let us also recall that a sage is not entirely oblivious to matters that touch upon his honor and, ultimately, the honor of the Torah.[21]

To regard ethics primarily from the standpoint of man's contemplative end is not to scant the moral needs of the community. This point can be further clarified by considering what Maimonides says in the *Logic* about political science, under whose aegis ethics falls. Political science takes its bearings from the goal of true happiness, which determines what states of character must be acquired by the community at large. The people in general should be educated in such a manner that they shun the things that bring about illusory happiness; thus, the moral requirements of both the community and man's contemplative end are taken into consideration (*Logic*, chap. 14). We are now in a position to supplement our earlier insistence that Maimonides largely abstracts from the political domain in his discussion of ethics in *EC*. By looking primarily to man's contemplative end, he simultaneously provides for the moral requirements of man's political nature.

In sum, a bridge between *theoria* and *praxis* can be built in a number of interrelated ways, which have been evident in the course of our study.

1. The contemplative life requires the sort of moral preparation that makes a man well disposed toward other people.
2. The moral virtues form the foundation within the soul for following the "generally accepted opinions" that are indispensable for the well-being of any society. A person with a good character will not be tempted to steal, or harm an innocent person, and so on.

20. See above, p. 29 and p. 109.
21. See, e.g., above, pp. 42–43; *MT*, H. Talmud Torah, 4.1. Regarding the significance of the fear of Heaven, as distinct from the love of honor, as the proper motivation for a ruler, see above, p. 111.

3. By following moral precepts that establish an equilibrium within his own soul, a sage can be a model for the conduct of other people. He, as it were, simultaneously discharges his responsibilities to himself and to the community.
4. In a law code, the stipulation of the middle way as the right ethical standard can produce a semblance of harmony among people with greatly divergent and potentially conflicting temperaments. It is, then, salutary for both the individual and the community.
5. Political science, by taking its bearings from the prerequisites for attaining true happiness, comprehends the well-being of the entire community. Even if most people are unable to attain true happiness, a political policy that opposes imaginary forms of happiness is beneficial for the community as a whole.
6. A devotion to *theoria* prevents contention for the things of this world, as Maimonides shows in his account of the Messianic era (*Guide*, 3.11). He says that "the great evils that come about among human individuals . . . are consequent upon a privation of knowledge." A devotion to theoretical knowledge prevents people "from doing harm to themselves and to others." The supremacy of *theoria* has a benign influence upon conduct.[22]

The trans-moral nature of the contemplative life could conceivably be highlighted in an examination of Maimonides' ethics. We have in fact seen that there are no actions or moral qualities associated with true happiness; the "second-rate" happiness that Aristotle ascribes to the purely moral man (the gentleman) simply drops out of the picture. The whole realm of moral virtue could appear to be questionable from the standpoint of the theoretical life. I have therefore taken pains to show how Maimonides produces or discovers a rapport between the self-centered character of the philosophic life and the requirements of the community.

Our references to *theoria* in this chapter and throughout are

22. See also *CM*, Sanhedrin, 10.1 (p. 209): When the human form has been perfected, it impedes the development of the vices.

admittedly fraught with a certain ambiguity. This equivoca-
tion, whatever its disadvantage, has the advantage of disclosing
common ground between the philosopher and the Jew. The domain of *theoria* encompasses a considerable range of issues germane to both philosophy and the Law; it even makes possible
the discussion of matters that are addressed in both traditions.
Its generality, though, also conceals differences between them.
Maimonides' use of the term *theoria* (*naẓar*) in the *Guide* is
instructive. Regarding a dispute between a philosopher and an
adherent of the Law concerning the nature of the beings and
whether existence can come into being from nonexistence,
Maimonides refers to a difficult "way of *theoria* [*naẓar*]" that
has arisen (1.73 [115b]). Those who think about the roots of the
Law are engaged in *theoria*; the "theologians" (Mutakallimūn),
too, are such theoreticians (1.73 [105b], 1.76 [127b], 1.69 [90b]).
Jews can certainly engage in *theoria* (e.g., 2.15 [32b]). But sometimes Maimonides designates the philosophers as men of
theoria, and in one passage he distinguishes "people of *theoria*
[*naẓar*]" from the "people of our religious community" (3.18,
end). *Theoria*, then, can refer to the sort of inquiry found in
"theology" or *kalām*, but it can also encompass philosophy in
the strict sense. The references to *theoria* in the *Guide* tend to
blur the differences between what is called for by philosophy
on the one hand and the Law on the other.

Our own references to *theoria* and the contemplative life
have intentionally skirted the pressing "theoretical questions,"
such as that concerning creation versus the eternity of the
world; such questions extend beyond the scope of this study. In
ethical matters, Maimonides by and large stresses the harmony
between philosophy and the Law, though the accord is produced on the basis of premises that stem from philosophy. Following Maimonides' own procedure in matters of *praxis*, I have
tended to emphasize the symmetry between the two traditions
and to gloss over the discordant features that he himself has
concealed in his articulation of practical matters. By remaining
close to the surface of his works, we can more clearly grasp
what the issues are as they come to light from the vantage
point of a "Platonic" modification of philosophic material

that goes hand-in-hand with a reinterpretation of the biblical-rabbinic tradition. For Maimonides, the relationship between Jerusalem and Athens is in the broad sense a political problem, which, as a live issue, requires taking account of the sensibilities of the community. Only through muting the discordant elements between Jerusalem and Athens could Maimonides effect an acceptable and persuasive "reform" of the ancient traditions of his people.

APPENDIX 1

Torah and *Mitsvah*

The reordering of Jewish law in the Code, which represents a departure from the *Talmud*, is a reflection of the flexibility that Maimonides assumed for himself as a philosophic codifier. His treatment of the commandments is a fundamental part of this remarkable latitude. The individual "elements" of his novel classification are the 613 commandments.[1] Maimonides both clarifies what should be included in the enumeration of the commandments and places them in a coherent order within an exhaustive classification of Jewish law. Since the commandments form an essential part of the classification, whose subject matter is the Oral Law, the 613 commandments are treated as belonging to the Oral Law. To justify his procedure, Maimonides makes a surprising distinction at the very beginning of the Code: the Torah is differentiated from the *mitsvot*. Torah is the Written Law; the *mitsvah* is the "explanation" of the Torah.[2]

1. The distinctive character of his procedure can be underscored by comparing the *Mishneh Torah* with the halakhic compilation of the renowed Alfasi (1013–1103), a code that adheres to the talmudic classification of the halakhah. Alfasi's code is not constructed on the basis of an enumeration of the 613 commandments. Rav Ḥefets, however, appears to have used such an enumeration for the organization of his law code. See Ḥefets ben Yatsliah, *Book of the Commandments*, ed. B. Halper; Mosheh Zucker, "New Fragments from the *Book of the Commandments* by R. Ḥefets ben Yatsliaḥ"; Isadore Twersky, *Introduction to the Code of Maimonides*, pp. 245–53.

2. *Sefer ha-Maddaʿ*, p. 1b.4. Maimonides relies here upon a biblical verse that tacitly distinguishes between Torah and *mitsvah*: "And I will give you tablets of stone and the Torah and the *mitsvah*" (Exod. 24.12). Cf. the commentary of ibn Ezra ad loc.; *BT*, Berakhot, 5a. See also Isadore Twersky, "Some Non-Halakic Aspects of the *Mishneh Torah*," pp. 108–9. Twersky calls attention to H. Sheḥiṭah, 1.4, where Maimonides makes a cross-reference to the beginning of the code and reiterates that the *mitsvah* is the Oral Law.

The term *mitsvah* as used by Maimonides is sufficiently comprehensive to cover laws in the Written as well as the Oral Law. He himself occasionally refers to the 613 commandments of the Torah; he also takes for granted that, for juridical purposes, they have the status of a law of the Torah.[3] Nevertheless, for the purpose of the Code's organization, the commandments are understood to be part of the Oral Law rather than the Written Law. It goes without saying that this is not a conventional view of the 613 commandments—which are usually regarded as part of the Pentateuch.

The importance of the distinction between Torah and *mitsvah* is evident from the format for the list of 613 commandments in the introduction to the Code. First, the commandment is stated, and then a verse (or part of a verse) from the Torah. The precise wording of the *mitsvah* always differs from the biblical verse; occasionally no biblical verse is given. It is quite evident from the very first commandment not only that the *mitsvah* is differentiated from the Torah but also that the *mitsvah* is indeed the "explanation" of the Written Law. "The first commandment of the positive commandments is to know that there is a God. As it is said, 'I am the Lord.'"[4] Maimonides thus abbreviates the first verse of the Ten Commandments in the Torah; the complete verse reads, "I am the Lord your God who brought you out of the land of Egypt, out of the house of bondage" (Exod. 20.2; Deut. 5.6). The Maimonidean "explanation" of the verse issues in the need, ultimately, to go beyond the brief sketch of physics and metaphysics in the Code and to study the theoretical sciences. At the same time, the "explanation," as befits a law code, imposes an obligation upon the addressee. And it is Maimonides himself who determines that it is a commandment to know that God exists.

The second of the Ten Commandments is divided into four *mitsvot:*

3. This agrees with the dictum of Maimonides in the *Book of the Commandments* that none of the commandments that stem from the rabbis should be counted among the 613 (Root 1).

4. *Sefer ha-Madda*ʿ, p. 5a.14–15.

a) "The first commandment of the negative commandments is that there not arise in [one's] thought that there exists a god besides the Lord. As it is said, 'You shall have no other gods before Me.'"

b) "Not to make a graven image; not to make it by oneself nor have others make it for him. As it is said, 'You shall not make for yourself a graven image nor any manner of likeness.'"

c) "Not to bow down to any idol, even though its manner of worship is not bowing down. As it is said, 'You shall not bow down to them.'"

d) "Not to worship an idol by means of the things that are its manner of worship. As it is said, 'And you shall not worship them.'" [5]

Maimonides clearly had the latitude to formulate these commandments as he saw fit. In the case of the first negative precept, his explanation prohibits any idolatrous "thought"; this requires an act of interpretation to be extracted from the original verse ("You shall have no other gods before Me").

His statement of the commandment generally adheres closely to the original verse of the Torah upon which it is based. When a change is introduced, it sometimes takes the form of broadening the literal meaning of the Torah (the formulation of the commandment, of course, often has a clear basis in the rabbinic tradition). Maimonides' procedure throws light upon the Pentateuch as well as the Oral Law.

For instance, he states as a commandment, "Do not eat or drink like a glutton or drunkard." The Torah, however, does not expressly forbid gluttony and drunkenness; the Maimonidean precept is based upon a biblical passage that condemns a rebellious son who commits such offenses: "This our son, etc. is a glutton and drunkard" (Deut. 21.20).[6] To take another example, the commandment forbids cursing "anyone from the family of Israel"; the Torah simply says, "You shall not curse

5. Ibid., pp. 9b.25–10a.2, 4–6 (negative precepts nos. 1, 2, 5, 6).
6. Ibid., p. 14a.1 (negative precept no. 195).

the deaf" (Lev. 19.14).[7] Further, Deuteronomy states, "and you shall *teach* them diligently to your children" (6.7), but it is a commandment "to *study* Torah and to teach it" (emphasis added).[8] In the body of the Code, in H. Talmud Torah (1.8), Maimonides bases this *mitsvah* upon a verse from the Book of Joshua (1.8): "And you shall meditate on it day and night." He implies that there is no verse in the Torah itself that requires the study of the Torah.

The difference betweeen Torah and *mitsvah* is also evident from the Maimonidean interpretation of the commandment, "To honor the wise men." This commandment is based upon the biblical verse, "You shall rise before the hoary head" (Lev. 19.32).[9] In the course of discussing the commandment in H. Talmud Torah, Maimonides at one point gives the plain meaning of the verse: "Whoever is an old man, extremely old, *even if he is not a wise man,* one stands before him. . . . And even to an aged Gentile one shows respect in speech and extends a hand to support him. As it is said, 'You shall rise before the hoary head'; every hoary head is the meaning (*mashma*ᶜ)" (6.9, emphasis added). The commandment itself, however, is to honor the wise.

Turning to the laws concerning ethics, we find that although the commandments of HD (as set forth in its heading) largely follow the plain meaning of the biblical verses upon which they are based, there are a few exceptions. There is a commandment "Not to afflict the distressed"; the Torah simply states, "You shall not afflict any widow or orphan" (Exod. 22.21). Further, we are commanded to cleave to certain exceptional human beings, that is, "those who know Him"; the biblical verse refers to cleaving to God ("And to Him shall you cleave" [Deut. 10.20]; Maimonides follows the *Sifre* in this instance). To take another example, the commandment "Not to put [anyone] to shame" is based upon the biblical verse, "And you shall not bear sin on account of him"; a man's "bearing of sin" is

7. Ibid., p. 16a.22–23 (negative precept no. 317).
8. Ibid., p. 5a.22 (positive precept no. 11).
9. Ibid., p. 9a.16 (positive precept no 209).

understood to result from putting another person to shame.
(The complete biblical verse reads: "You shall surely rebuke
your neighbor and you shall not bear sin on account of him"
[Lev. 19.17].) Maimonides himself observes in the *Book of the
Commandments* that this commandment does not follow the
literal ("manifest," *ẓāhir*) meaning of the biblical locution
(negative precept no. 303).

How to understand the difference between Torah and *mitsvah* is illuminated, finally, by the description of the Messianic
king. "He [the king] mediates [*hogeh*] on the Torah and labors
in the *mitsvot*" (H. Melakhim, 11.4). The Written Law is studied; the *mitsvot* are carried out in deed. Although the Written
Law is used to sanction the *mitsvot*, the laws to be followed are
the *mitsvot* themselves. This is the vantage point from which
the Oral Law is reconstituted in the Code. The commandments
set forth in the Code form the legal interpretation, the "explanation," of the Written Law.

APPENDIX 2

The Noahidic Commandments

The account of the "generally accepted opinions" in *EC* shows how the common rules of human conduct appear from the standpoint of philosophy. They are distinguishable from the seven Noahidic commandments, the *sheva᷄ mitsvot benei noah* (commandments whose observance is enjoined upon the descendants of Noah). These laws specify the obligations that are incumbent upon non-Jews from the viewpoint of the Torah; they are set forth in the final section of the Code, in the "Laws Concerning Kings and Their Wars."

The Noahidic commandments prohibit the following: idolatry, blasphemy, murder, illicit sexual unions, robbery, and eating the limb from a living animal; there is also a positive duty to establish courts of law (H. Melakhim, 9.1). The Noahidic laws do not expressly require that God's existence be acknowledged; it is assumed that the other nations recognize in one way or another that God exists. The nations of the world have gone astray in thinking that entities other than the deity deserve to be worshiped (H. ᷄Avodah Zarah, 1.1); hence, a prohibition against idolatry is needed, and its importance is underscored by being given the first position in the account of the Noahidic laws.

The "illicit sexual unions" found in the Noahidic code of conduct are not as extensive as those forbidden to Jews. The following are enjoined upon the descendants of Noah: prohibitions against sexual relations with one's mother, the wife of one's father (polygamy is not proscribed), a married woman, one's sister from the same mother; also prohibited are homosexuality and bestiality. As is evident from the way the prohibition against adultery is established, the determination of the Noahidic commandments sometimes relies upon legal inference. This prohibition is derived from the biblical verse, "Therefore a man shall leave his father and his mother and cleave unto his wife" (Gen. 2.24), that is, *his* wife and not another man's wife (H. Melakhim, 9.5).

The Noahidic commandments, like the "generally accepted opinions" of *EC*, imply a tacit rejection of natural law, that is, a law of reason that man knows by nature. Thus, if a man commits murder or adultery and then claims that he did not know that these acts are wrong, he is culpable because it was his responsibility to have learned that murder and adultery are forbidden (ibid., 10.1). It is not assumed that man naturally knows that such actions are wrong. A Gentile is, however, obliged to learn what the Noahidic precepts require or forbid.

A non-Jew who accepts the seven Noahidic commandments is called a "resident alien" (*ger toshav*). But if a man follows them "because the Holy One, blessed be He, commanded them in the Torah and made them known to us through Moses," he is among the "pious men of the nations of the world" (ibid., 8.11). How Maimonides understands the piety of these non-Jews can be clarified by comparing this statement with his rabbinic source, the *Mishnah of Rabbi Eliezer* (ed. H. Enelow, p. 121), which he follows quite closely on the whole. However, according to that rabbinic work, the pious Gentiles say, "Because our father Noah commanded us from God [*ha-gevurah*], we follow [the seven Noahidic commandments]." Maimonides does not refer to "our father Noah" in the above statement but to the revealed character of the Torah. In one of his letters, he indicates that the Sinaitic revelation is the source of what is known about Noah and the Patriarchs.[1] To be a pious Gentile, it is accordingly necessary to accept the prophecy of Moses.[2]

1. Letter to Joseph ibn Jabir, in *Qovets Teshuvot ha-Rambam*, pt. 2, p. 16a; cf. the letter to Ḥisdai Halevi, pt. 2, p. 23b.

2. See also *Teshuvot ha-Rambam*, vol. 1, p. 282: The reward for a Gentile who follows a commandment is the same as that for a Jew, provided that the Gentile obeys the commandment because "he acknowledges the prophecy of Moses our master, who commanded it from God."

Select Bibliography

The following list is limited to works cited in this book. The number of works on Maimonides is very extensive and continually growing, as new articles and books appear that reflect a renewed interest in his thought. The bibliography below does not attempt to record this development.

Editions of Works by Maimonides

Book of the Commandments. Judeo-Arabic text, with modern Hebrew translation, edited by Joseph Kafih. Jerusalem: Mossad Harav Kook, 1971.

Commentary on the Mishnah. 7 vols. Judeo-Arabic text, with modern Hebrew translation, edited by Joseph Kafih. Jerusalem: Mossad Harav Kook, 1963–68.

Einleitung in die Mischna. Judeo-Arabic text, with medieval Hebrew translation, edited by Bernhard Hamburger. Frankfurt: Kaufmann, 1902.

Ethical Writings of Maimonides. Edited by Raymond L. Weiss with Charles E. Butterworth. New York: New York University Press, 1975; paperback ed., Dover 1983. Contains English translations of various works referred to in the text.

Fī Tadbīr Aṣ-Ṣiḥḥat [On the Management of Health]. Edited by Hermann Kroner. Leiden: Brill, 1925. English translation by Bar-Sela, Hoff, and Faris, in *Transactions of the American Philosophical Society* 54, pt. 4 (1964).

Guide of the Perplexed. Judeo-Arabic text of S. Munk; edited by I. Joel. Jerusalem: Junovitch, 1929. English translation by Shlomo Pines. Chicago: University of Chicago Press, 1963.

ʾIggrot ha-Rambam. Edited by David Baneth. Jerusalem: Mekize Nirdamim, 1946.

ʾIggarot le-Rabbenu Mosheh ben Maimon. Edited by Joseph Kafih. Jerusalem: Mossad Harav Kook, 1972.

Letter on Astrology. Hebrew text edited by Alexander Marx, in *Hebrew Union College Annual* 3 (1926): 349–58. English translation by Ralph Lerner, in Ralph Lerner and Muhsin Mahdi, eds., *Medieval Political Philosophy: A Sourcebook.* New York: Free Press of Glencoe, 1963.

Mishneh Torah. Standard Warsaw-Vilna edition, with commentaries.

Moses Maimonides' Epistle to Yemen. Judeo-Arabic text, with medieval Hebrew translations, edited by Abraham Halkin; English translation by Boaz Cohen. New York: American Academy for Jewish Research, 1952.

Pirqei Mosheh. Edited by Suessman Muntner. Jerusalem: Mossad Harav Kook, 1958. English translation by Fred Rosner and Suessman Munter, *The Medical Aphorisms of Moses Maimonides.* New York: Yeshiva University Press, 1970. Arabic edition and English translation of chapter 25 (in part) by Joseph Schacht and Max Meyerhoff, in "Maimonides Against Galen, On Philosophy and Cosmogeny," *Bulletin of the Faculty of the Arts,* Cairo, 5, pt. 1 (May, 1937).

Qovets Teshuvot ha-Rambam. Edited by A. Lichtenberg. Leipzig, 1849.

Sefer ha-Maddaᶜ (The Book of Knowledge). Hebrew text, with English translation, edited by Moses Hyamson. Jerusalem: Boys Town, 1962.

Sefer ha-Qatseret [Treatise on Asthma]. Edited by Suessman Munter. Jerusalem: Ruben Mass, 1940.

Teshuvot ha-Rambam. 3 vols. Edited by Joshua Blau. Jerusalem: Mekize Nirdamim, 1958–61.

Treatise on the Art of Logic. Judeo-Arabic text edited by Israel Efros, "Maimonides' Arabic Treatise on Logic," in *Proceedings of the American Academy for Jewish Research* 34 (1966); Arabic text edited by Mubahat Türker, "Mūsā ibn-i Meymūn'un al-Makālā fī Ṣināᶜat al-Manṭik," in *Ankara Üniversitesi Dil ve Tarih-Coğrafya Fakültesi Dergisi* 18 (1960).

Other Works Cited
Primary Sources

Abraham ben Maimon. *The High Ways to Perfection of Abraham Maimonides.* 2 vols. Judeo-Arabic text, with English translation, edited by Samuel Rosenblatt. New York: Columbia University Press, 1927.

Abraham bar Ḥiyya. *Hegyon ha-Nefesh.* Edited by E. Freiman. Leipzig: Vollrath, 1860.

Alexander of Aphrodisias. *On Aristotle's Metaphysics 1.* Translated by W. E. Dooley. Ithaca: Cornell University Press, 1989.

Baḥya ibn Paqudah. *K. al-Hidāya ilā Farāʾiḍ al-Qulūb.* Judeo-Arabic text, with Hebrew translation, edited by Joseph Kafih. Jerusalem: Akiba Joseph, 1973. Judeo-Arabic text edited by A. S. Yahuda. Leiden: Brill, 1912.

Eliezer, Rabbi. *The Mishnah of Rabbi Eliezer.* Edited by H. G. Enelow. New York: Bloch, 1933.

al-Fārābī, Abū Naṣr Muḥammad. *Fīmā Yanbaghī an Yuqaddam qabl Taᶜallum al-Falsafa [Introduction to Aristotle].* In *Alfarabi's Philosophische Abhandlungen,* edited by Friedrich Dieterici. Leiden: Brill, 1890.

―――. *Fuṣūl Muntazaᶜa [Selected Chapters].* Edited by Fauzi M.

Najjar. Beirut: Dar el-Mashreq, 1971. Arabic text, with English translation, edited by D. M. Dunlop as *Aphorisms of the Statesman*. Cambridge: Cambridge University Press, 1961.

———. *Iḥṣāʾ al-ʿUlūm* [*Enumeration of the Sciences*]. Edited by Osman Amine. Cairo: Dar al-Fikr al-Arabi, 1949.

———. *Kitab al-Ḥurūf* [*Book of Letters*]. Edited by Muhsin Mahdi. Beirut: Dar el-Mashreq, 1970.

———. *Mabādiʾ Ārāʾ Ahl al-Madīna al-Faḍīla* [*The Principles of the Opinions of the People of the Virtuous City*]. Arabic text, with English translation, edited by Richard Walzer as *Al-Farabi on the Perfect State*. Oxford: Clarendon Press, 1985.

———. *Al-Siyāsa al-Madaniyya* [*The Political Regime*]. Edited by Fauzi M. Najjar. Beirut: Imprimerie Catholique, 1964.

———. *Taḥṣīl al-Saʿāda* [*Attainment of Happiness*]. Edited by Jafar Al-Yasin. Beirut: al-Andaloss, 1983. English translation by Muhsin Mahdi, in *Alfarabi's Philosophy of Plato and Aristotle*. New York: Free Press of Glencoe, 1962.

———. *Al-Tanbīh ʿalā Sabīl al-Saʿāda* [*Directive to the Path of Happiness*]. Edited by Jafar Al-Yasin. Beirut: Dar al-Manahel, 1985.

Galen. *De Placitis Hippocratis et Platonis* [*On the Doctrines of Hippocrates and Plato*]. Vol. 4, pts. 1, 2 of *Corpus Medicorum Graecorum*. Edited, with an English translation, by Phillip De Lacy. Berlin: Akadamie-Verlag, 1978.

al-Ghazālī, Abū Ḥāmid. *Al-Munqidh min al-Ḍalāl* [*Deliverance from Error*]. Beirut: al-Andaloss, 1967. English translation by W. Montgomery Watt, in *The Faith and Practice of Al-Ghazali*. London: George Allen & Unwin, 1953.

Giles of Rome. *Errores Philosophorum*. Edited by Josef Koch; English translation by John O. Riedl. Milwaukee: Marquette University Press, 1944.

Halakhot Gedolot. Edited by J. Hildesheimer. Berlin: Itzkowski, 1888.

Ḥefets ben Yatsliaḥ. *Book of the Commandments*. In *A Volume of the Book of Precepts*. Edited by B. Halper. Philadelphia: Dropsie College, 1915.

al-Hujwīrī, ʿAli ibn ʿUthman. *Kashf al-Maḥjūb* [*Unveiling the Hidden*]. Edited by V. A. Zhukowski. Leningrad, 1926. English translation by R. A. Nicholson. *The "Kashf al-Maḥjūb," the Oldest Persian Treatise on Sufism, by al-Hujwīrī*. E. J. W. Gibb Memorial Series, no. 17. Leiden: Brill, 1911.

Joseph ben Judah. *Sefer Musar*. Berlin: Itzkowski, 1910. Reprint. Jerusalem: Meqize Nirdamim, 1967.

Miskawayh, Aḥmad ibn Muḥammad. *Tahdhīb al-Akhlāq* [*The Refinement of Character*]. Edited by Constantine K. Zurayk. Beirut: American University of Beirut, 1967. English translation by Constantine K. Zurayk. Beirut: American University of Beirut, 1968.

Simon bar Tsemakh Duran. *Magen Avot*. Edited by Yeruham Halevi. Brooklyn: Sharga, 1946.

Spinoza, Benedict. *Theological-Political Treatise*. English translation by R. H. M. Elwes, in *The Chief Works of Benedict De Spinoza.* Vol. 1. New York: Dover, 1955.

Secondary Sources

Altmann, Alexander. *Von der mittelalterlichen zur modernen Aufklärung.* Tubingen: J. C. B. Mohr, 1987.

Arnold, Matthew. *Selections from the Prose Works of Matthew Arnold.* Edited by William Johnson. Cambridge, Mass.: Houghton Mifflin, 1913.

Assaf, David, ed. '*Otsar Leshon ha-Rambam.* Tel-Aviv: Heassor, 1960–.

Büchler, Adolph. *Types of Jewish-Palestinian Piety from 70 B.C.E. to 70 C.E.: The Ancient Pious Men.* 1922. Reprint. New York: Ktav, 1968.

Cohen, Boaz. "The Responsum of Maimonides Concerning Music." In *Law and Tradition in Judaism.* New York: Ktav, 1969, pp. 167–81.

Davidson, Herbert A. "Maimonides' *Shemonah Peraqim* and Alfarabi's *Fuṣūl al-Madanī.*" *Proceedings of the American Academy for Jewish Research* 36 (1963): 33–50.

———. "The Middle Way in Maimonides' Ethics." *Proceedings of the American Academy for Jewish Research* 54 (1987): 31–72.

Gauthier, R. A. *Magnanimité.* Paris: Vrin, 1951.

Goitein, S. D. "Moses Maimonides, Man of Action: A Revision of the Master's Biography in Light of Geniza Documents." In *Hommage à Georges Vajda,* ed. G. Nahon and C. Touati. Louvain, 1980, pp. 155–67.

Husik, Isaac. *A History of Medieval Jewish Philosophy.* Philadelphia: Jewish Publication Society of America, 1948.

Luzzatto, Samuel David. *Yesodei ha-Torah.* Edited by Aaron Zev Eshcoli. Jerusalem: Mossad Harav Kook, 1947. English translation by Noah H. Rosenbloom, in *Studies in Torah Judaism* (*Luzzatto's Ethico-Psychological Interpretation of Judaism*), no. 7. New York: Yeshiva University Press, 1965.

Macy, Jeffrey. "The Theological-Political Teaching of *Shemonah Peraqim:* A Reappraisal of the Text and of Its Arabic Sources." *Proceedings of the Eighth World Congress of Jewish Studies,* Division C, Jerusalem (1982): 31–40.

Pines, Shlomo. "Maimonides." In *The Encyclopaedia of Philosophy,* vol. 5. New York: Macmillan, 1967.

———. "The Limitations of Human Knowledge According to Al-Farabi, ibn Bajja, and Maimonides." In *Studies in Medieval Jewish History and Literature,* ed. Isadore Twersky. Cambridge, Mass.: Harvard University Press, 1979, pp. 82–109.

———. "The Philosophical Purport of Maimonides' Halachic Works and the Purport of *The Guide of the Perplexed.*" In *Maimonides and Philosophy,* ed. Shlomo Pines and Yirmiyahu Yovel. Dordrecht: Martinus Nijhoff, 1986, pp. 1–14.

Rosin, David. *Die Ethik des Maimonides.* Breslau: Jungfer, 1876.

Scheyer, Simon. *Das Psychologische System des Maimonides.* Frankfurt, 1845.

Shapiro, David. *Studies in Jewish Thought.* Vol. 1. New York: Yeshiva University Press, 1975.

Strauss, Leo. *Persecution and the Art of Writing.* Glencoe, Ill.: The Free Press, 1952.

———. *What Is Political Philosophy?* Glencoe, Ill.: The Free Press, 1959.

———. *Studies in Platonic Political Philosophy.* Chicago: University of Chicago Press, 1983.

Twersky, Isadore. *Introduction to the Code of Maimonides (Mishneh Torah).* New Haven: Yale University Press, 1980.

———. "Some Non-Halakic Aspects of the *Mishneh Torah.*" In *Jewish Medieval and Renaissance Studies,* ed. Alexander Altmann. Cambridge, Mass.: Harvard University Press, 1967, pp. 95–119.

Weiss, Raymond L. "Language and Ethics: Reflections on Maimonides' 'Ethics'." *Journal of the History of Philosophy* 9 (October 1971): 425–33.

———. "Some Notes on Twersky's *Introduction to the Code of Maimonides.*" *Jewish Quarterly Review* 74 (July 1983): 61–79.

———. "The Adaptation of Philosophic Ethics to a Religious Community: Maimonides' *Eight Chapters.*" *Proceedings of the American Academy for Jewish Research* 54 (1987): 261–87.

Wolfson, Harry A. *Philo: Foundations of Religious Philosophy in Judaism, Christianity, and Islam.* 2 vols. Cambridge Mass.: Harvard University Press, 1962.

Zucker, Mosheh. "New Fragments from the *Book of the Commandments* by R. Ḥefets ben Yatsliaḥ." (In Hebrew). *Proceedings of the American Academy for Jewish Research* 29 (1960–61): 1–68.

Index of Maimonidean Passages

The citations of passages from the *Commentary on the Mishnah* follow the order of the tractates of the *Mishnah*. The titles of the books of the *Mishneh Torah* (see pp. 214–16 below) are given below in English to assist the general reader. In this index only, page numbers are *italicized*.

A. MAJOR WORKS
Commentary on the Mishnah

Mishneh Torah

Guide of the Perplexed

General Index